AFTER THE FACT
The Art of Historical Detection

·*VOLUME II*

AFTER THE FACT

The Art of Historical Detection

THIRD EDITION

VOLUME II

James West Davidson

Mark Hamilton Lytle

Bard College

McGraw-Hill, Inc.

New York St. Louis San Francisco Auckland Bogotá
Caracas Lisbon London Madrid Mexico City Milan
Montreal New Delhi San Juan Singapore
Sydney Tokyo Toronto

AFTER THE FACT: The Art of Historical Detection, Volume II

5 6 7 8 9 0 DOC DOC 9 0 9 8 7 6 5

ISBN 0-07-015611-5

This book was set in Garamond Light by Better Graphics, Inc.
The editors were David C. Follmer, Niels Aaboe, and Sheila H. Gillams;
the designer was Joan Greenfield;
the production supervisor was Richard A. Ausburn.
R. R. Donnelley & Sons Company was printer and binder.

Library of Congress Cataloging-in-Publication Data
(Revised for vol. 2)

Davidson, James West.
  After the fact.

  Includes indexes.
    1. United States—Historiography.   2. United
States—History.   I. Lytle, Mark.   II. Title.
E179. D29   1992   973'.072   91-33803
ISBN 0-07-015610-7 (v. 1)
ISBN 0-07-015611-5 (v. 2)

About the Authors

James West Davidson received his A.B. from Haverford College and his Ph.D. from Yale University. A historian and full-time writer, he is the author of *The Logic of Millennial Thought: Eighteenth Century New England, Great Heart: the History of a Labrador Adventure* (with John Rugge), and other books. He is also one of the coauthors (along with Mark Lytle) of *Nation of Nations: A Narrative History of the American Republic*.

Mark Hamilton Lytle is Professor of History at Bard College. He received his B.A. from Cornell University and his Ph.D. from Yale University. He has written (with Davidson) *The United States: A History of the Republic; Shang* (with Dixon Merkt) and *The Origins of the Iranian-American Alliance, 1941-1953*. He is currently at work on *The Uncivil War: America in the Vietnam Era,* for McGraw-Hill.

For
Gretchen, Mike, and Rug
(first readers)
and Jesse and Kate
(future prospects)

Contents

Preface to the Third Edition

Ten years have passed since we shipped the final pages of this book's first edition to our copyeditor. Rereading the introduction, we are forced ruefully to admit that the description of ourselves as "young" historians has become somewhat antiquarian. The passage of time is inexorable: this, to be sure, is what keeps historians in business and our subject in constant need of revision.

The third edition reflects changes both large and small. We have added a new final chapter, in which we examine how historians can use dramatic films (and their larger-than-life myths) to explore the often painful realities of the Vietnam war. Chapter 5, which treats ecological transformations along the western frontier, has an expanded discussion of Indian demography and the racist assumptions that have sometimes influenced population estimates. Chapter 10 includes new material on the anarchist activities of Sacco and Vanzetti. Chapter 12, examining the decision to drop atomic bombs on Japan, has been rewritten to clarify our discussion of models. As in the second edition, we have revised our Additional Readings to take into account new materials and have made smaller alterations in other chapters.

Thanks are due to readers who have contributed support and insightful criticism. In particular, we have appreciated the counsel of Chris Rogers, David Follmer, and Niels Aaboe, our editors over the course of this revision. Others who have commented on all or part of our revised materials include James Crisp, William Gienapp, James Gilbert, Michael Stoff, Ken Ludwig, John Rugge, Daniel Beaver, Michael Welsh, Tom Terrill, Peter Sears, Michael Stoff, and Edward Tabor. Despite the changes, the passage of time has not altered the basic thrust of this book: that doing history, as well as simply reading it, can be both a challenge and a pleasure.

Acknowledgments

Because this book is as much about doing history as about history itself, we have drawn heavily on the research and methods of those scholars we most respect and whose history seems to us to provide excellent working models for any apprentice. These historians, past and present, demonstrate how exciting the pursuit of history can and ought to be. Because our narrative is written for lay readers and students as much as for professional scholars, we have omitted extensive footnotes and instead tried to acknowledge our many specific debts in the bibliographical essays that follow each chapter. These essays should provide scholars with the data needed to track down any specific points or issues of interest, as well as direct general readers and students to the primary and secondary sources needed for beginning their own investigations.

For the lay reader or student who comes to history only to sample the discipline or to fulfill distribution requirements, a confession of sorts is in order. Neither of us entered college with the idea of majoring in history, much less making a profession out of it. In the end it was good teachers who lured us into the vineyard. We had the fortune as undergraduates to study under some unusually exciting historians. At Cornell University, Donald Kagan made the ancient world come alive in a way that convinced Mark Lytle that history offered an indispensable way of organizing human knowledge. Walter LaFeber persuaded him that historians could have deep convictions, a powerful grasp of critical issues, and basic human decency. David Davis and Michael Kammen astonished him with the breadth and depth of their intellectual interests.

Jim Davidson's undergraduate years at Haverford College brought him the guidance and friendship of Wallace MacCaffery, whose judicious and eloquent lectures served as models not only for the department but for the rest of the college. In American history, Roger Lane's insights were by turns laconic (Vermont-style) and oratorical (the Irish mode), but always keenly analytical. And then there was William Smith—a colonial historian unaccountably serving in the English department and refusing to be digested by it. He taught unsuspecting freshmen the art of expository prose, a job he performed with more hard-nosed rigor (and consequent effect) than most of his suspicious colleagues.

Graduate school brought the authors together under the tutelage of many exceptional historians. To Edmund S. Morgan, David Davis, John Blum, Gaddis Smith, David Hall, Sydney Ahlstrom, Lawrence Chisolm, Donald Kagan, Firuz Kazemzadeh, Steven Ozment, C. Vann Woodward, and others who taught at Yale, we owe our belief that historians can adopt all manner of methodologies and still write with precision and eloquence. They demonstrated the value of imaginative approaches to evidence, at the same time insisting that history ought to be literate as well as accurate. To the extent that we have followed their precepts, we owe them our gratitude. Where we have not succeeded in following, we can at least say that the spirit was willing, if the flesh a little weak.

We have been fortunate, too, to have had graduate school friends who researched, wrote, kibitzed, and shared lunches along the way. Glenn May, Sherm Cochran, Alan Williams, Bill Gienapp, Jon Clark, Marie Caskey, Allan

Winkler, Alexis Pogerlskin, Jim Crisp, Steve Wiberley, Ellen Dwyer, Hal Williams, Rick Warch, and Elsa Dixler have now scattered across the nation, but they all contributed to the authors' present respect for the teaching and writing of history. Among our present colleagues and friends, we would like to thank Gretchen Lytle, Mike Stoff, Mary Keller, John Rugge, Avi Soifer, Christine Stansell, James Lytle, Tom Frost, Geoff Linburn, Eric Berger, Doug Baz, Sam Kauffmann, Irene Solet, Ellen Boyce, Ken Ludwig, Adrienne George, Robert Koblitz, Stephen Andors, David Pierce, Peter Skiff, John Fout, and Fred Crane. All of them responded generously with advice and comments, sharpened the authors' focus, lampooned their pretensions, and generated ideas and criticism that have kept this book alive.

There are many names here. But then, history has not proved a lonely business. For that, too, we remain grateful.

James West Davidson
Mark Hamilton Lytle

Introduction

This book began as an attempt to bring more life to the reading and learning of history. As young historians, we have been troubled by a growing disinterest in or even animosity toward the study of the past. How is it that when we and other historians have found so much that excites curiosity, other people find history irrelevant and boring? Perhaps, we thought, if lay readers and students understood better how historians go about their work—how they examine evidence, how they pose questions, and how they reach answers—history would engage them as it does us.

As often happens, it took a mundane event to focus and clarify our preoccupations. One day while working on another project, we went outside to watch a neighboring farmer cut down a large old hemlock that had become diseased. As his saw cut deeper into the tree, we joked that it had now bit into history as far back as the Depression. *"Depression?"* grunted our friend. "I thought you fellas were historians. I'm deep enough now, so's Hoover wasn't even a gleam in his father's eye."

With the tree down, the three of us examined the stump. Our woodcutter surprised us with what he saw.

"Here's when my folks moved into this place," he said, pointing to a ring. "1922."

"How do you know without counting the rings?" we asked.

"Oh, *well,*" he said, as if the answer were obvious. "Look at the core, here. The rings are all bunched up tight. I bet there's sixty or seventy—and all within a couple inches. Those came when the place was still forest. Then, you notice, the rings start getting fatter all of a sudden. That's when my dad cleared behind the house—in '22—and the tree started getting a lot more light. And look further out, here—see how the rings set together again for a couple years? That's from loopers."

"Loopers?" we asked cautiously.

"Sure—*loopers.* You know. The ones with only front legs and back." His hand imitated a looping, hopping crawl across the log. "Inchworms. They damn near killed the tree. That was sometime after the war—'49 or '50." As his fingers traced back and forth among the concentric circles, he spoke of other events from years gone by. Before we returned home, we had learned a good deal about past doings in the area.

Now, it occurs to us that our neighbor had a pretty good knack for putting together history. The evidence of the past, like the tree rings, comes easily enough to hand. But we still need to be taught how to see it, read it, and explain it before it can be turned into a story. Even more to the point, the explanations and interpretations *behind* the story often turn out to be as interesting as the story itself. After all, the fascination in our neighbor's account came from the way he traced his tale out of those silent tree rings.

Unfortunately, most readers first encounter history in school textbooks, and these omit the explanations and interpretations—the detective work, if you will. Textbooks, by their nature, seek to summarize knowledge. They have little interest and less space for looking at how that knowledge was gained. Yet the challenge of doing history, not just reading it, is what attracts so many historians. Couldn't some of that challenge be communicated in a concrete way? That was our first goal.

We also felt that the writing of history has suffered in recent years because some historians have been overly eager to convert their discipline into an unadulterated social science. Undeniably, history would lose much of its claim to contemporary relevance without the methods and theories it has borrowed from anthropology, psychology, political science, economics, sociology, and other fields. Indeed, such theories make an important contribution to these pages. Yet history is rooted in the narrative tradition. As much as it seeks to generalize from past events, as do the sciences, it also remains dedicated to capturing the uniqueness of a situation. When historians neglect the literary aspect of their discipline—when they forget that good history begins with a good story—they risk losing that wider audience which all great historians have addressed. They end up, sadly, talking to themselves.

Our second goal, then, was to discuss the methods of American historians in a way that would give proper due to both the humanistic and scientific sides of history. In taking this approach, we have tried to examine many of the methodologies that allow historians to unearth new evidence or to shed new light on old issues. At the same time, we selected topics that we felt were inherently interesting as stories.

Thus our book employs what might be called an apprentice approach to history rather than the synthetic approach of textbooks. A text strives to be comprehensive and broad. It presents its findings in as rational and programmatic a manner as possible. By contrast, apprentices are much less likely to receive such a formal presentation. They learn their profession from artisans who take their daily trade as it comes through the front door. A pewter pot is ordered? Very well, the pot is fashioned. Along the way, an apprentice is shown how to pour the mold. An engraving is needed? Then the apprentice receives his first taste of etching. While this method of teaching communicates a broad range of knowledge over the long run, it does so by focusing on specific situations.

So also this book. Our discussion of methods is set in the context of specific problems historians have encountered over the years. In piecing the individual stories together, we try to pause as an artisan might, and point out problems of evidence, historical perspective, or logical inference. Sometimes, we focus on problems that all historians must face, whatever their subjects. These include such matters as the selection of evidence, historical perspective, the analysis of a document, and the use of broader historical theory. In other cases, we explore problems not encountered by all historians, but characteristic of specific historical fields. These include the use of pictorial evidence, questions of psychohistory, problems encountered analyzing oral interviews, the value of decisionmaking models in political history, and so on. In each case, we have tried to provide the reader with some sense of vicarious participation—the savor of doing history as well as of reading it.

Given our approach, the ultimate success of this book can be best measured in functional terms—how well it works for the apprentices and artisans. We hope that the artisans, our fellow historians, will find the volume's implicit as well as explicit definitions of good history worth considering. In choosing our examples, we have naturally gravitated toward the work of those historians we most respect. At the same time we have drawn upon our own original research in many of the topics discussed; we hope those findings also may be of use to scholars.

As for the apprentices, we admit to being only modest proselytizers. We recognize that, of all the people who read this, only a few will go on to become professional historians. That is only natural. We do hope, however, that even casual readers will come to appreciate the complexity and excitement that go into the study of the past. History is not something that is simply brought out of the archives, dusted off, and displayed as "the way things really were." It is a painstaking construction, held together only with the help of assumptions, hypotheses, and inferences. Readers of history who push dutifully onward, unaware of all the backstage work, miss the essence of the discipline. They miss the opportunity to question and to judge their reading critically. Most of all, they miss the chance to learn how enjoyable it can be to go out and do a bit of digging themselves.

PROLOGUE

The Strange Death of Silas Deane

The writing of history is one of the most familiar ways of organizing human knowledge. And yet, if familiarity has not always bred contempt, it has at least encouraged a good deal of misunderstanding. All of us meet history long before we have heard of any of the social science disciplines, at a tender age when tales of the past easily blend with heroic myths of the culture. In Golden Books, Abe Lincoln looms every bit as large as Paul Bunyan, while George Washington's cherry tree gets chopped down yearly with almost as much ritual as St. Nick's Christmas tree goes up. Despite this long familiarity, or perhaps because of it, most students absorb the required facts about the past without any real conception of what history is. Even worse, most think they do know and never get around to discovering what they missed.

"History is what happened in the past." That is the everyday view of the matter. It supposes that historians must return to the past through the surviving records and bring it back to the present to display as "what really happened." The everyday view recognizes that this task is often difficult. But historians are said to succeed if they bring back the facts without distorting them or forcing a new perspective on them. In effect, historians are seen as couriers between the past and present. Like all good couriers, they are expected simply to deliver messages without adding to them.

This everyday view of history is profoundly misleading. In order to demonstrate how it is misleading, we would like to examine in detail an event that "happened in the past"—the death of Silas Deane. Deane does not appear in most American history texts, and rightly so. He served as a distinctly second-rate diplomat for the United States during the years of the American Revolution. Yet the story of Deane's death is an excellent example of an event that cannot be understood merely by transporting it, courier-like, to the present. In short, it illustrates the important difference between "what happened in the past" and what history really is.

An Untimely Death

Silas Deane's career began with one of those rags-to-riches stories so much appreciated in American folklore. In fact, Deane might have made a lasting place for himself in the history texts, except that his career ended with an equally dramatic riches-to-rags story.

He began life as the son of a humble blacksmith in Groton, Connecticut. The blacksmith had aspirations for his boy and sent him to Yale College, where Silas was quick to take advantage of his opportunities. After studying law, Deane opened a practice near Hartford; he then continued his climb up the social ladder by marrying a well-to-do widow, whose inheritance included the business of her late husband, a merchant. Conveniently, Deane became a merchant. After his first wife died, he married the granddaughter of a former governor of Connecticut.

Not content to remain a prospering businessman, Deane entered politics. He served on Connecticut's Committee of Correspondence and later as a delegate to the first and second Continental Congresses, where he attracted the attention of prominent leaders, including Benjamin Franklin, Robert Morris, and John Jay. In 1776 Congress sent Deane to France as the first American to represent the united colonies abroad. His mission was to purchase badly needed military supplies for the Revolutionary cause. A few months later Benjamin Franklin and Arthur Lee joined him in an attempt to arrange a formal treaty of alliance with France. The American commissioners concluded the alliance in March 1778.

Deane worked hard to progress from the son of a blacksmith all the way to Minister Plenipotentiary from the United States to the Court of France. Most observers described him as ambitious: someone who thoroughly enjoyed fame, honor, and wealth. "You know his ambition—" wrote John Adams to one correspondent, "his desire of making a Fortune. . . . You also know his Art and Enterprise. Such Characters are often useful, altho always to be carefully watched and contracted, specially in such a government as ours." One man in particular suspected Deane enough to watch him: Arthur Lee, the third member of the American mission. Lee accused Deane of taking unfair advantage of his official position to make a private fortune—as much as £50,000 pounds, some said. Deane stoutly denied the accusations and Congress engaged in a heated debate over his conduct. In 1778 it voted to recall its Minister Plenipotentiary, although none of the charges had been conclusively proved.

Deane embroiled himself in further controversy in 1781, having written friends to recommend that America sue for peace and patch up the quarrel with England. His letters were intercepted, and copies of them turned up in a New York Tory newspaper just after Cornwallis surrendered to Washington at Yorktown. For Deane, the timing could not have been worse. With American victory complete, anyone advocating that the United States rejoin Britain was considered as much a traitor as Benedict Arnold. So Deane suddenly found himself adrift. He could not return to America, for no one would have him. Nor could he go to England without confirming his reputation as a traitor. And he could not

Drawn from the life by Wm Simitier in Philadelphia.   *Engraved by B. L. Prevost at Paris.*

*"**You know his ambition**—his desire of making a Fortune. . . . You also know his Art and Enterprise. Such Characters are often useful, altho always to be carefully watched and contracted, specially in such a government as ours." —John Adams on Silas Deane*

stay in France, where he had injudiciously accused Louis XVI of aiding the Americans for purely selfish reasons. Rejected on all sides, Deane took refuge in Flanders.

The next few years of his life were spent unhappily. Without friends and with little money, he continued in Flanders until 1783, when the controversy had died down enough for him to move to England. There he lived in obscurity, took to drink, and wound up boarding at the house of an unsavory prostitute. The only friend who remained faithful to him was Edward Bancroft, another Connecticut Yankee who, as a boy, had been Deane's pupil and later his personal secretary during the Paris negotiations for the alliance. Although Bancroft's position as a secretary seemed innocent enough, members of the Continential Congress knew that Bancroft was also acting as a spy for the Americans, using his connections in England to secure information about the British ministry's war plans. With the war concluded, Bancroft was back in London. Out of kindness, he provided Deane with living money from time to time.

Finally, Deane decided he could no longer live in London and in 1789 booked passage on a ship sailing for the United States. When Thomas Jefferson heard the news, he wrote his friend James Madison: "Silas Deane is coming over to finish his days in America, not having one *sou* to subsist on elsewhere. He is a wretched monument of the consequences of a departure from right."

The rest of the sad story could be gotten from the obituaries. Deane boarded the *Boston Packet* in mid-September, and it sailed out of London down the estuary of the Thames. A storm came up, however, and on September 19 the ship lost both its anchors and beat a course for safer shelter, where it could wait out the storm. On September 22, while walking the quarter deck with the ship's captain, Deane suddenly "complain'd of a dizziness in his head, and an oppression at his stomach." The captain immediately put him to bed. Deane's condition worsened; twice he tried to say something, but no one was able to make out his words. A "drowsiness and insensibility continually incroached upon his faculties," and only four hours after the first signs of illness he breathed his last.

Such, in outline, was the rise and fall of the ambitious Silas Deane. The story itself seems pretty clear, although certainly people might interpret it in different ways. Thomas Jefferson thought Deane's unhappy career demonstrated "the consequences of a departure from right," whereas one English newspaper more sympathetically attributed his downfall to the mistake of "placing confidence in his [American] Compatriots, and doing them service before he had got his compensation, of which no well-bred Politician was before him ever guilty." Yet either way, the basic story remains the same—the same, that is, until the historian begins putting together a more complete account of Deane's life. Then some of the basic facts become clouded.

For example, a researcher familiar with the correspondence of Americans in Europe during 1789 would realize that a rumor had been making its way around London in the weeks following Deane's death. According to certain people, Deane had become depressed by his poverty, ill health, and low reputation, and consequently had committed suicide. John Cutting, a New England merchant and friend of Jefferson, wrote of the rumor that Deane "had predetermin'd to take a sufficient quantity of Laudanum [a form of opium] to ensure his dissolution" before the boat could sail for America. John Quincy Adams heard that "every probability" of the situation suggested Deane's death was "voluntary and self-administered." And Tom Paine, the famous pamphleteer, also reported the gossip: "Cutting told me he took poison."

At this point we face a substantial problem. Obviously, historians cannot rest content with the facts that come most easily to hand. They must search the odd corners of libraries and letter collections in order to put together a complete story. But how do historians know when their research is "complete?" How do they know to search one collection of letters rather than another? These questions point up the misconception at the heart of the everyday view of history. History is not "what happened in the past;" rather, it is *the act of selecting, analyzing, and writing about the past.* It is something that is done, that is constructed, rather than an inert body of data that lies scattered through the archives.

The distinction is important. It allows us to recognize the confusion in the question of whether a history of something is "complete." If history were merely "what happened in the past," there would never be a "complete" history of Silas Deane—or even a complete history of the last day of his life. The past holds an infinite number of facts about those last days, and they could never all be included in a historical account.

The truth is, no historian would *want* to include all the facts. Here, for example, is a list of items from the past which might form part of a history of Silas Deane. Which ones should be included?

Deane is sent to Paris to help conclude a treaty of alliance.
Arthur Lee accuses him of cheating his country to make a private profit.
Deane writes letters which make him unpopular in America.
He goes into exile and nearly starves.
Helped out by a gentleman friend, he buys passage on a ship for America
    as his last chance to redeem himself.
He takes ill and dies before the ship can leave; rumors suggest he may have
    committed suicide.

Ben Franklin and Arthur Lee are members of the delegation to Paris.
Edward Bancroft is Deane's private secretary and an American spy.
Men who know Deane say he is talented but ambitious, and ought to be
    watched.

Before Deane leaves, he visits an American artist, John Trumbull.
The *Boston Packet* is delayed for several days by a storm.
On the last day of his life, Deane gets out of bed in the morning.
He puts on his clothes and buckles his shoes.
He eats breakfast.
When he takes ill, he tries to speak twice.
He is buried several days later.

Even this short list of facts demonstrates the impossibility of including all of them. For behind each one lie hundreds more. You might mention that Deane put on his clothes and ate breakfast, but consider also: What color were his clothes? When did he get up that morning? What did he have for breakfast? When did he leave the table? All these things "happened in the past," but only a comparatively small number of them can appear in a history of Silas Deane.

It may be objected that we are placing too much emphasis on this process of selection. Surely, a certain amount of good judgment will suggest which facts are important. Who needs to know what color Deane's clothes were or when he got up from the breakfast table?

Admittedly this objection has some merit, as the list of facts about Deane demonstrates. The list is divided into three groups, roughly according to the way common sense might rank them in importance. The first group contains facts which every historian would be likely to include. The second group contains less important information, which could either be included or left out. (It might be useful, for instance, to know who Arthur Lee and Edward Bancroft were, but not essential.) The last group contains information that appears either too detailed or else unnecessary. Deane may have visited John Trumbull, but then, he surely visited other people as well—why include any of that? Knowing that the *Boston Packet* was delayed by a storm reveals little about Silas Deane. And readers will assume without being told that Deane rose in the morning, put on his clothes, and had breakfast.

But if common sense helps to select evidence, it also produces a good deal of pedestrian history. The fact is, the straightforward account of Silas Deane we have just presented has actually managed to miss the most fascinating parts of the story.

Fortunately, one enterprising historian named Julian Boyd was not satisfied with the traditional account of the matter. He examined the known facts of Deane's career and put them together in ways common sense had not suggested. Take, for example, two items on our list: (1) Deane was down on his luck and left in desperation for America; and (2) he visited John Trumbull. One fact is from the "important" items on the list and the other from items that seem incidental. How do they fit together?

To answer that, we have to know the source of information about the visit to Trumbull's, which is the letter from John Cutting informing Jefferson of Deane's rumored suicide.

> A subscription had been made here chiefly by Americans to defray the expense of getting [Deane] out of this country. . . . Dr. Bancroft with great humanity and equal discretion undertook the management of the *man* and his *business*. Accordingly his passage was engaged, comfortable cloaths and stores for his voyage were laid in, and apparently without much reluctance he embarked. . . . I happen'd to see him a few days since at the lodging of Mr. Trumbull and thought I had never seen him look better.

We are now in a better position to see how our two items fit together. And as Julian Boyd has pointed out, they don't fit. According to the first, Deane was depressed, dejected, almost starving. According to the second, he had "never looked better." An alert historian begins to get nervous when he sees contradictions like that, so he hunts around a little more. And finds, among the collection of papers published by the Connecticut and New York historical societies, that Deane had been writing letters of his own.

One went to his brother-in-law in America, who had agreed to help pay Deane's transportation over and to receive him when he arrived—something that nobody had been willing to do for years. Other letters reveal that Deane had plans for what he would do when he finally returned home. He had seen models in England of the new steam engines, which he hoped might operate gristmills in America. He had talked to friends about getting a canal built from Lake Champlain in New York to the St. Lawrence River, in order to promote trade. These were not offhand dreams. As early as 1785, Deane had been at work drumming up support for his canal project. He had even laboriously calculated the cost of the canal's construction. ("Suppose a labourer to dig and remove six feet deep and eight feet square in one day. . . . 2,933 days of labour will dig one mile in length, twenty feet wide and eight feet deep. . . .") Obviously, Deane looked forward to a promising future.

Lastly, Deane appeared to believe that the controversy surrounding his French mission had finally abated. As he wrote an American friend,

> It is now almost ten years since I have solicited for an impartial inquiry [into the dispute over my conduct]. . . . that justice might be done to my fortune and my character. . . . You can sufficiently imagine, without my attempting to describe, what I must have suffered on every account during so long a period of anxiety and distress. I hope that it is now drawing to a close.

Other letters went to George Washington and John Jay, reiterating Deane's innocence.

All this makes the two items on our list even more puzzling. If Deane was depressed and discouraged, why was he so enthusiastic about coming back to build canals and gristmills? If he really believed that his time of "anxiety and distress" was "drawing to a close," why did he commit suicide? Of course, Deane might have been subject to dramatic shifts in mood. Perhaps hope for the future alternated with despair about his chances for success. Perhaps a sudden fit of depression caused him to take his life.

But another piece of "unimportant" information, way down on our third list, makes this hypothesis difficult to accept. After Deane's ship left London, it was delayed offshore for more than a week. Suppose Deane did decide to commit suicide by taking an overdose of laudanum. Where did he get the drug? Surely not by walking up to the ship's surgeon and asking for it. He must have purchased it in London, before he left. Yet he remained on shipboard for more than a week. If Deane bought the laudanum during a temporary "fit" of depression, why did he wait a week before taking it? And if his depression was not just a sudden fit, how do we explain the optimistic letters to America?

This close look at three apparently unrelated facts indicates that perhaps Deane's story has more to it than meets the eye. It would be well, then, to reserve judgment about our first reconstruction of Silas Deane's career, and try to find as much information about the man as possible—regardless of whether it seems relevant at first. That means investigating not only Deane himself but also his friends and associates, like Ben Franklin, Arthur Lee, and Edward

Bancroft. Since it is impossible in this prologue to look closely at all of Deane's acquaintances, for purpose of example we will take only one: his friend Bancroft.

Silas Deane's Friend

Edward Bancroft was born in Westfield, Massachusetts, where his stepfather presided over a respectable tavern, the *Bunch of Grapes.* Bancroft was a clever fellow, and his father soon apprenticed him to a physician. Like many boys before him, Edward did not fancy his position and so ran away to sea. Unlike many boys, he managed to make the most of his situation. His ship landed in the Barbadoes, and there Bancroft signed on as the surgeon for a plantation in Surinam. The plantation owner, Paul Wentworth, liked the young man and let him use his private library for study. In addition, Bancroft met another doctor who taught him much about the area's exotic tropical plants and animals. When Bancroft returned to New England in 1766 and continued on to London the following year, he knew enough about Surinam's wildlife to publish a book entitled *An Essay on the Natural History of Guiana in South America.* It was well received by knowledgeable scholars and, among other things, established that an electric eel's shock was caused by electricity, a fact not previously recognized.

A young American bright enough to publish a book at age twenty-five and to experiment with electric eels attracted the attention of another electrical experimenter then in London, Ben Franklin. Franklin befriended Bancroft and introduced him to many influential colleagues, not only learned philosophers but also the politicians with whom Franklin worked as colonial agent for Pennsylvania. A second trip to Surinam produced more research on plants used in making color dyes; research so successful that Bancroft soon found himself elected to the prestigious Royal Society of Medicine. At the same time, Franklin led Bancroft into the political arena, both public and private. On the public side, Bancroft published a favorable review of Thomas Jefferson's pamphlet, *A Summary View of the Rights of British America;* privately, he joined Franklin and other investors in an attempt to gain a charter for land along the banks of the Ohio River.

Up to this point it has been possible to sketch Bancroft's career without once mentioning the name of Silas Deane. Common sense would suggest that the information about Bancroft's early travels, his scientific studies, his friends in Surinam, tell us little about Deane, and that the story ought to begin with a certain letter Bancroft received from Deane in June 1776. (Common sense is again wrong, but we must wait a little to discover why.)

The letter, which came to Bancroft in 1776, informed him that his old friend Silas Deane was coming to France as a merchant engaged in private business. Would Bancroft be interested in crossing over from England to meet Deane at Calais to catch up on news for old time's sake? An invitation like that would very likely have attracted Bancroft's curiosity. He did know Deane, who had been his teacher in 1758, but not very well. Why would Deane now write and suggest a meeting? Bancroft may have guessed the rest, or he may have known it from other contacts; in any case, he wrote his "old friend" that he would make all possible haste for Calais.

The truth of the matter, as we know, was the Deane had come to France to secure military supplies for the colonies. Franklin, who was back in Philadelphia, had suggested to Congress's Committee of Secret Correspondence that Deane contact Bancroft as a good source of information about British war plans. Bancroft could easily continue his friendship with English officials, because he did not have the reputation of being a hot-headed American patriot. So Deane met Bancroft at Calais in July and the two concluded their arrangements. Bancroft would be Deane's "private secretary" when needed in Paris and a spy for the Americans when in England.

It turned out that Deane's arrangement worked well—perhaps a little too well. Legally, Deane was permitted to collect a commission on all the supplies he purchased for Congress, but he went beyond that. He and Bancroft used their official connections in France to conduct a highly profitable private trade of their own. Deane, for instance, sometimes sent ships from France without declaring whether they were loaded with private or public goods. Then if the ships arrived safely, he would declare that the cargo was private, his own. But if the English navy captured the goods on the high seas, he labeled it government merchandise and the public absorbed the loss.

Deane used Bancroft to take advantage of his official position in other ways. Both men speculated in the London insurance markets, which were the eighteenth-century equivalent of gambling parlors. Anyone who wished could take out "insurance" against a particular event which might happen in the future. An insurer, for example, might quote odds on the chances of France going to war with England within the year. The insured would pay whatever premium he wished, say £1,000, and if France did go to war, and the odds had been five to one against it, the insured would receive £5,000. Wagers were made on almost any public event: which armies would win which battles, which politicians would fall from power, and even on whether a particular lord would die before the year was out.

Obviously, someone who had access to inside information—someone who knew in advance, for instance, that France was going to war with England—could win a fortune. That was exactly what Bancroft and Deane decided to do. Deane was in charge of concluding the French alliance, and he knew that if he succeeded Britain would be forced to declare war on France. Bancroft hurried across to London as soon as the treaty had been concluded and took out the proper insurance before the news went public. The profits shared by the two men from this and other similar ventures amounted to approximately £10,000. Like most gamblers, however, Deane also lost wagers. In the end, he netted little for his troubles.

Historians know these facts because they now have access to the papers of Deane, Bancroft, and others. Acquaintances of the two men lacked this advantage, but they suspected shady dealings anyway. Arthur Lee publicly accused Deane and Bancroft of playing the London insurance game. (Deane shot back that Lee was doing the same thing.) And the moralistic John Adams found Bancroft's conduct distasteful. Bancroft, according to Adams, was

> a meddler in stocks as well as reviews, and frequently went into the alley, and into the deepest and darkest retirements and recesses of the brokers and jobbers . . . and found amusement as well, perhaps, as profit, by listening to all the news and anecdotes, true or false, that were there whispered or more boldly pronounced. . . . This man had with him in France, a woman with whom he lives, and who by the French was called La Femme de Monsieur Bancroft. At tables he would season his foods with such enormous quantities of cayenne pepper which assisted by generous burgundy would set his tongue a running in the most licentious way both at table and after dinner. . . .

Yet for all Bancroft's dubious habits, and for all the suspicions of men like Lee and Adams, there was one thing that almost no one at the time suspected, and that not even historians discovered until the records of certain British officials were opened to the public more than a century later. Edward Bancroft was a double agent.

At the end of July 1776, after he had arranged to be Deane's secretary, Bancroft returned to England and met with Paul Wentworth, his friend from Surinam, who was then working in London for Britain's intelligence organization. Immediately Wentworth realized how valuable Bancroft would be as a spy and introduced him to two secretaries of state. They in turn persuaded Bancroft to submit reports on the American negotiations in France. For his services, he received a lifetime pension of £200 a year—a figure the British were only too happy to pay for such good information. So quick was Bancroft's reporting that the secretaries of state knew about the American mission to France even before the United States Congress could confirm that Deane had arrived safely!

Eventually, Bancroft discovered that he could pass his information directly to the British ambassador at the French court. To do so, he wrote innocent letters on the subject of "gallantry" and signed them "B. Edwards." On the same paper would go another note written in invisible ink, to appear only when the letter was dipped in a special developer held by Lord Stormont, the British ambassador. Bancroft left his letters every Tuesday morning in a sealed bottle in a hole near the trunk of a tree on the south terrace of the Tuileries, the royal palace. Lord Stormont's secretary would put any return information near another tree on the same terrace. With this system in operation Stormont could receive intelligence without having to wait for it to filter back from England.

Did any Americans suspect Bancroft of double dealing? Arthur Lee once claimed he had evidence to charge Bancroft with treason, but he never produced it. In any case, Lee had a reputation for suspecting everybody of everything. Franklin, for his part, shared lodgings with Deane and Bancroft during their stays in Paris. He had reason to guess that someone close to the American mission was leaking secrets—especially when Lord Stormont and the British newspapers made embarrassingly accurate accusations about French aid. The French wished to keep their assistance secret in order to avoid war with England as long as possible, but of course Franklin knew America would fare better with

The Tuileries, *such as it appeared when Bancroft and Lord Stormont used the south terrace as a drop for their secret correspondence. The royal palace overlooks a magnificent formal garden which, as a modern observer has noted, "seems so large, so full of surprising hidden corners and unexpected stairways, that its strict ground plan—sixteen carefully spaced and shaped gardens of trees, separated by arrow-straight walks—is not immediately discernable."*

France fighting, so he did little to stop the leaks. "If I was sure," he remarked, "that my *valet de place* was a spy, as he probably is, I think I should not discharge him for that, if in other respects I liked him." So the French would tell Franklin he *really* ought to guard his papers more closely, and Franklin would say yes, yes, he really would have to do something about that; and the secrets continued to leak. Perhaps Franklin suspected Deane and Bancroft of playing the London insurance markets, but there is no evidence that he knew Bancroft was a double agent.

What about Deane, who was closer to Bancroft than anyone else? We have no proof that he shared the double agent's secret, but his alliance with Bancroft in other intrigues tells against him. Furthermore, one published leak pointed to a source so close to the American commissioners that Franklin began to investigate. As Julian Boyd has pointed out, Deane immediately directed suspicion toward a man he knew perfectly well was not a spy. We can only conclude he did so to help throw suspicion away from Bancroft. Very likely, if Bancroft was willing to help Deane play his games with the London insurers, Deane was willing to assist Bancroft in his game with British intelligence.

Of the two, Bancroft seems to have made out better. While Deane suffered reproach and exile for his conduct, Bancroft returned to England still respected by both the Americans and the British. Not that he had been without narrow escapes. Some of the British ministry (the king especially) did not trust him, and he once came close to being hung for treason when his superiors rightly suspected that he had associated with John the Painter, an unbalanced fanatic who tried to set England's navy ablaze. But Bancroft left for Paris at the first opportunity, waited until the storm blew over, and returned to London at the end of the war with his lifetime pension raised to £1,000 a year. At the time of Deane's death, he was doing more of his scientific experiments, in hopes that Parliament would grant him a profitable monopoly on a new process for making dyes.

Deane's Death: A Second Look

So we finally arrive, the long way around, back where the story began: September 1789 and Deane's death. But now we have at hand a much larger store of information out of which to construct a narrative. Since writing history involves the acts of analyzing and selecting, let us review the results of our investigation.

We know that Deane was indeed engaged in dubious private ventures; ventures Congress would have condemned as unethical. We also have reason to suspect that Deane knew Bancroft was a spy for the British. Combining that evidence with what we already know about Deane's death, we might theorize that Deane committed suicide because, underneath all his claims to innocence, he knew he was guilty as Congress charged. The additional evidence, in other words, reveals a possible new motive for Deane's suicide.

Yet this theory presents definite problems. In the first place, Deane never admitted any wrongdoing to anyone—not in all the letters he wrote, not in any of his surviving papers. That does not mean he was innocent, nor even that he believed himself innocent. But often it is easier for a person to lie to himself than to his friends. Perhaps Deane actually convinced himself that he was blameless; that he had a right to make a little extra money from his influential position; that he did no more than anyone would in his situation. Certainly his personal papers point to that conclusion. And if Deane believed himself innocent—correctly or not—would he have any obvious motive for suicide? Furthermore, the theory does not explain the puzzle that started this investigation. If Deane felt guilty enough about his conduct to commit suicide, why did that guilt increase ten years after the fact? If he did feel suddenly guilty, why wait a week aboard ship before taking the fatal dose of laudanum? For that matter, why go up and chat with the captain when death was about to strike?

No, things still do not set quite right, so we must question the theory. What proof do we have that Deane committed suicide? Rumors about London. Tom Paine heard it from Cutting, the merchant. And Cutting reports in his letter to Jefferson that Deane's suicide was "the suspicion of Dr. Bancroft." How do we know the circumstances of Deane's death? The captain made a report, but for some reason it was not preserved. The one account that did survive was written by Bancroft, at the request of a friend. Then there were the anonymous obituaries in the newspapers. Who wrote them? Very likely Bancroft composed at least one; certainly, he was known as Silas Deane's closest friend and would have been consulted by any interested parties. There are a lot of strings here, which, when pulled hard enough, all run back to the affable Dr. Bancroft. What do we know about *his* situation in 1789?

We know Bancroft is dependent upon a pension of £1,000 a year, given him for his faithful service as a British spy. We know he is hoping Parliament will grant him a monopoly for making color dyes. Suddenly his old associate Deane, who has been leading a dissolute life in London, decides to return to America, vindicate himself to his former friends, and start a new life. Put yourself in Bancroft's place. Would you be just a little nervous about that idea? Here is a man down on his luck, now picking up and going to America to clear his reputation. What would Deane do to clear it? Tell everything he knew about his life in Paris? Submit his record books to Congress, as he had been asked to do so many years before? If Deane knew Bancroft was a double agent, would he say so? And if Deane's records mentioned the affair of John the Painter (as indeed they did), what would happen if knowledge of Bancroft's role in the plot reached England? Ten years earlier, Bancroft would have been hung. True, memories had faded, but even if he were spared death, would Parliament grant a monopoly on color dyes to a known traitor? Would Parliament continue the £1,000 pension? It was one thing to have Deane living in London, where Bancroft could watch him; it would be quite another to have him all the way across the Atlantic Ocean, ready to tell—who knows what?

Admit it: if you were Bancroft, wouldn't you be just a little nervous?

We are forced to consider, however reluctantly, that Deane was not expecting to die as he walked the deck of the *Boston Packet*. Yet if Bancroft did murder Deane, how? He was not aboard ship when death came and had not seen Deane for more than a week. That is a good alibi, but then, Bancroft was a clever man. We know (once again from the letters of John Cutting) that Bancroft was the person who "with great humanity and equal discretion undertook the management of the *man* and the *business*" of getting Deane ready to leave for America. Bancroft himself wrote Jefferson that he had been visiting Deane often "to assist him with advice, medicins, and money for his subsistence." If Deane were a laudanum addict, as Bancroft hinted to Cutting, might not the good doctor who helped with "medicins" also have procured the laudanum? And having done that, might he not easily slip some other deadly chemical into the mixture, knowing full well that Deane would not use it until he was on shipboard and safely off to America? That is only conjecture. We have no direct evidence to suggest this is what happened.

But there is one other fact we do know for sure; and in light of our latest theory, it is an interesting one. Undeniably, Edward Bancroft was an expert on poisons.

He did not advertise that knowledge, of course; few people in London at the time of Deane's death would have been likely to remember that fact. But twenty years earlier, the historian may recall, Bancroft wrote a book on the natural history of Guiana. At that time, he not only investigated electric eels and color dyes, but also the poisons of the area, particularly curare (or "Woowara" as Bancroft called it). He investigated it so well, in fact, that when he returned to England he brought samples of curare with him which (he announced in the book) he had deposited with the publishers so that any gentleman of "unimpeachable" character might use the samples for scientific study.

Furthermore, Bancroft seemed to be a remarkably good observer not only of the poisons but also of those who used them. His book described in ample detail the natives' ability to prepare poisons

> which, given in the smallest quantities, produce a very slow but inevitable death, particularly a composition which resembles wheat-flour, which they sometimes use to revenge past injuries, that have been long neglected, and are thought forgotten. On these occasions they always feign an insensibility of the injury which they intend to revenge, and even repay it with services and acts of friendship, until they have destroyed all distrust and apprehension of danger in the destined victim of the vengeance. When this is effected, they meet at some festival, and engage him to drink with them, drinking first themselves to obviate suspicion, and afterwards secretly dropping the poison, ready concealed under their nails, which are usually long, into the drink.

Twenty years later Bancroft was busy at work with the color dyes he had brought back from Surinam. Had he, by any chance, also held onto any of those poisons?

Unless new evidence comes to light, we will probably never know for sure. Historians are generally forced to deal with probabilities, not certainties, and we leave you to draw your own conclusions about the death of Silas Deane.

What does seem certain is that whatever "really happened" to Deane 200 years ago cannot be determined today without the active participation of the

> * As the Author has brought a confiderable quantity of this Poifon to *England*, any Gentleman, whofe genius may incline him to profecute thefe experiments, and whofe character will warrant us to confide in his hands a preparation, capable of perpetrating the moft fecret and fatal villainy, may be fupplied with a fufficient quantity of the *Woo-rara*, by applying to Mr. *Becket*, in the *Strand*.

An excerpt from An Essay on the Natural History of Guiana in South America, *by Edward Bancroft.*

historian. Being courier to the past is not enough. For better or worse, historians inescapably leave an imprint as they go about their business: asking interesting questions about apparently dull facts, seeing connections between subjects that had not seemed related before, shifting and rearranging evidence until it assumes a coherent pattern. The past is not history; only the raw material of it. How those raw materials come to be fashioned and shaped is the central concern of the rest of this book.

ADDITIONAL READING

The historian responsible for the brilliant detective work exposing the possibility of foul play on the *Boston Packet* is Julian Boyd. He makes his case, in much greater detail than can be summarized here, in a series of three articles entitled "Silas Deane: Death by a Kindly Teacher of Treason?" *William and Mary Quarterly*, 3rd Ser., XVI (1959), 165-187, 319-342, and 515-550. For additional background on Silas Deane, see the entry in the *Dictionary of American Biography* (New York, 1946). (The *DAB*, incidentally, is a good starting point for those seeking biographical details of American figures. It provides short sketches as well as further bibliographical references.) For details on additional intrigue surrounding the American mission to France, see Samuel F. Bemis, "The British Secret Service and the French-American Alliance," *American Historical Review*, XXIX (1923-1924), 474-495.

Interested readers who wish to examine some of the primary documents in the case may do so easily enough. Much of Deane's correspondence is available in *The Deane Papers*, published as part of the New York Historical Society's *Collections*, XIX-XXIII (New York, 1887-1891) and in *The Deane Papers: Correspondence between Silas Deane, His Brothers . . . 1771-1795*, Connecticut Historical Society *Collections*, XXIII (Hartford, Conn., 1930). These volumes shed helpful light on Deane's state of mind during his London years. The London obituary notices are reprinted in the *American Mercury* (Hartford, Conn., December 28, 1789), the *Gazette of the United States* (Philadelphia, Pa., December 12, 1789), and other newspapers in New York and Boston. See also the *Gentleman's Magazine* of London, LIX, Pt. ii (September 1789), 866. American colonial newspapers are available in many libraries on microprint, published by the Readex Microprint Corporation in conjunction with the American Antiquarian Society.

Edward Bancroft's role as double agent was not established conclusively until the private papers of William Eden (Lord Auckland) were made public in the 1890s. As director of the British Secret Service during the Revolution, Eden and his right-hand man, Paul Wentworth, were in close touch with Bancroft. The details of the Bancroft-Wentworth-Eden connection are spelled out in Paul L. Ford, *Edward Bancroft's Narrative of the Objects and Proceedings of Silas Deane* (Brooklyn, N.Y., 1891). Further information on Bancroft may be found in Sir Arthur S. MacNalty, "Edward Bancroft, M.D., F.R.S. and the War of American Independence," Royal Society of Medicine *Proceedings*, XXXVIII (1944), 7-15. The Historical Society of Pennsylvania, in Philadelphia, has a collection of Bancroft's papers. And further background may be gained, of course, from the good doctor's own writings, chief among them the *Essay on the Natural History of Guiana in South America . . .* (London, 1769).

We have pointed out that no evidence in the historical record conclusively links Edward Bancroft with Silas Deane's death. In an eminently fair-minded manner, we left you to draw your own conclusions. Yet, as the lesson of this chapter makes clear, every historical narrative is bound to select facts in shaping its story—including this narrative. Given our limitations of space, we chose to concentrate on the evidence and arguments which illuminated Boyd's hypothesis most forcibly. So we suspect that most readers, if left to draw their "own" conclusions, will tend to find Bancroft guilty as charged.

Boyd's case strikes us as impressive too, but it certainly can be questioned. How sound, for instance, is the hypothesis about Deane's depression (or lack of it)? Many people who have contemplated suicide, it could be argued, do so over an extended period of time, and their moods of depression may alternate with happier periods. Perhaps Deane toyed with the idea, put it away, then returned to it in the gloomy confines of the *Boston Packet.* If Deane were a laudanum addict and had a large quantity of the drug on hand, might he not easily take an overdose during a sudden return of severe depression? For that matter, if he were a careless addict, might he not have taken an *accidental* overdose?

In another area, William Stinchcombe has suggested that, contrary to Julian Boyd's suggestion, Deane did not face any really hopeful prospects for success in America. If Deane continued to be destitute and down on his luck when he departed for America, then the suicide theory again becomes more probable. Stinchcombe's article, "A Note on Silas Deane's Death," may be found in the *William and Mary Quarterly,* 3rd Ser., XXXII (1975), 619-624.

We can also report with pleasure that the first edition of this book sparked an interesting counter to Boyd's thesis. Dr. Guido Gianfranceschi, a surgeon from Danbury, Connecticut, read our Prologue in a course on historical methods he was taking at Western Connecticut State College. He points out to us that a check of the standard medical reference, *Goodman and Gilman's Pharmacological Basis of Therapeutics* (Sixth Edition; New York, 1980), reveals that Deane was not likely done in by curare. Though quite toxic when entering the bloodstream, curare is "poorly and irregularly absorbed from the gastrointestinal tract. d-Tubocurarine is inactive after oral administration, unless huge doses are ingested; this fact was well known to the South American Indians, who ate with impunity the flesh of game killed with curare-poisoned arrows." (It was also known to Bancroft, who notes in this own work that, "when received by the alimentary passage," the poison "is subdued by the action of the digestive organs. . . .")

Of course, curare was only one of many poisons Bancroft learned about from the natives of Guiana. "I have spent many days in a dangerous and almost fruitless endeavor to investigate the nature and qualities of these plants," he reported in 1769, "and by handling, smelling, tasting, etc. I have frequently found, at different times, almost all the several senses, and their organs either disordered or violently affected. . . ." Could it have been another one of those deadly substances which Deane ingested? Perhaps; Boyd makes no guess what the poison might have been. But while Bancroft indicated he had brought home snake specimens, curare is the only poison he specifically mentions having in London. Furthermore, Dr. Gianfranceschi points out that the symptoms of opium overdose are similar to those Deane is said to have experienced prior to his death. Finally, for a third opinion, consult D. K. Anderson and G. T. Anderson, "The Death of Silas Deane," *New England Quarterly,* LVII (1984), 98-105. The Andersons surveyed several medical authorities and concluded that Deane may well have suffered from chronic tuberculosis and died from a stroke or some other acute attack.

Murder, suicide, stroke, or accidental overdose? We eagerly await new evidence that our readers may turn up.

AFTER THE FACT
The Art of Historical Detection

VOLUME II

CHAPTER SEVEN

The View from the Bottom Rail

Thunder. From across the swamps and salt marshes of the Carolina coast came the distant, repetitive pounding. Thunder out of a clear blue sky. Down at the slave quarters, young Sam Mitchell heard the noise and wondered. In Beaufort, the nearby village, planter John Chaplin heard too, and dashed for his carriage. The drive back to his plantation was as quick as Chaplin could make it. Once home, he ordered his wife and children to pack; then looked for his slaves. The flatboat must be made ready, he told them; the family was going to Charleston. He needed eight men at the oars. One of the slaves, Sam Mitchell's father, brought the news to his wife and son at the slave quarters. "You ain't gonna row no boat to Charleston," the wife snapped, "you go out dat back door and keep a-going." Young Sam was mystified by all the commotion. How could it thunder without a cloud in the sky? "Son, dat ain't no t'under," explained the mother, "dat Yankee come to gib you freedom."

The pounding of the guns came relatively quickly to Beaufort—November of 1861, only seven months after the first hostilities at Fort Sumter. Yet it was only a matter of time before the thunder of freedom rolled across the rest of the south, from the bayous and deltas of Louisiana in 1862 to the farms around Richmond in 1865. And as the guns of the Union spoke, thousands of Sam Mitchells experienced their own unforgettable moments. Freedom was coming to a nation of four million slaves.

To most slaves, the men in the blue coats were foreigners. As foreigners, they were sometimes suspect. Many southern masters painted the prospect of northern invasion in deliberately lurid colors. Union soldiers, one Tennessee slave was told, "got long horns on their heads, and tushes in their mouths, and eyes sticking out like a cow! They're mean old things." A terrified Mississippi slave refused to come down out of a tree until the Union soldier below her took off his cap and demonstrated he had no horns. Many slaves, however, took such tales with more than a grain of salt. "We all hear 'bout dem Yankees," a Carolina slave told his overseer. "Folks tell we they has horns and a tail . . . W'en I see dem coming I shall run like all possess." But as soon as the overseer fled, leaving

This slave family *lived on a plantation at Beaufort, South Carolina, not far from the plantation where Sam Mitchell heard the thunder of northern guns in 1861. The photograph was taken after northern forces had occupied the Sea Island area.*

the plantation in the slaves' care, the tune changed: "Good-by, ole man, good-by. That's right. Skedaddle as fast as you kin. . . . We's gwine to run sure enough; but we knows the Yankees, an' we runs that way."

For some slaves, the habit of long years, the bond of loyalty, or the fear of alternatives led them to side with their masters. Faithful slaves hid valuable silver, persuaded Yankees that their departed masters were actually Union sympathizers, or feigned contagious illness in order to scare off marauding soldiers. One pert slave even led Yankees right to the plantation beehives. "De Yankees forgot all about de meat an' things dey done stole," she noted with satisfaction; "they took off down de road at a run." But in many cases, the conflict between loyalty and freedom caused confusion and anguish. An older Georgia couple, both over sixty, greeted the advance of Sherman's soldiers calmly and with apparent lack of interest. They seemed entirely content to remain under the care of their master instead of joining the mass of slaves flocking along behind Sherman's troops. As the soldiers prepared to leave, however, the old woman suddenly stood up, a "fierce, almost devilish" look in her eyes, and turned to her husband. "What you sit dar for?" she asked vehemently. "You s'pose I wait sixty years for nutten? Don't yer see de door open? I'se follow my child; I not stay. Yes, anudder day I goes 'long wid dese people; yes, sar, I walks till I drop in my tracks."

Other slaves felt no hesitation about choosing freedom; indeed, they found it difficult to contain the joy within them. One woman, who overheard the news of emancipation just before she was to serve her master's dinner, asked to be excused because she had to get water from a nearby spring. Once she had reached the seclusion of the spring, she allowed her feelings free rein.

> I jump up and scream, "Glory, glory hallelujah to Jesus! I'se free! I'se free! Glory to God, you come down an' free us; no big man could do it." An' I got sort o' scared, afeared somebody hear me, an' I takes another good look, an' fall on de goun' an' roll over, an' kiss de gound' fo' de Lord's sake, I's so full o' praise to Masser Jesus.

To the newly freed slaves, it seemed as if the world had been turned upside down. Rich and powerful masters were fleeing before Yankees, while freed slaves were left with the run of the plantation. The situation was summed up succinctly by one black soldier who was surprised—and delighted—to find that his former master was among the prisoners he was guarding. "Hello, massa!" he said cheerfully, "bottom rail top dis time!"

In Search of the Freedmen's Point of View

The freeing of four million black slaves surely ranks as one of the major events in American history. Yet the story has not been an easy one to tell. To understand the personal trials and triumphs of the newly liberated slaves, or freedmen as they came to be called, historians must draw upon the personal experiences of those at the center of the drama. They must re-create the freedman's point of view. But slaves had occupied the lowest level of America's social and economic scale. They sat, as the black soldier correctly noted, on the bottom rail of the fence. For several reasons, that debased position has made it unusually difficult for historians to recover the freedman's point of view.

In the first place, most histories suffer from a natural "top-rail" bias. They tend to take as their subjects members of the higher social classes. Histories cannot be written without the aid of documentary raw material, left in the historical record by participants. The more detailed the records, the easier it is to write a history. By and large, those on the top rails of society produce the best and most voluminous records. Having been privileged to receive an education, they are more apt to publish memoirs, keep diaries, or write letters. As leaders of society who make decisions, they are the subjects of official minutes and records. They are more often written about and commented on by their contemporaries.

At the other end of the social spectrum, "bottom-rail" people lead lives that are commonly repetitious. While political leaders involve themselves in what appears to be one momentous issue after another, a farmer most often plants the same crop and follows the ritual of the seasons year after year. Furthermore, the individual actions of the anonymous majority seem to have little effect on the course of history. Biographical details of such people appear both uninspiring and unavailable, at first glance anyway, when compared to the bustling lives of the powerful. Thus the elites of any society have long been the natural subjects of historians.

The decade of the 1970s saw an increasing interest by historians in the writing of social histories that would shed greater light on the activities and feelings of bottom-rail people. We saw, for example, that a knowledge of the social and economic position of the serving class was essential to understanding the volatile society of early Virginia. Similarly, we turned to the social tensions of ordinary farmers in order to explain the alliances behind the witchcraft controversy at Salem. Often enough, social historians have found it difficult to piece together the lives of any anonymous class of Americans; yet reconstructing the perspective of the black slave or freedman has proved particularly challenging, simply because few written source materials are available. Black slaves were not only discouraged from learning to read and write, southern legislatures passed slave codes which flatly forbade whites to teach them.

The laws were not entirely effective; a few blacks employed as drivers on large plantations learned to read and correspond so that their absent masters might send them instructions. Some black preachers were also literate. Still, most reading remained a clandestine affair, done out of sight of the master or other whites. During the war, a literate slave named Squires Jackson was eagerly scanning a newspaper for word of northern victories when his master unexpectedly entered the room and demanded to know what the slave was doing. The surprised reader deftly turned the newspaper upside down, put on a foolish grin, and said, "Confederates done won the war!" The master laughed and went about his business.

Even though most slaves never wrote letters, kept diaries, or left any other written records, it might at first seem easy enough to learn about slave life from accounts written by white contemporaries. Slavery, after all, was an institution whose faults and alleged virtues were hotly debated by nineteenth-century Americans. Any number of letters, books, travelers' accounts, and diaries survive, full of descriptions of life under slavery and of the experiences of freedmen after the war. Yet here too, the question of perspective raises serious problems. The vantage point of white Americans observing slavery was emphatically not that of slaves who lived under the "peculiar institution," nor of those freedmen forced to cope with their dramatically changed circumstances. The marked differences between the social and psychological positions of blacks and whites make it extremely difficult to reconstruct the black point of view solely from white accounts.

Consider, first, the observations of those white people who associated most often and most closely with black slaves: their masters. The relation between master and slave was inherently unequal. Blacks were at the mercy of their owners' whims. Slaves could be whipped for trifling offenses; they could be sold or separated from their families and closest friends; even under "kind" masters, they were bound to labor as ordered if they wanted their ration of food and clothing. With slaves so dependent on the master's authority, they were hardly likely to reveal their true feelings; the dangerous consequences of such indiscretion were too great.

In fact, we have already encountered an example where a slave was forced to deceive his master, the case of Squires Jackson and his newspaper. A moment's reflection will indicate that we narrated that story from Jackson's point of view, not the master's. Our impression of the slave's conduct would have been remarkably different if we had access only to a diary kept by Jackson's master. "A humorous incident occurred today," the entry might have read.

> While entering the woodshed to attend some business, I came upon my slave Squires. His large eyes were fixed with intense interest upon an old copy of a newspaper he had come upon, which alarmed me some until I discovered the rascal was reading its contents upside down. "Why Squires," I said innocently. "What is the latest news?" He looked up at me with a big grin and said, "Massa, de 'Federates jes' won de war!" It made me laugh to see the darkey's simple confidence. I wish I could share his optimism.

This entry is fictional, but having Jackson's version of the story serves to cast suspicion on similar entries in real planter diaries. One Louisiana slaveowner, for instance, marveled that his field hands went on with their Christmas party apparently unaware that Yankee raiding parties had pillaged a nearby town. "We have been watching the negroes dancing for the last two hours. . . . They are having a merry time, thoughtless creatures, they think not of the morrow." It apparently never occurred to the planter that the "thoughtless" merriment may have been especially great because of the northern troops nearby.[1]

The harsh realities of the war brought many southerners to realize for the first time just how little they really knew about their slaves. In areas where Union troops were near, slaves ran for freedom—often the very servants masters had deemed most loyal. Mary Chesnut, whose house was not far from Fort Sumter, sought in vain to penetrate the blank expressions of her slaves. "Not by one word or look can we detect any change in the demeanor of these Negro servants. . . . You could not tell that they even hear the awful noise that is going on in the bay [at Fort Sumter], though it is dinning in their ears night and day. . . . Are they stolidly stupid, or wiser than we are, silent and strong, biding their time?"

It is tempting to suppose that northerners, as liberators of slaves, might

---

[1] Readers who review the opening narrative of this chapter will discover that they have already encountered quite a few other examples of blacks concealing their true feelings. In fact, except for the black soldier's comment about the bottom rail being top, every example of white-black relations cited in the opening section has some element of concealment or deception, either by blacks toward whites, or by whites toward blacks. It may be worth noting that we did not select the opening incidents with that fact in mind. The preponderance of deception was noted only when we reviewed the draft several days after it had been written.

"They are having a merry time, thoughtless creatures, they think not of the morrow." This scene of a Christmas party, similar to the one described by the Louisiana planter, appeared with an article written by a northern correspondent for Frank Leslie's Illustrated Newspaper *in 1857. The picture, reflecting the popular stereotype of slaves as cheerful and ignorantly content with their lot, suggests that the social constraints of the times made it as difficult for southern African Americans to be completely candid with their northern liberators as it had been to be candid with their southern masters.*

provide more sympathetic or accurate accounts of freedmen's attitudes. But that is a dangerous assumption to make. Although virtually all northern slaves had been freed by 1820, race prejudice remained overwhelmingly evident. Antislavery forces often combined a vehement dislike of slavery with an equally vehement desire to keep the freedmen out of the North. For African Americans who did live there, most housing and transportation facilities were segregated. Whites and blacks had much less contact than afforded by the easy, if unequal, familiarity common in the South.

Consequently, while some Union soldiers went out of their way to be kind to the slaves they encountered, many more looked upon African Americans with distaste and open hostility. Many Yankees strongly believed that they were fighting a war to save the Union, not to free the "cursed Nigger," as one recruit put it. Even white officers who commanded black regiments could be remarkably unsympathetic. "Any one listening to your shouting and singing can see how grotesquely ignorant you are," one officer lectured his troops, when they refused to accept less than the pay promised them upon enlistment. Missionaries and other sympathetic northerners who came to occupied territory understood the slaves better, but even they had preconceptions to overcome. "I saw some very low-looking women who answered very intelligently, contrary to my expectations," noted Philadelphia missionary Laura Towne. Where she was serving, in the Carolina sea-islands near Beaufort, she observed that "some, indeed most of [the slaves], were the real bullet-headed negroes." Another female missionary, much less sympathetic than Laura Towne, bridled when a black child greeted her with too much familiarity. "I say good-mornin' to my young missus," recounted the child to a friend, "and she say, 'I slap your mouth for your impudence, you nigger.'" Such callousness underlines the need for caution when dealing with northern accounts.

Indeed, the more perceptive northern observers recognized that black people would continue to be circumspect around white people. Just as the slave had been dependent on his southern masters, so the freedmen found themselves similarly vulnerable to the new class of conquerors. The newly liberated often responded to questions with answers carefully designed to please. "One of these blacks, fresh from slavery, will most adroitly tell you precisely what you want to hear," noted northerner Charles Nordhoff.

> To cross-examine such a creature is a task of the most delicate nature; if you chance to put a leading question he will answer to its spirit as closely as the compass needle answers to the magnetic pole. Ask if the enemy had fifty thousand men, and he will be sure that they had at least that many; express your belief that they had not five thousand, and he will laugh at the idea of their having more than forty-five hundred.

Samuel Gridley Howe, a wartime commissioner investigating the freedmen's condition, saw the situation clearly. "The negro, like other men, naturally desires to live in the light of truth," he argued, "but he hides in the shadow of falsehood, more or less deeply, according as his safety or welfare seems to require it. Other things equal, the freer a people, the more truthful; and only the perfectly free and fearless are perfectly truthful."

Even sympathetic northerners were at a disadvantage in recounting the freedmen's point of view, simply because black culture was so foreign to them. The world of the southern field hand, black religious culture, surviving African folk customs and songs—all these were unfamiliar to northern observers. Black dialect too created problems. Charles Nordhoff noted that often he had the feeling that he was "speaking with foreigners." The slaves' phrase "I go shum" puzzled him until he discovered it to be a contraction of "I'll go see about it." Another missionary was "teaching the little darkies gymnastics and what various things were for, eyes, etc. He asked what ears were made for, and when they said, 'To yer with,' he could not understand them at all."

If black dialect was difficult to understand, black culture and religion could appear even more unfathomable. Although most slaves nominally shared with northerners a belief in Christianity, black methods of worship shocked more than one staid Unitarian. After church meetings, slaves often participated in a singing and dancing session known as a "shout," where the leader would sing out a line of song and the chorus respond, dancing in rhythm to the music. As the night proceeded, the music became more vocal and the dancing more vigorous. "Tonight I have been to a 'shout,'" reported Laura Towne, "which seems to me certainly the remains of some old idol worship . . . I never saw anything so savage." Another missionary noted, "It was the most hideous and at the same time the most pitiful sight I ever witnessed."

Thus, as sympathetic as many northerners wished to be, significant obstacles prevented them from fully appreciating the freedman's point of view. With race prejudice so prevalent, with black people in such a vulnerable position, with black culture so much at odds with white, it is not surprising that perceptive observers like Nordhoff felt as if they were speaking with "foreigners." The nature of slave society and the persistence of race prejudice made it virtually impossible for blacks and whites to deal with one another in open, candid ways.

The Freedmen Speak

Given the scarcity of first-person African-American accounts, how can we fully recover the freedman's point of view? From the very beginning, some observers recognized the value that black testimony would have and worked to collect it. If few black people could write, their stories could be written down by others and made public. Oral testimony, transcribed by literate editors, would allow black Americans to speak out on issues that affected them most closely.

The tradition of oral evidence began even before the slaves were freed. Abolitionists recognized the value of firsthand evidence against the slave system. They took down the stories of fugitive slaves who had safely made their way North, and published the accounts. During the war, Congress also established the Freedman's Inquiry Commission, which collected information about blacks that might aid the government in formulating policies toward the newly freed slaves.

In the half-century following Reconstruction, however, interest in preserving black history generally languished. An occasional journalist or historian traveled through the South to interview former slaves. Educators at black schools, such as the Hampton Institute, published a few recollections. But a relatively small number of subjects were interviewed. Often the interviews were published in daily newspapers whose standards of accuracy were not high and where limitations of space required that the interviews be severely edited.

Furthermore, the vast majority of professional historians writing about Reconstruction ignored these interviews, as well as the freedmen's perspective in general. They most often relied on white accounts which, not unexpectedly, painted a rather partial picture. William A. Dunning, a historian at Columbia University, was perhaps the most influential scholar in setting forth the prevalent viewpoint. He painted the freedmen as childish, happy-go-lucky creatures who failed to appreciate the responsibilities of their new status. "As the full meaning of [emancipation] was grasped by the freedmen," Dunning wrote, "great numbers of them abandoned their old homes, and, regardless of crops to be cultivated, stock to be cared for, or food to be provided, gave themselves up to testing their freedom. They wandered aimless but happy through the country. . . ." At the same time Dunning asserted that Confederate soldiers and other southern whites had "devoted themselves with desperate energy to the procurement of what must sustain the life of both themselves and their former slaves." Such were the conclusions deduced without the aid of the freedmen's perspectives.

Only in the twentieth century were systematic efforts made to question blacks about their experiences as slaves and freedmen. Interest in the African-American heritage rose markedly during the 1920s, in great part spurred by the efforts of black scholars like W. E. B. Du Bois, Charles Johnson, and Carter Woodson, the editor and founder of the *Journal of Negro History*. Those scholars labored diligently to overturn the Reconstruction stereotypes promoted by the Dunning school. Moreover, the growth of both sociology and anthropology departments at American universities encouraged scholars to analyze Southern culture using the tools of the new social sciences. By the beginning of the 1930s historians at Fisk and Southern universities had instituted projects to collect oral evidence.

Ironically, it was the economic adversity of the Depression that sparked the greatest single effort to gather oral testimony from the freedmen. One of the many alphabet-soup agencies chartered by the Roosevelt administration was the Federal Writers' Project (FWP). Primarily, the project sought to compile cultural guides to each of the forty-eight states, using unemployed writers and journalists to collect and edit the information. But under the direction of folklorist John Lomax, the FWP also organized staffs in many states to interview former slaves.

Although Lomax's project placed greatest emphasis on collecting black folklore and songs, the FWP's directive to interviewers included a long list of historical questions that interviewers were encouraged to ask. The following sampling gives an indication of the project's interests:

> What work did you do in slavery days? Did you ever earn any money?
> What did you eat and how was it cooked? Any possums? Rabbits? Fish?
> Was there a jail for slaves? Did you ever see any slaves sold or auctioned off?
>   How and for what causes were the slaves punished? Tell what you saw.
> What do you remember about the war that brought you your freedom?
>   When the Yankees came what did they do or say?
> What did the slaves do after the war? What did they receive generally?
>   What do they think about the reconstruction period?

The results of these interviews are remarkable, if only in terms of sheer bulk. More than 2,300 were recorded and edited in state FWP offices and then sent to Washington, assembled in 1941, and published in typescript. A facsimile edition, issued during the 1970s, takes up nineteen volumes. Supplementary materials, including hundreds of interviews never forwarded to Washington during the project's life, comprise another twelve volumes, with additional materials forthcoming. Benjamin Botkin, the series' original editor, recognized the collection's importance:

> These life histories, taken down as far as possible in the narrator's words, constitute
> an invaluable body of unconscious evidence or indirect source material, which

scholars and writers dealing with the South, especially, social psychologists and cultural anthropolgists, cannot afford to reckon without. For the first and last time, a large number of surviving slaves (many of whom have since died) have been permitted to tell their own story, in their own way.

At first glance, the slave narrative collection would appear to fulfill admirably the need for a guide to the freedmen's point of view. But even Botkin, for all his enthusiasm, recognized that the narratives could not simply be taken at face value. Like other primary source materials, they need to be viewed in terms of the context in which they originated.

To begin with, no matter how massive the nineteen volumes of interviews may appear on the library shelf, they still constitute a small sampling of the original four million freedmen. What sort of selection bias might exist? Geographic imbalance comes quickly to mind. Are the slave interviews drawn from a broad cross section of southern states? Counting the number of slaves interviewed from each state, we discover that there are only 155 interviews from black people living in Virginia, Missouri, Maryland, Delaware, and Kentucky— about 6 percent of the total number of interviews published. Yet in 1860, 23 percent of the southern slave population lived in those states. Thus the upper South is underrepresented in the collection. For researchers who wished to investigate whether conditions varied from the border states to the deep south, this geographic bias would have to be taken into account.[2]

What about age? Since the interviews took place primarily between 1936 and 1938, ex-slaves were fairly old: fully two-thirds of them were over 80. The predominance of elderly interviewees raises several questions. Most obviously, the Civil War was already seventy years in the past. How sharp were the informants' memories? Ability to recall accurately varies from person to person, but common sense suggests that the further away from an event, the less detailed one's memory is likely to be. In addition, age may have biased the *type* of recollections as well as their accuracy. Historian John Blassingame has noted that the average life expectancy of a slave in 1850 was less than 50 years. Those who lived to a ripe old age might well have survived because they were treated better than the average slave. If so, their accounts would reflect some of the milder experiences of slaves.

Secondly, if those interviewed were predominantly old in 1936, they were predominantly young during the Civil War. Almost half (43 percent) were less than ten years old in 1865. Sixty-seven percent were under fifteen years old, and 83 percent were under twenty. Thus, many remembered slavery as it would have been experienced by a child. Since the conditions of bondage were relatively less harsh for a child than for an adult slave, once again the FWP narratives may be somewhat skewed toward an optimistic view of slavery. (On the other hand, it might be argued that since children are so impressionable, memories both good and bad might have been vividly magnified.)

---

[2] Statistics quoted are for the original slave narrative interviews only. They do not include materials issued in the supplementary volumes, which are helping to rectify the imbalance.

Other possible sampling biases come to mind—the sex of the subjects or the kinds of labor they performed as slaves. But distortions may be introduced into the slave narratives in ways more serious than sample bias. Interviewers, simply by choosing their questions, define the kinds of information a subject will volunteer. We have already seen that sensitive observers, such as Charles Nordhoff, recognized how important it was not to ask leading questions. But even Nordhoff may not have realized how many unconscious cues the most innocent questions carry.

Social scientists specializing in interviewing have pointed out that even the grammatical form of a question will influence a subject's response. Take, for example, the following questions:

> Where did you hear about this job opening?
> How did you hear about this job opening?
> So you saw our want ad for this job?

Each question is directed at the same information, yet each suggests to the subject a different response. The first version ("*Where* did you hear . . .") implies that the interviewer wants a specific, limited answer. ("Down at the employment center.") The second question, by substituting *how* for *where,* invites the subject to offer a longer response. ("Well, I'd been looking around for a job for several weeks, and I was over at the employment office when . . . .") The final question signals that the interviewer wants only a yes or no confirmation to a question whose answer he believes he already knows.

Interviewers, in other words, constantly communicate to their subjects the kinds of evidence they want, the length of the answers, and even the manner in which answers ought to be offered. If such interviewing "cues" influence routine conversations, they prove even more crucial when a subject as controversial as slavery is involved, and where relations between blacks and whites continue to be strained. In fact, the most important cue an interviewer was likely to have given was one presented before any conversation took place. Was the interviewer white or black? William Ferris, a sociologist obtaining oral folklore in the Mississippi Delta region in 1968, discussed the problem. "It was not possible to maintain rapport with both Whites and Blacks in the same community," he noted,

> for the confidence and cooperation of each was based on their belief that I was "with them" in my convictions about racial taboos of Delta society. Thus when I was "presented" to Blacks by a white member of the community, the informants regarded me as a member of the white caste and therefore limited their lore to noncontroversial topics. . . .

Such tensions were even more prevalent throughout the South during the 1930s. In hundreds of ways, black people were made aware that they were still considered inferior to white people, and that they were to remain within strictly segregated and subordinate bounds. From 1931 to 1935, more than seventy African Americans were lynched in the South, often for minor or nonexistent crimes. Black prisoners found themselves forced to negotiate grossly unfavorable labor contracts if they wished to be released. Many sharecroppers and other poor farmers were constantly in debt to white property owners.

Smaller matters of etiquette reflected the larger state of affairs. A white southerner would commonly address black adults by their first names, or as "boy," "auntie," "uncle," regardless of the black person's status and even if the white person knew the black person's full name. Black people were required to address white people as "ma'am" or "mister." Such distinctions were maintained even on the telephone. If an African American placed a long-distance call for "Mr. Smith" in a neighboring town, the white operator would ask, "Is he colored?" The answer being yes, her reply would be, "Don't you say 'Mister' to me. He ain't 'Mister' to me." Conversely, an operator would refuse to place a call by a black caller who did not address her as "Ma'am."

In such circumstances, most African Americans were naturally reticent about volunteering information to white FWP interviewers. "Lots of old slaves closes the door before they tell the truth about their days of slavery," noted one black Texan to an interviewer. "When the door is open, they tell how kind their masters was how rosy it all was . . . ." Samuel S. Taylor, a skilled black interviewer in Arkansas, found that he had to reassure informants that the information they were giving would not be used against them. "I've told you too much," one subject concluded. "How come they want all this stuff from the colored people anyway? Do you take any stories from the white people? They know all about it. They know more about it than I do. They don't need me to tell it to them."

Often the whites who interviewed blacks lived in the same town and were long acquaintances. "I 'members when you was barefoot at de bottom," one black interviewee told his white (and balding) interviewer; "now I see you a settin' dere, gittin' bare at de top, as bare as de palm of my hand." Another black man revealed an even closer relationship when he noted that his wife Ellen " 'joy herself, have a good time nussin' [nursing] white folks chillun. Nussed you; she tell me 'bout it many time." In such circumstances African Americans could hardly be expected to speak frankly. One older woman summed up the situation quite cheerfully. "Oh, I know your father en your granfather en all of dem. Bless Mercy, child, I don't want to tell you nothin' but what to please you."

Although such statements put a researcher on guard, readers who are new to this field may still find it difficult to appreciate the varying responses that different interviewers might elicit. In order to bring home the point more forcibly, it may be helpful to analyze an interview that we came across during our own research in the slave narrative collection. The interview is with Susan Hamlin, a black woman who lived in Charleston, and we reprint it below exactly as it appears in typescript.

Interview With Ex-Slave

On July 6th, I interviewed Susan Hamlin, ex-slave, at 17 Henrietta street, Charleston, S. C. She was sitting just inside of the front door, on a step leading up to the porch, and upon hearing me inquire for her she assumed that I was from the Welfare office, from which she had received aid prior to its closing. I did not correct this impres-

"I've told you too much. How come they want all this stuff from the colored people anyway? Do you take any stories from the white people? . . . They don't need me to tell it to them." This Georgia woman, like many of the subjects interviewed for the Federal Writers' Project, was still living in the 1930s on the plantation where she had grown up as a slave child. The plantation was still owned by descendants of her former master. Under such conditions suspicion toward Project interviewers was a predictable reaction, even if the interviewer was black; doubly so if he or she was white and a resident of the community.*

sion, and at no time did she suspect that the object of my visit was to get the story of her experience as a slave. During our conversation she mentioned her age. "Why that's very interesting, Susan," I told her, "If you are that old you probably remember the Civil War and slavery days." "Yes, Ma'am, I been a slave myself," she said, and told me the following story:

"I kin remember some things like it was yesterday, but I is 104 years old now, and age is starting to get me, I can't remember everything like I use to. I getting old, old. You know I is old when I been a grown woman when the Civil War broke out. I was hired out then, to a Mr. McDonald, who lived on Atlantic Street, and I remembers when de first shot was fired, and the shells went right over de city. I got seven dollars a month for looking after children, not taking them out, you understand, just minding them. I did not got the money, Mausa got it." "Don't you think that was fair?" I asked. "If you were fed and clothed by him, shouldn't he be paid for your work?" Course it been fair," she answered, "I belong to him and he got to get something to take care of me."

"My name before I was married was Susan Calder, but I married a man named Hamlin. I belonged to Mr. Edward Fuller, he was president of the First National Bank. He was a good man to his people till de Lord took him. Mr. Fuller got his slaves by marriage. He married Miss Mikell, a lady what lived on Edisto Island, who was a slave owner, and we lived on Edisto on a plantation. I don't remember de name cause when Mr. Fuller got to be president of de bank we come to Charleston to live. He sell out the plantation and say them (the slaves) that want to come to Charleston with him could come and them what wants to stay can stay on the island with his wife's people. We had our choice. Some is come and some is stay, but my ma and us children come with Mr. Fuller.

We lived on St. Philip street. The house still there, good as ever. I go 'round there to see it all de time; the cistern still there too, where we used to sit 'round and drink the cold water, and eat, and talk and laugh. Mr. Fuller have lots of servants and the ones he didn't need hisself he hired out. The slaves had rooms in the back, the ones with children had two rooms and them that didn't have any children had one room, not to cook in but to sleep in. They all cooked and ate downstairs in the hall that they had for the colored people. I don't know about slavery but I know all the slavery I know about, the people was good to me. Mr. Fuller was a good man and his wife's people been grand people, all good to their slaves. Seem like Mr. Fuller just git his slaves so he could be good to dem. He made all the little colored chillen love him. If you don't believe they loved him what they all cry, and scream, and holler for when dey hear he dead? 'Oh, Mausa dead my Mausa dead, what I going to do, my Mausa dead.' Dey tell dem t'aint no use to cry, dat can't bring him back, but de chillen keep on crying. We used to call him Mausa Eddie but he named Mr. Edward Fuller, and he sure was a good man.

"A man come here about a month ago, say he from de Government, and dey send him to find out 'bout slavery. I give him most a book, and what he give me? A dime. He ask me all kind of questions. He ask me dis and he ask me dat, didn't de white people do dis and did dey do dat but Mr. Fuller was a good man, he was sure good to me and all his people, dey all like him, God bless him, he in de ground now but I ain't going to let nobody lie on him. You know he good when even the little chillen cry and holler when he dead. I tell you dey couldn't just fix us up any kind of way when we going to Sunday School. We had to be dressed nice, if you pass him and you ain't dress to suit him he send you right back and say tell your ma to see dat you dress right. Dey couldn't send you out in de cold barefoot neither. I 'member one day my ma want to send me wid some milk for her sister-in-law what live 'round de corner. I fuss cause it cold and say 'how you going to send me out wid no shoe, and it cold?' Mausa hear how I talkin and turn he back and laugh, den he call to my ma to gone in de house and find shoe to put on my feet and don't let him see me barefoot again in cold weather.

When de war start going good and de shell fly over Charleston he take all us up to Aiken for protection. Talk 'bout marching through Georgia, dey sure march through Aiken, soldiers was everywhere.

"My ma had six children, three boys and three girls, but I de only one left, all my white people and all de colored people gone, not a soul left but me. I ain't been sick in 25 years. I is near my church and I don't miss service any Sunday, night or morning. I kin walk wherever I please, I kin walk to de Battery if I want to. The Welfare use to help me but dey shut down now, I can't find out if dey going to open again or not. Miss (Mrs.) Buist and Miss Pringle, dey help me when I can go there but all my own dead."

"Were most of the masters kind?" I asked. "Well you know," she answered, "times den was just like dey is now, some was kind and some was mean; heaps of wickedness went on just de same as now. All my people was good people. I see some wickedness and I hear 'bout all kinds of t'ings but you don't know whether it was lie or not. Mr. Fuller been a Christian man."

"Do you think it would have been better if the Negroes had never left Africa?" was the next question I asked. "No Ma'am," (emphatically) dem heathen didn't have no religion. I tell you how I t'ink it is. The Lord made t'ree nations, the white, the red and the black, and put dem in different places on de earth where dey was to stay. Dose black ignoramuses in Africa forgot God, and didn't have no religion and God blessed and prospered the white people dat did remember Him and sent dem to teach de black people even if dey have to grab dem and bring dem into bondage till dey learned some sense. The Indians forgot God and dey had to be taught better so dey land was taken away from dem. God sure bless and prosper de white people and He put de red and de black people under dem so dey could teach dem and bring dem into sense wid God. Dey had to get dere brains right, and honor God, and learn uprightness wid God cause ain't He make you, and ain't His Son redeem you and save you wid His precious blood. You kin plan all de wickedness you want and pull hard as you choose but when the Lord mek up His mind you is to change, He can change you dat quick (snapping her fingers) and easy. You got to believe on Him if it tek bondage to bring you to your knees.

You know I is got converted. I been in Big Bethel (church) on my knees praying under one of de preachers. I see a great, big, dark pack on my back, and it had me all bent over and my shoulders drawn down, all hunch up. I look up and I see de glory, I see a big beautiful light, a great light, and in de middle is de Sabior, hanging so (extending her arms) just like He died. Den I gone to praying good, and I can feel de sheckles (shackles) loose up and moving and de pack fall off. I don't know where it went to, I see de angels in de Heaven, and hear dem say 'Your sins are forgiven.' I scream and fell off so. (Swoon.) When I come to dey has laid me out straight and I know I is converted cause you can't see no such sight and go on like you is before. I know I is still a sinner but I believe in de power of God and I trust his Holy name. Den dey put me wid de seekers but I know I is already saved."

"Did they take good care of the slaves when their babies were born?" she was asked. "If you want chickens for fat (to fatten) you got to feed dem," she said with a smile, "and if you want people to work dey got to be strong, you got to feed dem and take care of dem too. If dey can't work it come out of your pocket. Lots of wickedness gone on in dem days, just as it do now, some good, some mean, black and white, it just dere nature, if dey good dey going to be kind to everybody, if dey mean dey going to be mean to everybody. Sometimes chillen was sold away from dey parents. De Mausa would come and say "Where Jennie," tell um to put clothes on dat baby, I want um. He sell de baby and de ma scream and holler, you know how dey carry on. Geneally (generally) dey sold it when de ma wasn't dere. Mr. Fuller didn't sell none of us, we stay wid our ma's till we grown. I stay wid my ma till she dead.

"You know I is mix blood, my grandfather bin a white man and my grandmother a mulatto. She been marry to a black so dat how I get fix like I is. I got both blood, so how I going to quarrel wid either side?"

SOURCE: Interview with Susan Hamlin, 17 Henrietta Street.

NOTE * Susan lives with a mulatto family of the better type. The name is Hamlin not Hamilton, and her name prior to her marriage was Calder not Collins. I paid particular attention to this and had them spell the names for me. I would judge Susan to be in the late nineties but she is wonderfully well preserved. She now claims to be 104 years old.

From the beginning, the circumstances of this conversation arouse suspicion. The white interviewer, Jessie Butler, mentions that she allowed Hamlin to think she was from the welfare office. Evidently, Butler thought Hamlin would speak more freely if the real purpose of the visit was hidden. But surely the deception had the opposite effect. Hamlin, like most of the black people interviewed, was elderly, unable to work, and dependent on charity. If Butler appeared to be from the welfare office, Hamlin would likely have done whatever she could to ingratiate herself. Many black interviewees consistently assumed that their white interviewers had influence with the welfare office. "You through wid me now, boss? I sho' is glad of dat," concluded one subject. "Help all you kin to get me dat pension befo' I die and de Lord will bless you, honey. . . . Has you got a dime to give dis old nigger, boss?"

Furthermore, Butler's questioning was hardly subtle. When Hamlin noted that she had to give her master the money she made from looking after children, Butler asked, "Don't you think that was fair?" "Course it been fair," came the quick response. Hamlin knew very well what was expected, especially since Butler had already answered the question herself: "If you were fed and clothed by him, shouldn't he be paid for your work?"

Not surprisingly, then, the interview paints slavery in relatively mild colors. Hamlin describes in great detail how good her master was and how she had shoes in the winter. When asked whether most masters were kind, Hamlin appears eminently "fair"—"some was kind and some was mean." She admits hearing "all kinds of t'ings but you don't know whether it was lie or not." She does note that slave children could be sold away from parents and that black mothers protested; but she talks as if that were only to be expected. ("De ma scream and holler, you know how dey carry on.")

Equally flattering is the picture Hamlin paints of relations between the races. "Black ignoramuses" in Africa had forgotten about God, she explains, just as the Indians had; but "God sure bless and prosper de white people." So Africans and the Indians are placed under white supervision, "to get dere brains right, and honor God, and learn uprightness." Those were not exactly the words proslavery apologists would have used to describe the situation, but they were the same sentiments. Defenders of slavery constantly stressed that Europeans served as benevolent models ("parents," Andrew Jackson might have said) leading Africans and Indians on the slow upward road to civilization.

All these aspects of the interview led us to be suspicious about its content. Moreover, there were several additional clues in the document that puzzled us. Hamlin had mentioned a man who visited her "about a month ago, say he from de Government, and dey send him to find out 'bout slavery." Apparently her interview with Jessie Butler was the second she had given. Butler, for her part, made a fuss at the end of the transcript over the spelling of Hamlin's name. ("I paid particular attention to this.") It was "Hamlin not Hamilton" and her maiden name was "Calder not Collins." The phrasing indicates that somewhere else Butler had seen Hamlin referred to as "Susan Hamilton." If someone had interviewed Hamlin earlier, we wondered, could Hamilton have been the name on that original report?

We found the answer when we continued on through the narrative collection. The interview following Butler's was conducted by a man named Augustus Ladson, with a slave named "Susan Hamilton." When compared with Jessie Butler's interview, Augustus Ladson's makes absorbing reading. Here it is, printed exactly as it appears in the collection:

Ex-Slave 101 Years of Age

Has Never Shaken Hands Since 1863
Was on Knees Scrubbing when Freedom Gun Fired

I'm a hund'ed an' one years old now, son. De only one livin' in my crowd frum de days I wuz a slave. Mr. Fuller, my master, who was president of the Firs' National Bank, owned the fambly of us except my father. There were eight men an' women with five girls an' six boys workin' for him. Most o' them wus hired out. De house in which we stayed is still dere with de sisterns an' slave quarters. I always go to see de old home which is on St. Phillip Street.

My ma had t'ree boys an' t'ree girls who did well at their work. Hope Mikell, my eldest brodder, an' James wus de shoemaker. William Fuller, son of our Master, wus de bricklayer. Margurite an' Catharine wus de maids an' look as de children.

My pa b'long to a man on Edisto Island. Frum what he said, his master was very mean. Pa real name wus Adam Collins but he took his master' name; he wus de coachman. Pa did supin one day en his master whipped him. De next day which wus

Monday, pa carry him 'bout four miles frum home in de woods an' give him de same 'mount of lickin' he wus given on Sunday. He tied him to a tree an' unhitched de horse so it couldn't git tie-up an' kill e self. Pa den gone to de landin' an' cetch a boat dat wus comin' to Charleston wood fa'm products. He (was) permitted by his master to go to town on errands, which helped him to go on de boat without bein' question'. W'en he got here he gone on de water-front an' ax for a job on a ship so he could git to de North. He got de job an' sail' wood de ship. Dey search de island up an' down for him wood houndogs en w'en it wus t'ought he wus drowned, 'cause dey track him to de river, did dey give up. One of his master' friend gone to New York en went in a store w'ere pas wus employed as a clerk. he reconize' pa is easy is pa reconize' him. He gone back home an' tell pa master who know den dat pa wusn't comin' back an' before he died he sign' papers dat pa wus free. Pa' ma wus dead an' he come down to bury her by de permission of his master' son who had promised no ha'm would come to him, but dey wus' fixin' plans to keep him, so he went to de Work House an' ax to be sold 'cause any slave could sell e self if e could git to de Work House. But it wus on record down dere so dey couldn't sell 'im an' told him his master' people couldn't hold him a slave.

People den use to do de same t'ings dey do now. Some marry an' some live together jus' like now. One t'ing, no minister nebber say in readin' de matrimony "let no man put asounder" 'cause a couple would be married tonight an' tomorrow one would be taken away en be sold. All slaves wus married in dere master house, in de livin' room where slaves an' dere missus an' mossa wus to witness de ceremony. Brides use to wear some of de finest dress an' if dey could afford it, have de best kind of furniture. Your master nor your missus objected to good t'ings.

I'll always 'member Clory, de washer. She wus very high-tempered. She was a mulatto with beautiful hair she could sit on; Clory didn't take foolishness frum anybody. One day our missus gone in de laundry an' find fault with de clothes. Clory didn't do a t'ing but pick her up bodily an' throw 'er out de door. Dey had to sen' fur a doctor 'cause she pregnant an' less than two hours de baby wus bo'n. Afta dat she begged to be sold fur she didn't [want] to kill missus, but our master ain't nebber want to sell his slaves. But dat didn't keep Clory frum gittin' a brutal whippin'. Dey whip' 'er until dere wusn't a white spot on her body. Dat wus de worst I ebber see a human bein' got such a beatin'. I t'ought she wus goin' to die, but she got well an' didn't get any better but meaner until our master decide it wus bes' to rent her out. She willingly agree' since she wusn't 'round missus. She hated an' detest' both of them an' all de fambly.

W'en any slave wus whipped all de other slaves wus made to watch. I see women hung frum de ceilin' of buildin's an' whipped with only supin tied 'round her lower part of de body, until w'en dey wus taken down, dere wusn't breath in de body. I had some terribly bad experiences.

Yankees use to come t'rough de streets, especially de Big Market, huntin' those who want to go to de "free country" as dey call' it. Men an' women wus always missin' an' nobody could give 'count of dere disappearance. De men wus train' up North fur sojus.

De white race is so brazen. Dey come here an' run de Indians frum dere own lan', but dey couldn't make dem slaves 'cause dey wouldn't stan' for it. Indians use to git up in trees an' shoot dem with poison arrow. W'en dey couldn't make dem slaves den dey gone to Africa an' bring dere black brother an' sister. Dey say 'mong themselves, "we gwine mix dem up en make ourselves king. Dats d only way we'd git even with de Indians."

All time, night an' day, you could hear men an' women screamin' to de tip of dere voices as either ma, pa, sister, or brother wus take without any warnin' an' sell. Some time mother who had only one chile wus separated fur life. People wus always dyin' frum a broken heart.

One night a couple married an' de next mornin' de boss sell de wife. De gal ma got in in de street an' cursed de white woman fur all she could find. She said: "dat damn white, pale-face bastard sell my daughter who jus' married las' night," an' other t'ings. The white man tresten' her to call de police if she didn't stop, but de collud woman said: "hit me or call de police. I redder die dan to stan' dis any longer." De police took her to de Work House by de white woman orders an' what became of 'er, I never hear.

W'en de war began we wus taken to Aiken, South Ca'lina were we stay' until de Yankees come t'rough. We could see balls sailin' t'rough de air w'en Sherman wus comin'. Bumbs hit trees in our yard. W'en de freedom gun wus fired, I wus on my 'nees scrubbin'. Dey tell me I wus free but I didn't b'lieve it.

In de days of slavory woman wus jus' given time 'nough to deliver dere babies. Dey deliver de baby 'bout eight in de mornin' an' twelve had to be back to work.

I wus a member of Emmanuel African Methodist Episcopal Church for 67 years. Big Zion, across de street wus my church before den an' before Old Bethel w'en I lived on de other end of town.

Sence Lincoln shook hands with his assasin who at de same time shoot him, frum dat day I stop shakin' hands, even in de church, an' you know how long dat wus. I don't b'lieve in kissin' neider fur all carry dere meannesses. De Master wus betrayed by one of his bosom frien' with a kiss.

SOURCE: Interview with (Mrs.) Susan Hamilton, 17 Henrietta Street, who claims to be 101 years of age. She has never been sick for twenty years and walks as though just 40. She was hired out by her master for seven dollars a month which had to be given her master.

Susan Hamlin and Susan "Hamilton" are obviously one and the same; yet by the end of Ladson's interview, we are wondering if we have been listening to the same person! Kindness of the masters? We hear no tales about old Mr. Fuller; only vivid recollections of whippings so harsh "dere wusn't a white spot on her body." To Butler, Hamlin had mentioned only cruelties that she had heard about secondhand ("you don't know whether it was lie or not"); to Ladson, she recounts firsthand experiences ("I see women hung from de ceilin' of buildin's an' whipped with only supin tied 'round her lower part of de body.").

Discussions of happy family relations? Instead of tales about shoes in the winter, we hear of Hamlin's father, whipped so severely, he rebels and flees. We hear of family separations, not downplayed with a "you know how dey carry on," but with all the bitterness of mothers whose children had been taken "without any warnin'." We hear of a couple married one night, then callously separated and sold the next day. In the Butler account, slave babies are fed well, treated

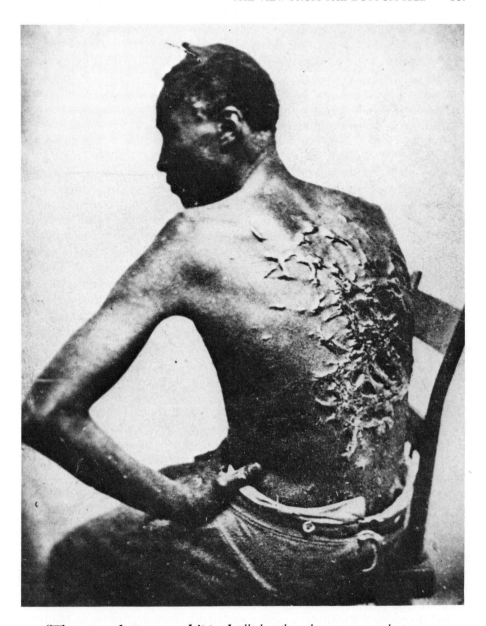

"W'en any slave wus whipped all de other slaves was made to watch. . . . I had some terribly bad experiences." The scars from whippings on this slave's back were recorded in 1863 by an unknown photographer traveling with the Union army.

nicely; in the Ladson account, the recollection is of mothers who were given only a few hours away from the fields in order to deliver their children.

Benevolent white paternalism? This time Hamlin's tale of three races draws a different moral. The white race is "brazen," running the Indians off their land. With a touch of admiration, she notes that the Indians "wouldn't stan' for" being made slaves. White motives are seen not as religious but exploitative and vengeful: "Dey say 'mong themselves, 'we gwine mix dem up and make ourselves king. Dats de only way we'll git even with de Indians.'" The difference between the two interviews, both in tone and substance, is astonishing.

How do we account for this? Nowhere in the South Carolina narratives is the race of Augustus Ladson mentioned, but internal evidence would indicate he is black. In a culture where blacks usually addressed whites respectfully with a "Sir," "Ma'am," or "Boss," it seems doubtful that Susan Hamlin would address a white man as "son." ("I'm a hund'ed an' one years old now, son.") Furthermore, the content of the interview is just too consistently anti-white. Hamlin would never have remarked, "De white race is so brazen," if Ladson had been white, especially given the reticence demonstrated in her interview with Butler. Nor would she have been so specific about the angry mother's curses ("damn white, pale-face bastard"). It would be difficult to conceive of a more strikingly dramatic demonstration of how an interviewer can affect the responses of a subject.

Freedom and Deception

The slave narrative collection, then, is not the direct, unfiltered perspective that it first appears to be. In fact, interviews like the ones with Susan Hamlin seem to suggest that the search for the "true" freedmen's perspective is bound to end in failure and frustration. We have seen, first, that information from planters and other white sources must be treated with extreme skepticism; second, that northern white sources deserve similar caution. Finally, it appears that even the oral testimony of African Americans themselves must be questioned, given the circumstances under which much of it was gathered. It is as if a detective discovered that all the clues he had carefully pieced together were hopelessly biased, leading his investigation down the wrong path.

The seriousness of the problem should not be underestimated. It is fundamental. We can try to ease out of the dilemma by noting that there are doubtless differing degrees of bias—that some accounts, relatively speaking, are likely to be less deceptive than others. It can be argued, for instance, that Susan Hamlin's interview with Ladson is a more accurate portrayal of her feelings than the interview with Butler. In large measure that is probably true. But does that mean we must reject all of the Butler interview? Presumably, Susan Hamlin's master did give her a pair of shoes one cold winter day. Are we to assume, because of Ladson's interview, that the young child felt no gratitude or obligation to "kind old" Mr. Fuller? Or that the old woman did not look back on those years with some ambivalence? For all her life, both slave and free, Susan Hamlin lived in a world where she was required to "feel" one set of emotions when dealing with some people and a different set when dealing with other people. Can we rest completely confident in concluding that the emotions she expressed to Ladson were her "real" feelings, while the ones to Jessie Butler were her "false" feelings? How can we possibly arrive at an objective conclusion about "real" feelings in any social situation where such severe strains existed?

Yet putting the question in this light offers at least a partial way out of the dilemma. If so many clues in the investigation are hopelessly "biased"—that is, distorted by the social situation in which they are set—then the very per-vasiveness of the distortion may serve as a key to understanding the situation. The evidence in the case is warped precisely because it accurately reflects a distortion in the society itself. The elements of racism and slavery determined a culture where personal relations were necessarily grounded in mistrust and deception; where slaves could survive only if they remained acutely conscious of the need to adapt their feelings to the situation. The distortion in the evidence, in other words, speaks eloquently of the hurt inflicted in a society where personal behavior routinely operated under an economy of deception.

The deception was mutual—practiced by both sides upon each other. Susan Hamlin was adapting the story of her past to the needs of the moment, at the same time that Jessie Butler was letting Hamlin believe her to be a welfare agent. White masters painted lurid stories of Yankee devils with horns while slaves, playing roles they were expected to play, rolled their eyes in fear until they had the chance to run straight for Union lines. The deceptions fed upon each other and were compounded, becoming an inextricable part of daily life.

It would be tempting, given our awareness of this situation, simply to turn previous historical interpretations on their heads. Where William Dunning and his disciples took most of their primary sources at face value and thus saw only cheerful, childlike Sambos, an enlightened history would read the documents upside down, so to speak, stripping away the camouflage to reveal slaves who, quite rationally, went about the daily business of "puttin' on ole massa." And of course we have already seen abundant evidence that slaves did use calculated deception in order to protect themselves.

But simply to replace one set of feelings with another is to ignore the intricate and tense relationships between them. It drastically underestimates the strains that arose out of an economy of deception. The longer and more consistently masters and slaves were compelled to live false and inauthentic lives, the easier it must have been for them to mislead themselves as well as others. Where white and black people alike engaged in daily dissimulation, some of the deception was inevitably directed inward, simply to preserve the fiction of living in a tolerable, normally functioning society.

When the war came, shattering that fiction, whites and blacks were exposed in concrete and vivid ways to the deception that had been so much a part of their lives. For white slaveholders, the revelation usually came when Union troops entered a region and slaves deserted the plantations in droves. Especially demoralizing was the flight of slaves whom planters had believed most loyal. "He was about my age and I had always treated him more as a companion than a slave," noted one planter, of the first defector from his ranks. Mary Chesnut, the woman near Fort Sumter who had tried to penetrate the blank expressions of her slaves, discovered how impossible the task had been. "Jonathan, whom we trusted, betrayed us," she lamented, while "Claiborne, that black rascal who was suspected by all the world," faithfully protected the plantation.

Many slaveholders, when faced with the truth, refused to recognize the role that deception had played in their lives, so deceiving themselves further. "The poor negroes don't do us any harm except when they are put up to it," concluded one Georgia woman. A Richmond newspaper editor demanded that a slave who had denounced Jefferson Davis "be whipped every day until he confesses what white man put these notions in his head." Yet the war brought painful insight to others. "We were all laboring under a delusion," confessed one South Carolina planter. "I believed that these people were content, happy, and attached to their masters. But events and reflection have caused me to change these opinions. . . . If they were content, happy and attached to their masters, why did they desert him in the moment of his need and flock to an enemy, whom they did not know . . . ?"

For slaves, the news of emancipation brought an entirely different reaction, but still one conditioned by the old habits. We have already seen how one old Georgia slave couple remained impassive as Sherman's troops passed through, until finally the wife could restrain herself no longer. Even the servant who eloquently shouted the praises of freedom at a secluded brook instinctively remembered the need for caution: "I got sort o' scared, afeared somebody hear me, an' I takes another good look. . . ." Although emancipation promised a society founded upon equal treatment and open relations, slaves could not help wondering whether the new order would fully replace the old. That would occur only if the freedmen could forge relationships that were no longer based on the customs of deception nor rooted in the central fiction of slavery—that blacks were morally and intellectually incapable of assuming a place in free society.

No historian has more vividly conveyed the freedmen's attempts to achieve that goal than Leon Litwack. Having recognized the substantial value of the slave narrative collection, Litwack drew upon its evidence as well as the standard range of primary sources to recreate the freedmen's perspectives as they sought the real meaning of their new freedom. Certainly that meaning was by no means evident once the first excitement of liberation had passed. James Lucas, a slave of Jefferson Davis, recalled the freedmen's confusion: "Dey all had diffe'nt ways o' thinkin' 'bout it. Mos'ly though dey was jus' lak me, dey didn' know jus' zackly what it meant. It was jus' somp'n dat de white folks an' slaves all de time talk 'bout. Dat's all. Folks dat ain' never been free don' rightly know de *feel* of bein' free. Dey don' know de meanin' of it." But former slaves were not long in taking their first steps toward defining freedom. On the surface, many of these seemed small. But however limited, they served to distance the freedmen in significant ways from the old habits of bondage.

The taking of new names was one such step. As slaves, African Americans often had no surname, or took the name of their master. Equally demeaning, given names were often casually assigned by their owners. Cicero, Pompey, and other Latin or Biblical names were commonly bestowed in jest. And whether or not slaves had a surname, they were always addressed familiarly, by their given names. Such customs were part of the symbolic language of deception, promoting the illusion that black people were helpless and even laughable dependents of the planter's family.

Thus many freedmen took for themselves new names, severing the symbolic tie with their old masters. "A heap of people say they was going to name their selves over," recalled one freedman. "They named their selves big names. . . . Some of the names was Abraham an' some called their selves Lincum. Any big name 'ceptin' their master's name. It was the fashion." Even former slaves who remained loyal to their masters recognized the significance of the change. "When you'all had de power you was good to me," an older freedman told his master, "an I'll protect you now. No niggers nor Yankees shall touch you. If you want anything, call for Sambo. I mean, call for Mr. Samuel— that's my name now."

Just as freedmen took new names to symbolize their new status, so also many husbands and wives reaffirmed their marriages in formal ceremonies. Under slavery, many marriages and family ties had been ignored through the convenient fiction that Africans were morally inferior. Black affections, the planters argued, were dominated by impulse and the physical desires of the moment. Such self-deception eased many a master's conscience when slave families were separated and sold. Similarly, many planters married slaves only informally, with a few words sufficing to join the couple. "Don't mean nuthin' less you say, "What God done jined, cain't no man pull asunder," noted one Virginia freedman. "But dey never would say dat. Jus' say, 'Now you married.'" For obvious reasons of human dignity, black couples moved to solemnize their marriage vows. There were practical reasons for an official ceremony too: it might qualify families for military pensions, or the division of lands that were widely rumored to be coming.

Equally symbolic for most former slaves was the freedom to travel where they wished. As we have seen, historian William Dunning recognized this fact, but interpreted it from the viewpoint of his southern white sources as "aimless but happy" wandering. Black accounts make abundantly clear how travel helped freedmen to rid themselves of the role they had been forced to play during their bondage. Richard Edwards, a preacher in Florida, explicitly described the symbolic nature of such a move:

> You ain't, none o' you, gwinter feel rale free till you shakes de dus' ob de Old Plantashun offen yore feet an' goes ter a new place whey you kin live out o' sight o' de gret house. So long ez de shadder ob de gret house falls acrost you, you ain't gwine ter feel lak no free man, an' you ain't gwine ter feel lak no free 'oman. You mus' all move—you mus' move clar away from de ole places what you knows, ter de new places what you don't know, whey you kin raise up yore head douten no fear o' Marse Dis ur Marse Tudder.

And so, in the spring and summer of 1865, southern roads were filled with black people, hiving off "like bees trying to find a setting place," as one ex-slave recalled. Generally freedmen preferred to remain within the general locale of family and friends, merely leaving one plantation in search of work at another. But a sizable minority traveled farther, to settle in cities, move west, or try their fortunes at new occupations.

Many ex-slaves traveled in order to reunite families separated through previous sales. Freedmen "had a passion, not so much for wandering, as for getting together," a Freedman's Bureau agent observed; "and every mother's son among them seemed to be in search of his mother; every mother in search of her children." Often, relatives had only scanty information; in other cases, so much time had passed that kin could hardly recognize each other, especially when young children had grown up separated from their parents.

A change of name or location, the formalization of marriages, reunion with relatives—all these acts demonstrated that freedmen wanted no part of the old constraints and deceptions of slavery. But as much as these acts defined black freedom, larger issues remained. How much would emancipation broaden economic avenues open to African Americans? Would freedom provide an opportunity to rise on the social ladder? The freedmen looked anxiously for signs of significant changes.

Perhaps the most commonly perceived avenue to success was through education. Slavery had been rationalized, in part, through the fiction that blacks were incapable of profiting from an education. The myth of intellectual inferiority stood side by side with that of moral inferiority. Especially in areas where masters had energetically prevented slaves from acquiring skills in reading, writing, and arithmetic, the freedmen's hunger for learning was intense. When northerners occupied the Carolina Sea Islands during the war, Yankee plantation superintendents found that the most effective way to force unwilling laborers to work was to threaten to take away their schoolbooks. "The Negroes . . . will do anything for us, if we will only teach them," noted one missionary stationed on the islands.

After the war, when the Freedman's Bureau sent hundreds of northern school teachers into the South, black students flocked enthusiastically to the makeshift schoolhouses. Often, classes could be held only at night, but the freedmen were willing. "We work all day, but we'll come to you in the evening for learning," Georgia freedmen told their teacher, "and we want you to make us learn; we're dull, but we want you to beat it into us!" Some white plantation owners discovered that if they wished to keep their field hands, they would have to provide a schoolhouse and teacher.

Important as education was, the freedmen were preoccupied even more with their relation to the lands they had worked for so many years. The vast majority of slaves were field hands. The agricultural life was the one they had grown up with, and as freedmen, they wanted the chance to own and cultivate their own property. Independent ownership would lay to rest the lie that black people were incapable of managing their own affairs; but without land, the idea of freedom would be just another deception. "Gib us our own land and we take care of ourselves; but widout land, de ole massas can hire us or starve us, as dey please," noted one freedman.

"My Lord, ma'am, what a great thing larning is!" *a freedman exclaimed to a white teacher. Many white people were surprised by the intensity of the ex-slaves' desire for an education. To say that the freedmen were "anxious to learn" was not strong enough, one Virginia school official noted; "they are crazy to learn." This woodcut, drawn in 1867, depicts several youngsters studying their lessons along a village street.*

In the heady enthusiasm at the close of the war, many ex-slaves were convinced that the Union would divide up confiscated Confederate plantations. Each family, so the persistent rumor went, would receive forty acres and a mule. "This was no slight error, no trifling idea," reported one white observer, "but a fixed and earnest conviction as strong as any belief a man can ever have." Slaves had worked their masters' lands for so long without significant compensation, it seemed only fair that recompense should finally be made. Further, the liberated had more than hopes to rely on. Ever since southern planters had fled from invading Union troops, some black workers had been allowed to cultivate the abandoned fields.

The largest of such occupied regions was the Sea Islands along the Carolina coast, where young Sam Mitchell had first heard the northern guns. As early as March 1863, freedmen were purchasing confiscated lands from the government. Then in January 1865, after General William Sherman completed his devastating march to the sea, he extended the area which was open to confiscation. In his

Special Field Order No. 15, Sherman decreed that a long strip of abandoned lands, stretching from Charleston on the north to Jacksonville on the south, would be reserved for the freedmen. The lands would be subdivided into forty-acre tracts, which could be rented for a nominal fee. After three years, the freedmen had the option to purchase the land outright.

Sherman's order was essentially a tactical maneuver, designed to deal with the overwhelming problem of refugees in his path. But black workers widely perceived this order and other promises by enthusiastic northerners as a foretaste of Reconstruction policy. Consequently, when white planters returned to their plantations, they often found blacks who no longer bowed obsequiously and tipped their hats. Thomas Pinckney of South Carolina, having called his former slaves together, asked them if they would continue to work for him. "O yes, we gwi wuk! we gwi wuk all right . . ." came the angry response. "We gwi wuk fuh ourse'ves. We ain' gwi wuk fuh no white man." Where would they go to work, Pinckney asked—seeing as they had no land? "We ain't gwine nowhar," they replied defiantly. "We gwi wuk right here on de lan' whar we wuz bo'n an' whar belongs tuh us."

Despite the defiance, Pinckney prevailed, as did the vast majority of southern planters. Redistribution of southern lands was an idea strongly supported only by more radical northerners. Thaddeus Stevens introduced a confiscation bill in Congress, but it was swamped by debate and never passed. President Johnson, whose conciliatory policies pleased southern planters, determined to settle the issue as quickly as possible. He summoned General O. O. Howard, head of the Freedman's Bureau, and instructed Howard to reach a solution "mutually satisfactory" to both blacks and planters. Howard, though sympathetic to the freedmen, could not mistake the true meaning of the President's order.

Regretfully, the general returned to the Sea Islands in October and assembled a group of freedmen on Edisto Island. The audience, suspecting the bad news, was restless and unruly. Howard tried vainly to speak, and made "no progress" until a woman in the crowd began singing, "Nobody knows the trouble I've seen." The crowd joined, then was silent while Howard told them they must give up their lands. Bitter cries of "No! No!" came from the audience. "Why, General Howard, why do you take away our lands?" called one burly man. "You take them from us who have always been true, always true to the Government! You give them to our all-time enemies! That is not right!"

Reluctantly, and sometimes only after forcible resistance, African Americans lost the lands to returning planters. Whatever else freedom might mean, it was not to signify compensation for previous labor. In the years to come Reconstruction would offer freedom of another sort, through the political process. By the beginning of 1866, the radicals in Congress had charted a plan that gave African Americans basic civil rights and political power. Yet even that avenue of opportunity was quickly sealed off. In the decades that followed the first thunder of emancipation, black people would look back on their early experiences almost as if they were part of another, vanished world. The traditions of racial oppression and the daily deceptions that went with them were too strong to be thoroughly overturned by the war. It is perhaps significant that the term "freedman" uses a past participle. Despite the best efforts of black citizens, American society found it impossible to define them without reference to the fictions of their past.

"I was right smart bit by de freedom bug for awhile," Charlie Davenport of Mississippi recalled.

> It sounded pow'ful nice to be tol: "You don't have to chop cotton no more. You can th'ow dat hoe down an' go fishin' whensoever de notion strikes you. An' you can roam 'roun' at night an' court gals jus' as you please. Aint no marster gwine a-say to you, 'Charlie, you's got to be back when de clock strikes nine.'" I was fool 'nough to b'lieve all dat kin' o' stuff.

Both perceptions—the first flush of the "freedom bug" as well as Davenport's later disillusionment—accurately reflect the black experience. Freedom had come to a nation of four million slaves, and it changed their lives in deep and important ways. But for many years after the war put an end to human bondage, the freedmen still had to settle for the view from the bottom rail.

ADDITIONAL READING

Leon Litwack's superb *Been In the Storm So Long: the Aftermath of Slavery* (New York, 1979) serves as an excellent starting point for background on the freedmen's experience after the war. Litwack supplies an interpretive framework that moves the book from topic to topic, but the material is kaleidoscopic in detail, story after story tumbling onto the page and threatening to overwhelm the book's structure. The result is a rich and vibrant portrait. A general history of Reconstruction that emphasizes black contributions is Eric Foner, *Reconstruction: America's Unfinished Revolution* (New York, 1988). African-American experiences can also be traced in state histories, where more attention is given to grass-roots effects of the new freedom. Joel Williamson, *After Slavery* (Chapel Hill, 1965), covers South Carolina; Peter Kolchin, *First Freedom* (Westport, Conn., 1972), treats Alabama; William C. Harris, *Day of the Carpetbagger* (Baton Rouge, 1979), examines Mississippi. Herbert Gutman, *The Black Family in Slavery and Freedom, 1750-1925* (New York, 1976), covers the Reconstruction era as well. Willie Lee Rose, *Rehearsal for Reconstruction: the Port Royal Experiment* (Indianapolis, 1964), tells the story of the Union occupation of the Carolina Sea Islands, where the North first attempted to forge a coherent Reconstruction policy. For information about the Freedmen's Bureau, see William O. McFeely's biography of its leader, General O. O. Howard, *Yankee Stepfather* (New Haven, 1968) and Donald Nieman, *To Set the Law in Motion: The Freedmen's Bureau and the Legal Rights of Blacks* (Millwood, N.Y., 1979).

Contemporary white accounts of the slaves' first days of freedom abound. Litwack, cited above, has a helpful bibliography. Among those sources we found useful: Rupert S. Holland, ed., *Letters and Diary of Laura M. Towne* (Cambridge, Mass., 1912); Charles Nordhoff, *The Freedmen of South-Carolina* (New York, 1863); C. Vann Woodward, ed., *Mary Chesnut's Civil War* (New Haven, Conn. 1981); and Arney R. Childs, ed., *The Private Journal of Henry William Ravenel, 1859-1887* (Columbia, S.C., 1947). James L. Roark, *Masters without Slaves* (New York, 1977), provides an account of the postwar perceptions of the planter class. In addition to the slave narrative collection discussed below, other sources for the freedmen's perspective include Octavia V. Rogers Albert, *The House of Bondage* (New York, 1891); Orland K. Armstrong, *Old Massa's People* (Indianapolis, Ind., 1931); M. F. Armstrong and Helen W. Ludlow, *Hampton and Its Students* (New York, 1875); and Laura Haviland, *A Woman's Life Work* (Cincinnati, Ohio, 1881). In addition, a massive project is in progress at the University of Maryland, under the direction of historian Ira Berlin, to publish *A Documentary History of Emancipation, 1861-1867* (New York, 1982-) based on government records by and about freedmen, now housed in the National Archives. This material should provide an unsurpassed wealth of contemporary primary sources, including testimony before Freedman's Bureau courts, petitions, letters, and military files. Three volumes have been issued thus far.

The Federal Writers' Project interviews are found in George P. Rawick, *The American Slave: A Composite Autobiography,* 19 vols. & supplements (Westport, Conn., 1972-). The collection invites use in many ways. Intriguing material is available on the relations between African Americans and Indians, for example, especially in the Oklahoma narratives. Because one interviewer often submitted many interviews, readers may wish to analyze strengths and weaknesses of particular interviewers. The Library of Congress, under Benjamin Botkin's direction, began such an analysis; its records can be examined at the National Archives, catalogued under Correspondence Pertaining to Ex-Slave Studies, Records of the Federal Writers' Project, Records Group 69, Works Progress Administration.

Further information on the slave narratives may be found in Norman Yetman, "The Background of the Slave Narrative Collection," *American Quarterly,* 19 (Fall 1967), 534-553. John Blassingame has an excellent discussion of oral history and its pitfalls in "Using the Testimony of Ex-slaves: Approaches and Problems," *Journal of Southern History,* XLI (November 1975), 473-492, available in expanded form in his introduction to *Slave Testimony* (Baton Rouge, La., 1977). Paul D. Escott, *Slavery Remembered: A Record of Twentieth-Century Slave Narratives* (Chapel Hill, N.C. 1979), provides interested researchers with helpful data. Escott's quantitative analysis of the narratives includes the percentage of interviews with field hands, house servants, and artisans; the occupations they took up as freedmen, and the destinations of those who migrated. The race of many of the project's interviewers is also included [although not always accurately—see Jerrold Hirsch's review of the book in *Reviews in American History,* VIII (September 1980), 312-317].

Finally, those who wish to do their own oral history should consult Stephen A. Richardson et al., *Interviewing: Its Forms and Functions* (New York, 1965), for an introduction to that art. More specific, nuts-and-bolts information can be found in James Hoopes's excellent *Oral History: An Introduction for Students* (Chapel Hill, N.C., 1979). See also Cullom Davis et al., *Oral History: From Tape to Type* (Chicago, Ill., 1977) and Ramon I. Harris, et al., *The Practice of Oral History* (Glen Rock, N.J., 1975). The latter book has erred in at least one pertinent fact, however: in the area of libel, it blithely assures would-be publishers of oral history that truth is always a sufficient defense. Truth may suffice when it comes to history, but not invariably so in the courts of law.

CHAPTER EIGHT

The Mirror with a Memory

At the same time that freedmen all across the South were struggling to become an integral part of a free and equal society, millions of other Americans in the urbanized North and Midwest were searching for a place in the new industrial society of the late nineteenth century. In the forty years following the Civil War over 24 million people flooded into American cities. While the population of the agricultural hinterlands doubled during these years, urban population increased by more than 700 percent. Sixteen cities could boast of populations over 50,000 in 1860; by 1910 over a hundred could make that claim. New York City alone grew by 2 million.

Urban areas changed not only in size but also in ethnic composition. While many of the new city-dwellers had migrated from rural America, large numbers came from abroad. Where most antebellum cities had been relatively homogeneous, with perhaps an enclave of Irish or German immigrants, the metropolises at the turn of the century were home to large groups of southern as well as northern European immigrants. Again, New York City provides a striking example. By 1900 it included the largest Jewish population of any city in the world, as many Irish as Dublin, and more Italians and Poles than any city outside Rome or Warsaw. Enclaves of Bohemians, Slavs, Lithuanians, Chinese, Scandinavians, and other nationalities added to the ethnic mix.

The quality of living in cities changed too. As manufacturing and commerce crowded into city centers, the wealthy and middle classes fled along newly constructed trolley and rail lines to the quiet of developing suburbs. Enterprising realtors either subdivided or replaced the mansions of the rich with tenements where a maximum number of people could be packed into a minimum of space. Crude sanitation transformed streets into breeding grounds for typhus, scarlet fever, cholera, and other epidemic diseases. Few tenement rooms had outside windows; less than ten percent of all buildings had either indoor plumbing or running water.

The story of the urban poor and their struggle against the slum's cruel waste of human beings is well-known today—as it was even at the turn of the century—because of a generation of social workers and muckrakers who studied the slums firsthand and wrote indignantly about what they found. Not only did they collect statistics to document their general observations, they compiled numerous case studies that described the collective experience in compelling stories about individuals. The pioneer in this endeavor was Jacob Riis. Few books have had as much impact on social policy as his landmark study of New York's Lower East Side, *How the Other Half Lives*. It was at once a shocking revelation of the conditions of slum life and a call for reform. As urban historian Sam Bass Warner concluded, "Before Riis there was no broad understanding of urban poverty that could lead to political action."

Riis had come to know firsthand the degrading conditions of urban life. In 1870 at the age of twenty-one he joined the growing tide of emigrants who fled the poverty of the Scandinavian countryside for the opportunities offered in America. Riis was no starving peasant; in fact his father was a respected schoolmaster and his family comfortably middle class. But Jacob had rejected professional training in order to work with his hands as a carpenter. Unable to find a job in his home town, and rejected by his local sweetheart, he set out for the United States.

Once there, Riis retraced the pattern that millions of immigrants before him had followed. For three years he wandered in search of the promise of the new land. He built workers' shacks near Pittsburgh, trapped muskrats in upstate New York, sold furniture, did odd jobs, and occasionally returned to carpentry. In none of those lines of work did he find either satisfaction or success. At one point poverty reduced him to begging for crumbs outside New York City restaurants and spending nights in a police lodging house. His health failed. He lingered near death until the Danish consul in Philadelphia took him in. At times his situation grew so desperate and his frustration so intense that he contemplated suicide.

Riis, however, had a talent for talking and the hard sell. Eventually he landed a job with a news association in New York and turned his talent to reporting. The direction of his career was determined in 1877 when he became the police reporter for the *New York Tribune*. He was well suited for the job, his earlier wanderings having made him all too familiar with the seamy side of urban life. The police beat took him to headquarters near "The Bend," what Riis referred to as the "foul core of New York's slums." Every day he observed the symptoms of urban poverty. Over the course of a year police dragnets collected some forty thousand indigents who were carted off to the workhouses and asylums. And at night Riis shadowed the police to catch a view of the neighborhood "off its guard." He began to visit immigrants in their homes, where he observed their continual struggle to preserve a measure of decency in an environment of chronic unemployment, disease, crime, and cultural dislocation.

As a *Tribune* reporter, Riis published exposé after exposé on wretched slum conditions. In so doing he followed the journalistic style of the day. Most reporters had adopted the strategies found in Charles Dickens's novels, personifying social issues through the use of graphic detail and telling vignettes. Such concrete examples involved readers most directly with the squalor of city slums.

The issue of female exploitation in sweat shops became the story of an old woman Riis discovered paralyzed by a stroke on her own doorstep. The plight of working children, who had neither education nor more than passing familiarity with the English language, was dramatized by the story of Pietro, the young Italian boy who struggled to keep awake at night school. Touching stories brought home the struggles of the poor better than general statistics. They also sold newspapers.

But Riis found the newspaper life frustrating. His stories may have been vivid, but apparently not vivid enough to shock anyone to action. New York authorities had made token efforts at slum clearance, but by 1890 the conditions about which Riis had protested had grown steadily worse. The Lower East Side had a greater population density than any neighborhood in the world—335,000 people to one square mile of the tenth ward and as many as one person per square foot in the worst places.[1]

In frustration Riis left the *Tribune* to write *How the Other Half Lives*. He wanted to make a case for reform that even the most callous officials could not dismiss, and a full-length book was more likely to accomplish what a series of daily articles could not. The new format enabled Riis to weave his individual stories into a broader indictment of urban blight. It allowed him to buttress concrete stories with collections of statistics. And perhaps most important, it inspired him to provide documentary proof of a new sort—proof so vivid and dramatic that even the most compelling literary vignettes seemed weak by comparison. Riis sought to document urban conditions with the swiftly developing techniques of photography.

From the experience of other urban reformers, Riis had learned that photographs could be powerful weapons to arouse popular indignation. In a book on London slums, *Street Life in London* (1877), authors John Thompson and Adolph Smith had decided to include photographs because, as they explained, "The unquestionable accuracy of this testimony will enable us to present true types of the London poor and shield us from accusations of either underrating or exaggerating individual peculiarities of appearance." For Riis that was a compelling argument. If photographs accompanied *How the Other Half Lives*, no corrupt politician could dismiss its arguments as opinionated word-paintings spawned by the imagination of an overheated reformer. Photography indisputably showed life as it really was.

"Reality" and Photographic Evidence

From the moment in 1839 when the French pioneer of photography Louis Jacques Daguerre announced his discovery of a process to fix images permanently on a copper plate, observers repeatedly remarked on the camera's

---

[1] Those readers conjuring up a picture of slum-dwellers standing like sardines row on row, each with his or her own square foot, must remember that tenement space reached upward through several stories. The statistic refers to square footage of ground area, not square footage of actual floor space.

capacity to record reality. More than anything else, the seeming objectivity of the new medium caught the popular imagination. The camera captured only those objects that appeared before the lens, nothing more, nothing less. So faithful was the camera that people often commented that the photographic image recorded the original with an exactness "equal to nature itself." Indeed, one of the attractions of the new medium was that it could accurately reveal the look of other parts of the United States and the world. Nineteenth-century Americans were hungry for visual images of unseen places. Few had ever seen the trans-Mississippi West, much less Europe or the South Pacific. Almost no one had access to pictures that satisfied curiosity about exotic lands or people. As a result, crowds flocked to the galleries of a painter like Alfred Bierstadt when he displayed his grand landscapes of the Rocky Mountains. Even Bierstadt's paintings, though, were colored by his romantic vision of the West, just as all artists' work reflected their own personal styles and quirks.

The new photography seemed to have no style—that was its promise. It recorded only what was before the camera. Reproductions were so faithful to the original that close observation with a magnifying glass often revealed details which had been invisible to the naked eye. The American writer and physician Oliver Wendell Holmes summed up the popular conception when he noted that the camera was even more than "the mirror of reality"; it was "the mirror with a memory."

Certainly, there was no denying the camera's unprecedented ability to record detail in a way that paintings could not. Yet, from today's vantage point, it is easier to see the limits of the camera's seeming objectivity. Any modern amateur photographer who is familiar with the features of a single-lens reflex camera will appreciate immediately how deceptive the camera's claim to mirroring reality can be. Merely to sight through the viewfinder reminds us that every photograph creates its own frame, including some objects and excluding others. The problem of selection of evidence, which is at the heart of the historian's task, remains of paramount importance in photography.

The situation becomes even more complex when we begin to make simple photographic adjustments once the frame has been selected. Far from recording every detail within the lens's reach, we immediately begin excluding details by turning the focusing ring. In choosing a closeup, background details blur; if aiming for a distant subject, it is the foreground that becomes hazy. The technical constraints of the camera thus limit what can be recorded on the negative's frame. If we close down the aperture of the camera's lens (the circular hole that allows light to pass through the lens), the camera's depth of field is increased, bringing into focus a larger area within the path of the lens. On the other hand, photographers who wish to concentrate the viewer's attention on a central subject will eliminate cluttering detail by decreasing their depth of field.

Of course, it may be argued with a good deal of justice that many if not all of these distorting capabilities of the camera are irrelevant when discussing the work of Jacob Riis. Riis worked with neither a sophisticated single-lens reflex camera nor a particularly extensive knowledge of photographic principles. His primary goals were not to record scenes aesthetically and artistically, but to

The cumbersome technology of early photography restricted its use largely to professionals. Field photographers had to take along darkrooms in which they prepared the photographic plates which went into a heavy box camera. The van pictured here was used by a photographer during the Crimean War. Matthew Brady and his assistants employed similar large wagons during the Civil War. They soon discovered, much to their chagrin, that such rolling darkrooms made uncomfortably obvious targets for enemy artillery and sharpshooters.

capture the subject matter before his camera. The niceties of art would have to wait.

Indeed, when Riis began his photographic efforts he quickly discovered that the primitive nature of photography precluded too much attention to aesthetic details, especially in his line of work. In the 1880s, taking pictures was no simple matter. Each step in the photographic process presented formidable obstacles. First, would-be photographers had to learn to prepare a light-sensitive chemical mixture and spread it evenly on the glass plates that served as photographic negatives. For work in the field, they had to take along a portable darkroom, usually a clumsy tent perched on a tripod. Here the negatives were taken from the cumbersome box camera and developed in chemical baths. Additional solutions were necessary to transfer the image from the plate to the final paper print. Such a process taxed the ingenuity and dedication of even the most avid practitioners.

Fortunately, advances in chemistry, optics, and photographic technology had given birth to a new generation of equipment, the "detective camera." To ease the burden of field photographers and make possible the "candid" shot, a number of companies had introduced small cameras about the size of a cigar box. Some carried as many as twelve photographic plates that could be used before the camera required reloading. Wily photographers took to disguising cameras as doctors' satchels, briefcases, books, revolvers, and vest buttons— hence the nickname "detective camera."

George Eastman simplified the process even further with his "Kodak" camera. Introduced to the public in 1888, the Kodak was more than an improved detective camera; it was the first model that replaced glass negatives with a photographic emulsion coated on paper rolls. For twenty-five dollars an aspiring photographer could acquire the camera loaded with 100 shots. Once the film had been exposed, the owner simply returned the camera to the dealer, who removed the spool in a darkroom and shipped it to Eastman's factory for processing. For an additional ten dollars, the dealer would reload the camera with new film. So successfully had Eastman reduced the burden on amateur photographers that his ads could boast, "You press the button, we do the rest."

But even the advances in photographic technology did not eliminate Riis's difficulties. When he began his photographic work, he knew nothing of photography. To help him he enlisted the assistance of several friends in the Health Department who also happened to be amateur photographers. Together they set out to catch their subjects unaware. That meant skulking around "the Bend" in the dead of night, with the normal photographic paraphernalia increased by bulky and primitive flash equipment. For a flash to work, a highly combustible powder was spread along a pan. The pan was then held up and Riis exploded a blank cartridge from a revolver to ignite the powder. This photographic entourage sneaking about town after hours made a remarkable sight, as the *New York Sun* reported:

> Somnolent policemen on the street, denizens of the dives in their dens, tramps and bummers in their so-called lodgings, and all the people of the wild and wonderful variety of New York night life have in turn marvelled at and been frightened by the phenomenon. What they saw was three or four figures in the gloom, a ghostly tripod, some weird and uncanny movements, the blinding flash, and then they heard the patter of retreating footsteps and their mysterious visitors were gone before they could collect their scattered thoughts.

The results from using such finicky equipment were not always predictable. Sometimes the noise would awaken unsuspecting subjects and create a disturbance. On one particularly unfortunate occasion Riis had gone to "Blind Man's Alley" to photograph five sightless men and women living in a cramped attic room. Soon after his eyes cleared from the blinding flash, he saw flames climbing up the rags covering the walls. Fear gripped him as he envisioned the blaze sweeping through twelve rickety flights of stairs between the attic and

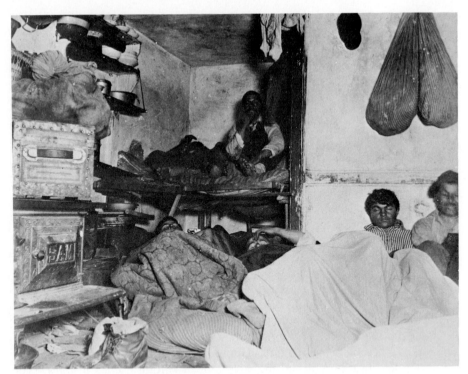

Lodgers in a crowded Bayard Street tenement—*"Five Cents a Spot."*

safety. Fighting the impulse to flee, he beat out the flames with his coat, then rushed to the street seeking help. The first policeman who heard his story burst out laughing. "Why, don't you know that's the Dirty Spoon?" he responded. "It caught fire six times last winter, but it wouldn't burn. The dirt was so thick on the walls it smothered the fire."

Under such precarious circumstances, it might be argued that Riis's photography more closely mirrored reality precisely because it was artless, and that what it lacked in aesthetics it gained in documentary detail. Above, for example, we see a picture taken on one of Riis's night expeditions, of lodgers at one of the crowded "five cents a spot" tenements. The room itself, Riis informs us in *How the Other Half Lives*, is "not thirteen feet either way," in which "slept twelve men and women, two or three in bunks in a sort of alcove, the rest on the floor." The sleepy faces and supine bodies reflect the candid nature of the picture; indeed, Riis had followed a policeman who was raiding the room in order to drive the lodgers into the street. The glare of the flash, casting distinct shadows, reveals all of the crowding, dirt, and disorder. This is no aesthetic triumph, perhaps, but it does reveal a wealth of details that prove most useful to the curious historian.

We notice, for instance, that the stove in the foreground is a traditional wood-burning model, with its fuel supply stacked underneath. Space in the

In the original edition *of* How the Other Half Lives, *seventeen of
the photographs appeared as blurry halftones and nineteen as artists'
engravings, such as this rendering of the "Five Cents a Spot"
photograph. A comparison of the two pictures quickly demonstrates
how much more graphically the photograph presented Riis's
concerns. Riis continued to take photographs for other books
he published, although it was not until well into the twentieth century
that mass reproduction techniques could begin to do justice to
them.*

apartment is so crowded that footlockers and bundles have been piled directly
on top of the stove. (Have they been moved from their daytime resting places on
the bunks? Or do these people carry their possessions onto the street during the
day?) The dishes and kitchen utensils are piled high on shelves next to the stove.
The bedding is well-used, dirty, and makeshift. Such details are nowhere near as
faithfully recorded in the line drawing originally published in *How the Other
Half Lives.*

Yet no matter how "artless" the photographs of Jacob Riis may be in terms of
their aesthetic control of the medium, to assume they are bias-free seriously
underestimates their interpretive content. However primitive a photographer
Riis may have been, he still influenced the messages he presented through an

appropriate selection of details. Even the most artless photographers make such interpretive choices in every snapshot they take.

Let us look, for example, at the most artless photographic observations of all: the ordinary family scrapbook found in most American homes. When George Eastman marketed his convenient pocket camera, he clearly recognized the wide appeal of his product. At long last the ordinary class of people, and not just the rich and well-born, would create for themselves a permanent documentary record of their doings. "A collection of these pictures may be made to furnish a pictorial history of life as it is lived by the owner," proclaimed one Kodak advertisement.

But while family albums provide a wide-ranging "pictorial history," they are still shaped by conventions every bit as stylized as the romantic conventions of Bierstadt or other artists with equally distinct styles. The albums are very much ceremonial history—birthdays, anniversaries, vacations. Life within their covers is a succession of proud achievements, celebrations, and uncommon moments. A father's retirement party may be covered, but probably not his routine day at the office. We see the sights at Disney World, not the long waits at the airport. Arguments, rivalries, and the tedium of the commonplace are missing.

If the artless photographers of family life unconsciously shape the records they leave behind, then we must expect those who self-consciously use photography to be even more interpretive with their materials. And this is not a matter of knowing the tricks of the trade about depth of field or shutter speed, but simply the fact that intelligent people will wish to convey a coherent message with their photographs. Civil War photographer Matthew Brady wanted to capture the horrific carnage of the war. To achieve it, he did not hesitate to drag dead bodies to a scene in order to further the composition or the effect he desired.

But to point out such literal examples of the photographer's influence almost destroys the point by caricaturing it. One need not rearrange compositions in order to be photographing for interpretive, even propagandistic purposes. The western land surveys of the 1860s and 1870s, for instance, discovered that their photographs had social uses that extended beyond the narrowly geologic. Though the surveys' missions were ostensibly scientific, they required the financial patronage of Congress. As rival surveys vied for an adequate share of the limited funds, they discovered that photographs of scenic wonders produced the desired results back East. The survey headed by F. V. Hayden in 1871 documented the tall tales, which had long circulated, rumoring natural wonders in northwest Wyoming. The photographs of spectacular vistas, towering waterfalls, Mammoth Hot Springs, Old Faithful, and the geyser basins justified survey appropriations, as well as helped persuade Congress to establish Yellowstone as the first national park safe from commercial development.

A later generation of government photographers, who worked during the Great Depression of the 1930s, also viewed photographs as vehicles to convey their social messages. Few photographers were more dedicated to the ideal of documentary realism than Walker Evans, Dorothea Lange, Ben Shahn, and others who photographed tenant farmers and sharecroppers for the Farm

"A collection of these pictures may be made to furnish a pictorial history of life as it is lived by the owner." Following the dictum in the Kodak advertisement, these two men pose happily, one holding one of the new Kodak cameras, while a friend uses another to record the scene. Like so many family album "candids," this shot follows the tradition of ceremonial history—proud achievements, celebrations, and uncommon moments. Dressed in their best, these are tourists from Pennsylvania enjoying spring on the White House lawn in April 1889.

"Photographing in High Places," *Teton Range, 1872; by William Henry Jackson. A member of John Wesley Powell's earlier expedition down the Colorado River recalled the effort involved in handling the unwieldy photographic equipment: "The camera in its strong box was a heavy load to carry up the rocks, but it was nothing to the chemical and plate-holder box, which in turn was feather weight compared to the imitation hand organ which served as a darkroom." Mishaps along the way were not uncommon. "The silver bath had gotten out of order," reported one of Powell's party, "and the horse bearing the camera fell off a cliff and landed on top of the camera . . . with a result that need not be described."*

Security Administration. Yet these photographers too brought to their work preconceived notions about how poverty should look. As critic Susan Sontag has noted, they "would take dozens of frontal pictures of one of their sharecropper subjects until satisfied that they had gotten just the right look on film—the precise expression on the subject's face that supported their own notions about poverty, light, dignity, texture, exploitation, and geometry. In deciding how a picture should look . . . photographers are always imposing standards on their subjects."

Thus any series of photographs—including those Jacob Riis took for his books—must be analyzed in the same way a written narrative is. We can appreciate the full import of the photographs only by establishing their historical context. What messages are they meant to convey? What are the premises—stated or unstated—which underlie the presentation of photographs? Ironically, in order to evaluate the messages in the Riis photographs, we must supplement our knowledge of his perspectives on the city by turning to his writings.

Images of the Other Half

Jacob Riis was an immigrant to America, like so many of those he wrote about. He had tasted poverty and hardship. Yet in a curious way, Riis the social reformer might best be understood as a tourist of the slums, wandering from tenement to tenement, camera in hand. To classify him as such is to suggest that despite his immigrant background, he maintained a distance between himself and his urban subjects.

In part, that distance can be explained by Riis's own background as an immigrant. Despite his tribulations, he came from a middle-class family, which made it easy to choose journalism as a career. As a boy, in fact, Riis had helped his family prepare copy for a weekly newspaper. Once established in a job commensurate with his training, Riis found it easy to accomplish the goal of so many immigrants—to rise to middle-class dignity and prosperity and to become, in the most respectable sense, not a newcomer but an American.

Furthermore, because Riis emigrated from Denmark, his northern European background made it more difficult for him to empathize with the immigrant cultures of southern and eastern Europe, increasingly the source of new immigrants in the 1880s and 1890s. Like many native-born Americans, Riis found most of their customs distasteful and doubted whether they could successfully learn the traditional American virtues. As Sam Warner remarked, Riis ascribed a "degree of opprobrium to each group directly proportional to the distance from Denmark. . . ."

Yet for all that, Riis retained a measure of sympathy and understanding for the poor. He did not work his way out of poverty only to find a quiet house far from the turmoil of the urban scene. He was unable to ignore the squalor that so evidently needed the attention of concerned Americans. Thus an ambivalence permeated Riis's writings. On the one hand he sympathized with the plight of the poor and recognized how much they were the victims of their slum environment. "In the tenements all the elements make for evil," he wrote. He struggled to maintain a distinction between the "vicious" classes of beggars, tramps, and thieves, and the working poor who made the slum their home because they had no other choice. On the other hand, Riis could not avoid using language that continuously dismissed whole classes of immigrants as inherently unable to adapt themselves to what he considered acceptable American behavior.

When he visited "Jewtown," for example, Riis scarcely commented on the strong bonds of faith and loyalty that held families and groups together in the face of all the debilitating aspects of slum life. Instead, he dwelt on the popular "Shylock" stereotype. "Money is their God," he wrote. "Life itself is of little value compared to even the leanest bank account." Upon the Irish, of course, he bestowed a talent for politics and drink. "His genius runs to public affairs rather than domestic life," said Riis of the Irish politician; "wherever he is mustered in force the saloon is the gorgeous center of political activity."

To southern and eastern Mediterranean people, Riis was least understanding. The "happy-go-lucky" Italians he observed were "content to live in a pig sty." Not only did they "come in at the bottom," but also they managed to stay there. They sought to reproduce the worst of life in Italy by flocking to slum tenements. When an Italian found better housing, "he soon reduced what he did find to his own level, if allowed to follow his natural bent." These affable and malleable souls "learned slowly, if at all." And then there was the passion for gambling and murder: "[The Italian's] soul is in the game from the moment the cards are on the table, and very frequently his knife is in it too before the game is ended." Such observations confirm our sense of Riis as a tourist in the slums, for he seemed only to have educated his prejudices without collecting objective information.

A second quality that strikes the reader of *How the Other Half Lives* is its tone of Christian moralism. Riis blamed the condition of the urban poor on the sins of individuals—greedy landlords, petty grafters, corrupt officials, the weak character of the poor, and popular indifference. Insensitive to the economic forces that had transformed cities, he never attempted a systematic analysis of urban classes and institutional structures. Instead, he appealed to moral regeneration as the means of overcoming evil, and approvingly cited the plea of a philanthropic tenement builder: "How are these men and women to understand the love of God you speak of, when they see only the greed of men?" In his own ominous warning to his fellow New Yorkers, Riis struck an almost apocalyptic note. "When another generation shall have doubled the census of our city," he warned, "and to the vast army of workers, held captive by poverty, the very name of home shall be a bitter mockery, what will the harvest be?" If conditions worsened, the violence of labor strikes during the 1870s and 1880s might seem quite tame in comparison.

Given those predispositions, how do we interpret Riis's photographs? Like the arrangers of family albums, his personal interests dictated the kind of photographs he included in his books. And as with the family albums, by being aware of these predispositions we can both understand Riis better by con-

Bohemian cigarmakers *at work in their tenement.*

sciously examining his photographic messages and at the same time transcend
the original intent of the pictures.

For example, Riis's Christian moralism led him to emphasize the need for
stable families as a key to ameliorating slum conditions. Many American Protestants in his audience thought of the home and family as a "haven" from the
bustle of the working world, as well as a nursery of piety and good morals.
Fathers could return at the end of the day to the warm, feminine environment in
which their children were carefully nurtured. Thus the picture we have already
examined of the "five cents a spot" lodgings takes on added significance in light
of these concerns. It is not simply the lack of cleanliness or space that would
make such an apartment appalling to many viewers, but the corrosive effect of
such conditions on family life. Yet this was a family dwelling, for Riis heard a
baby crying in the adjoining hall-room. How could a family preserve any
semblance of decency, Riis asked his readers, in a room occupied by twelve
single men and women?

Let us turn from that photograph to another, shown above, which is much
more obviously a family portrait. The middle-class Protestant viewer of Riis's day
would have found this picture shocking for the same reasons. The home was
supposed to be a haven away from the harsh workaday world, yet here the
factory has invaded the home. This is the small room of an immigrant Bohemian

Room in a tenement flat, *1910 (The Jacob A. Riis Collection, Museum of the City of New York).*

family, crowded with the tools and supplies needed to make a living. The business is apparently a family enterprise, since the husband, wife, and at least one child assist in the work. Though the young boy cannot keep his eyes off the camera, he continues to stretch tobacco leaves from the pile on his lap.

The room speaks of a rather single-minded focus on making a living. All the furnishings are used for cigarmaking, not for creature comforts or living after work. The only light comes from a small kerosene lamp and the indirect sunlight from two windows facing out on the wall of another building. Yet Riis had a stronger message for the picture to deliver. The text stresses the exploitation of Bohemians in New York, most of whom worked at cigarmaking in apartments owned by their employers, generally Polish Jewish immigrants.

The cigar trade dominated all aspects of life: "The rank smell that awaited us on the corner of the block follows us into the hallways, penetrates every nook and cranny of the house." This particular family, he noted, turned out 4,000 cigars a week, for which it was paid fifteen dollars. Out of that amount the landlord-employer deducted $11.75 in rent for three small rooms, two of which had no windows for light or air. The father was so tied to his workbench that in six years he had learned no English and, therefore, made no attempt to assimilate into American life.

It is interesting to contrast the portrait of the Bohemian family with a different family portrait, this one taken by another reforming photographer, but still often published in reprints of *How the Other Half Lives*.² Unlike the photograph of the cigarmakers' lodgings, this is a more formal family portrait. Very much aware of the camera's presence, everyone is looking directly at the lens. Perhaps the photographer could gain consent to intrude on their privacy only by agreeing to do a formal photograph. The children have been scrubbed and dressed in what appear to be their good clothes—the oldest son in his shirt and tie, his sister in a taffeta dress, and a younger girl in a frock. Unlike the "five cents a spot" lodging, where dishes were stacked one upon the other, here the family china is proudly displayed in the cabinet. Perhaps it was a valued possession carefully guarded on the journey from Europe.

Other details in the picture suggest that this family enjoyed a more pleasant environment than seen in the previous photos. Moving from left to right, we notice first a gas stove, a relatively modern improvement in an age when coal and wood were still widely used for heating and cooking. Perhaps these people had found a room in a once-elegant home divided by the realtor into a multiple dwelling. Certain details suggest that may be the case. Few tenements would have gas, much less built-in cupboards or the finished moldings around doors and windows. The window between the kitchen-bedroom and closet-bedroom indicates that the room may have once looked out on open space.

By contrast, the picture communicates a sense of crowding. This hardly seems an accident. Had the photographer wished to take only a family portrait, she could have clustered her subjects in the center of her lens. Instead, she placed them around the room, so that the camera would catch all the details of their domestic circumstance. We see not just a family, but the conditions of their lives in an area far too small for their needs. Each space and almost all the furnishings are used for more than one purpose. The wash tub just before the window and washboard behind it indicate that the kitchen doubles as laundry room—and the tub was probably used for baths as well. The bed serves during the day as a sofa. To gain a measure of privacy the parents have crowded their bed into a closet stuffed with family possessions. Seven people seem to share a room perhaps no more than 250 square feet in total. The children appear to range in age from one to twelve. If the mother is again pregnant as the picture hints, that means every two years another person enters that cramped space.

This portrait, then, does not conform to the typical stereotype we would expect to find of urban immigrant slum dwellers. In the first place, many immigrants came to America without families. Of those, a majority were young men who hoped to stay just long enough to accumulate a small savings with which to improve their family fortunes upon returning to Europe. On the other hand, immigrant families tended to be much larger than those of middle-class

---

² The photographer is Jessie Tarbox Beals, and the picture was taken in 1910. Although not included in the original edition of *How the Other Half Lives*, it is among the photographs in the Riis collection held by the Museum of the City of New York.

native-born Americans. Rather than evoking a sympathetic response among an American audience, the picture might, instead, reinforce the widespread fear that prolific breeding among foreign elements threatened white Protestant domination of American society.

What then does the modern viewer derive from this family portrait? Over all, it seems to say that immigrants, like other Americans, prized family life. The father perches at the center almost literally holding his family together, though with a rather tenuous grip. The son with his tie appears to embody the family's hopes for a better future. His mother securely holds the baby in her arms. Each element, in fact, emphasizes the virtues of the domestic family as it was traditionally conceived in America. The picture, while sending a mixed message, conveys less a sense of terrible slum conditions than a sense of the middle-class aspirations among those forced to live in inadequate housing.

Does the fact that this picture is posed make it less useful as historical evidence? Not at all. Even when people perform for the camera, they communicate information about themselves. There is no hiding the difficulty of making a decent life for seven people in a small space. Nor can the viewer ignore the sense of pride of person and place, no matter how limited the resources. What remains uncertain, however, is what message the photographer meant to convey. The scene could serve equally well to arouse nativist prejudice or to extol the strength of family ties in the immigrant community. Both were concerns that Riis addressed in his writing and photographs.

Concern over the breakdown of family life drew Riis to children. They are among his most frequently photographed subjects. He shared the Victorian

Street arabs *in sleeping quarters (The Jacob A. Riis Collection, Museum of the City of New York).*

notion of childhood innocence and, therefore, understood that nothing could be more disturbing to his middle-class audience than scenes of homeless children, youth gangs, and "street arabs" sleeping in alleys, gutters, and empty stairways. At first glance, the three "street arabs" on page 194 appear as if they might even be dead. A closer look suggests helpless innocence—children alone and unprotected as they sleep. Their ragged clothes and bare feet advertise poverty and the absence of parents to care for them. In each other, though, they seem to have extracted a small measure of warmth, belonging, and comfort. It would be almost impossible for any caring person to view the picture without empathy for its subjects and anger at a society that cares so little for its innocent creatures.

Riis hints at his sympathies through the location of the camera. He did not stand over the boys to shoot the picture from above. That angle would suggest visually the superiority of the photographer to his subjects. From ground level, however, observer and subject are on the same plane. We look at the boys, not

Hell's kitchen boys—"*Showing Their Tricks*" (*The Jacob A. Riis Collection, Museum of the City of New York*).

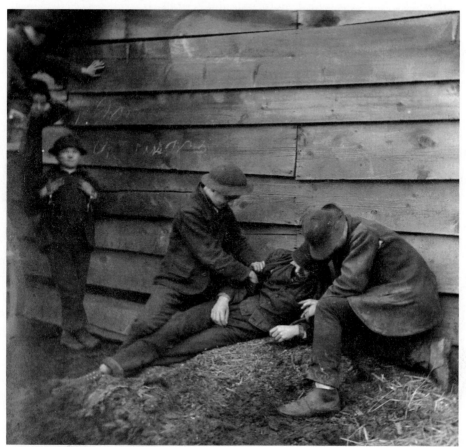

down on them. And should we dismiss as accidental his inclusion of the prisonlike bars over the small window? From another angle Riis could have eliminated that poignant symbol from his frame.

Certainly, we know that Riis feared that all too soon those "innocents" would become the members of slum gangs, operating outside the law with brazen disregard for society or its values. In this second picture of lost innocence (on page 195) Riis persuaded some gang members to demonstrate how they "did the trick"—that is, robbed the pockets of a drunk lying in an alley. The mere fact that Riis had obviously arranged the content of the picture, indicating that some relationship existed between the photographer and his subjects, would have made the image even more shocking. These young men were clearly proud of their acts and so confident that they were beyond the reach of the law that they could show off for the camera. We see smiles and smug satisfaction on several faces. Other members gather around to enjoy the novelty of the situation. Riis's audience would have understood quite clearly that the slums as breeding grounds for crime drove the innocence out of childhood.

Space was scarce not only in the homes of the poor. Crowding extended into public places as well. Without parks or wide streets children were forced to play in filthy alleys and garbage heaps. Adults had no decent communal space in which to make contact with the community. The picture of a tenement yard (page 197) immediately reveals a scene of chaos and crowding. As in slum apartments, every open area had to serve more than one purpose. Women doing the wash and children playing appear to fall all over one another. The fire escape doubles as a balcony. Any readers with a small yard, separate laundry room or laundress, and nearby park surely thanked their good fortune not to be part of this confusion.

Once again, however, closer scrutiny may lead us to reconsider our initial impressions. This place seems alive with energy. We see that the women and children are all part of a community. They have given their common space, restricted as it may be, to shared activities. Everyone seems to have a place in the scheme of things. All that laundry symbolizes a community concern with cleanliness and decency. On the balcony some people have flower boxes to add a touch of color and freshness to the drab landscape. Our initial shock gives way to a more complex set of feelings. We come to respect the durability of spirit that allowed people to struggle for a small measure of comfort amid such harsh surroundings. The message which at first seemed obvious is not so clear after all.

In the picture of "Bottle Alley" (page 198), Riis has editorialized on the same theme with more telling effect. In this dingy slum, along the infamous Bend, we are still among tenements. Laundry again hangs from the balcony. A few isolated men look upon the camera as it takes in the scene. Their presence during the day suggests they are among the army of unemployed who sit aimlessly waiting for time to pass. They seem oblivious to the filth that surrounds them. We cannot help but feel that they are as degraded as the conditions in which they live. The dilapidated buildings and rickety stairs create an overall sense of decay; nothing in the picture relieves the image of poverty and disorder Riis wanted to capture. The message is all too clear.

Tenement-house yard *(The Jacob A. Riis Collection, Museum of the City of New York).*

As the case of Jacob Riis demonstrates, photography is hardly a simple "mirror of reality." The meanings behind each image must be unncovered through careful exploration and analysis. On the surface, certainly, photographs often provide the historian with a wealth of concrete detail. In that sense they do convey the reality of a situation with some objectivity. Yet Riis's relative inexperience with a camera did not long prevent him from learning how to frame

"Bottle Alley" *(The Jacob A. Riis Collection, Museum of the City of New York).*

the content to create a powerful image. The photographic details communicate a stirring case for social reform, full of subjective as well as objective intent. Riis did not simply want us to see the poor or the slums; he wanted us to see them as he saw them. His view was that of a partisan, not an unbiased observer.

In that sense the photographic "mirror" is silvered on both sides: catching the reflections of its user as well as its subjects. The prints which emerge from the twilight of the darkroom must be read by historians as they do all evidence—appreciating messages that may be simple and obvious or complex and elusive. Once these evidentiary limits are appreciated and accepted, one can recognize the rueful justice in Oliver Wendell Holmes's definition of a photograph: an illusion with the "appearance of reality that cheats the senses with its seeming truth."

ADDITIONAL READING

Given the importance this chapter has placed on photographic evidence, readers wishing to examine more visual evidence of how Jacob Riis's other halves lived should consult the Dover Publications edition of his book. It has a good introduction by Charles Madison, but, most important, includes 100 photographs and several reproductions of line illustrations included in the original version. Another edition of *How the Other Half Lives* (Cambridge, Mass., 1970) has an excellent introduction by urban historian Sam Bass Warner, but suffers because of the limited number of photos included. The complete archive of Riis photographs are available on michrofiche from the International Archives of Photography (New York, 1981). Peter B. Hales, *Silver Cities: Photography of Urban America, 1839-1915* (Philadelphia, 1984), has offered a persuasive interpretation of Riis's place in the tradition of urban photography and social reform. Hales makes clear how much Riis redirected both traditions—urban photography away from the celebration of an idealized urban order, social reform away from its ignorance of slum conditions and its sentimentalized view of the poor.

Riis's own account of his life is found in *The Making of an American*, Roy Lubove, ed. (New York, 1966). An interesting but dated biography exists in Louise Ware, *Jacob A. Riis, Police Reporter* (New York, 1938); see also the more recent study by Edith P. Mayer, *"Not Charity but Justice:" The Story of Jacob A. Riis* (New York, 1974). One of America's finest photographers and critics, Ansel Adams, has also done the preface to an important book on Riis, Alexander Alland, *Jacob Riis: Photographer and Citizen* (Millerton, N.Y., 1974).

Even for those whose photographic expertise is limited to a mastery of George Eastman's injunction ("You press the button . . "), a number of excellent books provide clear discussions of the photographic medium, its potentialities, and its limitations. Susan Sontag, *On Photography* (New York, 1977), provides many stimulating ideas, particularly in her first essay, "In Plato's Cave." All followers of photographic art owe a debt to Beaumont Newhall, *The History of Photography from 1839 to the Present Day* (New York, 1964). Besides his work as photo-historian and critic, Newhall helped to establish the photographic wing of the Museum of Modern Art. Also useful for background on the technical and aesthetic developments in photography is Robert Taft, *Photography and the American Scene* (New York, 1938; reissued in 1964). For views that contrast with Riis's scenes of New York, see the Museum of the City of New York's *Once Upon a City: New York from 1890 to 1910* (New York, 1958), which features images captured by the photographer Byron.

Many photographs of historic value are on file and readily available to the public in the Library of Congress Prints and Photographs Division and the National Archives Still Picture Branch. At quite reasonable prices, interested researchers may obtain their own 8 × 10″ glossy reproductions, printed from copy negatives made of the original photographs. Of the two institutions, the

Library of Congress is the easier for novices to use, although the staffs at both institutions are extremely helpful. Two books provide a sampling from their collections: from the Library of Congress, *Viewpoints* (Washington, D.C., 1975); from the National Archives, *The American Image* (New York, 1979). The latter volume contains an excellent introduction by Alan Trachtenberg, whose discussions of photographic images planted the seed for this essay. Both books provide ordering numbers for the photographs reproduced, so that interested readers may order their own prints.

Excellent discussions of immigration, urbanization, and industrialization abound; here we mention only a representative and useful sampling. Among the histories and novels of the immigration experience, few have the impact of Anzia Yezierska, *Breadgivers* (New York, 1925), recently reissued with a fine introduction by Alice Kessler Harris. Umberto Nelli, *Italians of Chicago* (New York, 1972), is worth reading as a corrective to Riis's stereotypes of Italians. To appreciate Riis's impact on other urban reformers we suggest Robert Hunter, *Poverty* (New York, 1904; reissued 1965). Two brief yet informed analyses of late nineteenth-century economic development are Stuart Bruchey, *The Growth of the American Economy* (New York, 1975), and Robert Heilbroner, *The Economic Transformation of America* (New York, 1977). For the concurrent transformation of cities, see Zane Miller, *The Urbanization of Modern America* (New York, 1973), and even more stimulating, Sam Bass Warner, *The Urban Wilderness* (New York, 1972). Nor should readers miss Ray Ginger's lively discussion of urban Chicago in *Altgeld's Illinois* (Chicago, Ill., 1958). The problems and challenges of technology are treated in Nathan Rosenberg, *Technology and American Growth* (White Plains, N.Y., 1972).

One significant pleasure in a field as untapped as photographic evidence comes from doing original research yourself. Michael Lesey, *Wisconsin Death Trip* (New York, 1973), opened up the possibilities, though not without disturbing other historians. The field remains largely unexplored. Almost all readers will have access to their own family albums, local and neighborhood collections, yearbooks, newspaper files, and other sources with which to do their own investigating.

CHAPTER NINE

USDA Government Inspected

All of our essays tell a story and this one is no exception. But our present tale, by its very nature, partakes in large measure of the epic and the symbolic. It is a political tale, compiled largely from the accounts of politicians and the journalists who write about politicians; which is to say, it possesses much of the charm and innocence of a good, robust fairy tale. As we shall shortly discover, there are logical reasons for such larger-than-life overtones, and they deserve serious scrutiny. But the story must come first: an exciting tale of a bold president, an earnest reformer, some evil political bosses, and a lot of pork and beef.

It begins ("once upon a time") with the president, Teddy Roosevelt, who turns out to be the hero of the tale. There was nothing ordinary about Teddy, including the fact he was ever president at all. People from the Roosevelts' social class disdained politics and would never encourage their sons to take it up as a profession. But then again Teddy was not like other members of his social class nor his fellow students at Harvard. Anything he did, he did with gusto, and if being the best meant being president, then Teddy would not stop short of the White House.

His path to success was not an easy one. As a child Teddy was sickly, asthmatic, and nearsighted. He spent long hours pummelling punching bags, swinging on parallel bars, doing pushups, and boxing in the ring to build a body as active as his mind. When he went west in the 1880s to take up ranching, he had to overcome his image as an effete eastern "dude." He soon amazed many a grizzly cowboy by riding the Dakota badlands in spring mud, blasts of summer heat, and driving winter storms. He fought with his fists and once rounded up a band of desperados at gunpoint.

Back East, when Teddy played tennis, he showed the same determination, his record being 91 games in a single day. When he led the Rough Riders through Cuba in 1898, he raised troop morale by walking the sentry line whistling cheerfully while his men crouched low to avoid the bullets flying overhead. As President he advised others to speak softly and carry a big stick,

TR, displaying characteristic gritted teeth and holding a
moderately big stick. When he spoke, Roosevelt chopped every word into
neat, staccato syllables, with a rhythm that bore no resemblance to the
ordinary cadences of the English language. "I always think of a man
biting tenpenny nails when I think of Roosevelt making a speech,"
remarked one acquaintance.

though he himself more often observed only the latter half of his maxim.
Teddy's favorite expressions, seldom spoken softly, were "Bully!" and "Dee-
lighted!"—uttered because he usually got his way.

By 1906 Teddy had the White House firmly in his grasp. Just two years
earlier he had engineered an impressive victory to become president in his own
right. He had behind him a record of achievements to which he would soon add
the Nobel Peace Prize for his role in bringing an end to the Russo-Japanese war.
But Teddy could never rest on his laurels. In February a storm broke that
challenged his skill as leader of both the nation and the Republican Party.

The thunder clap that shattered the calm was the publication of *The Jungle.*
The book told a lurid tale about Chicago's meatpacking industry. Its author,
Upton Sinclair, was not only a reformer but a socialist as well. Most Americans of
the day believed that socialists were subversives who held extreme and imprac-
tical opinions. Despite that skepticism, readers could not ignore the grisly
realities recounted in *The Jungle.* It related, in often revolting detail, the conditions under which the packers processed pork and beef, adulterated it, and
shipped it to millions of American consumers.

Breakfast sausage, Sinclair revealed, was more than a tasty blend of ground
meats and spices. "It was too dark in these storage spaces to see clearly," he
reported,

Hogs being scalded *preparatory to scraping at a Swift and Company plant, 1905. The packers boasted that they used every bit of the pig "except the squeal," and they were probably more than right, given some of the extraneous ingredients that went into the canned goods of the period. Although modern viewers may be taken aback at the unsanitary appearance of the plant, this photograph was a promotional shot illustrating some of the better conditions in packing facilities.*

but a man could run his hands over the piles of meat and swap off handfulls of dry dung of rats. These rats were nuisances, and the packers would put out poisoned bread for them; they would die; and then rats, bread, and meat would go in the hoppers together. This is no fairy story and no joke; the meat would be shoveled into carts, and the man who did the shoveling did not trouble to lift out a rat, even when he saw one.

Rats were but one tasty additive in the meat sent to dinner tables. Potted chicken contained no chicken at all, only beef suet, waste ends of veal, and tripe. Most shocking of all, Sinclair told of men in cooking rooms who fell into vats and, after being cooked for days, "all but the bones had gone out into the world as Durham's Pure Leaf Lard!"

In just one week a scandalized public had snapped up some 25,000 copies of *The Jungle*. Almost all of those readers missed the socialist message. Sinclair had hoped to draw their attention to "the conditions under which toilers get their bread." The public had responded instead to the disclosures about corrupt federal meat inspectors, unsanitary slaughterhouses, tubercular cattle, and the packers' unscrupulous business practices.

One of the most outraged readers was President Theodore Roosevelt. Few politicians have ever been as well-informed as TR, who devoured books at over 1,500 words per minute, published works of history, and corresponded regularly with leading business, academic, and public figures. Roosevelt recognized immediately that the public would expect government at some level—local, state, or federal—to clean up the meat industry. He invited Sinclair for a talk at the White House, and though he dismissed the writer's "pathetic belief" in socialism, he promised that "the specific evils you point out shall, if their existence be proved, and if I have the power, be eradicated."

Roosevelt kept his promise. With the help of allies in Congress, he quickly brought out a new bill, along with the proverbial big stick. Only four months later, on June 30, he signed into law a Meat Inspection Act that banned the packers from using any unhealthy dyes, chemical preservatives, or adulterants. The bill provided $3 million toward a new, tougher inspection system, where government inspectors could be on hand day or night to condemn animals unfit for human consumption. Senator Albert Beveridge of Indiana, Roosevelt's progressive ally in Congress, gave the president credit for the new bill. "It is chiefly to him that we owe the fact that we will get as excellent a bill as we will have," he told reporters. Once again, Americans could put canned meats and sausages on the dinner table and eat happily ever after. Or so it would seem.

The Symbols of Politics

The story you have just read is true—as far as it goes. If it has taken on a legendary, even mythic quality in the telling, that is understandable given the nature of the American political system. Politics is, after all, public business. And the tales of national politics almost inescapably take on epic proportions. In such situations, symbolic language serves to simplify highly complex realities. It makes them more comprehensible by substituting concrete and recognizable actors and objects in the place of complicated, though often banal, situations. In doing so, symbols and symbolic language serve as a means of communication between political leaders and their constituencies. Skillful politicians generally have the ability to cast their actions in dramatic terms that speak to deeply felt public concerns.

Jacksonian Democrats pioneered many of the modern uses of campaign imagery. They touted their candidate, "Old Hickory," as the symbolic embodiment of the American frontier tradition. In their hands Jackson became the

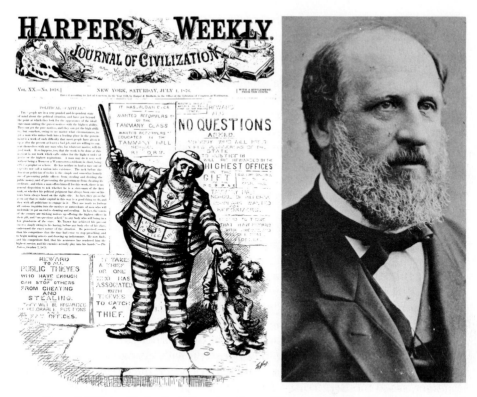

Boss William Tweed of New York, *in life and in art. During the latter half of the nineteenth century, cartoons played an important part in defining the symbols of political discourse. Occasionally the representations were readily recognizable in more than a symbolic sense. When Tweed fled the United States to escape a jail term, he was arrested in an out-of-the-way Spanish village. The Spanish constables, it turned out, had recognized him from this Thomas Nast cartoon. The symbolic aspect of the drawing escaped them, however; they thought they had apprehended a notorious child kidnapper.*

uncommon "Common Man." As president, he waged war against the Second Bank of the United States, fittingly symbolized by its enemies as the "Monster Bank." His Whig opposition had quickly grasped the use of such symbols; they nominated a popular general of their own, William Henry "Tippecanoe" Harrison. Their campaign rhetoric invoked the "log cabin" motif and other appropriate frontier images, even though Harrison came from a distinguished Virginia family and lived in an elegant house. Thus along with a two-party system of politics, Americans had developed a body of symbols to make complex political issues familiar and comprehensible to the voters.

Symbols as a mode of political discourse took on a new meaning with an art form that reached maturity in the late nineteenth century—the political cartoon.

Earlier cartoonists had portrayed Old Hickory's epic struggle with the Monster Bank, but they lacked the sophistication and draftsmanship achieved by Gilded Age caricaturists like Thomas Nast. Week after week, newspapers carried cartoons which established readily identifiable symbols. Nast conceived the elephant as a representation of the GOP (the Republicans, or Grand Old Party) and the donkey for the Democrats. To Nast and his fellow cartoonists we owe our image of the political boss, decked out in his gaudy suit that assumes a striking resemblance to a convict's striped outfit. So too, we have the Monopolist or greedy capitalist, his huge, bloated waistline taking on the aspect of a bag of silver dollars. A scraggly beard, overalls, and wild, crazed eyes denoted the Populist. In place of the Monster Bank stood the Trust, vividly pictured as a grasping octopus. Such cartoons by their very nature communicated the political symbolism of their day.

The cartoonists seldom had a better subject than Teddy Roosevelt with his gleaming, oversized front teeth, bull neck, pince-nez glasses, and, of course, his big stick. Caricaturists did not have to stretch the imagination much to cast Teddy larger than life; he specialized in that department long before he reached the White House. There was the gun-toting cowboy, the New York police commissioner in his long, black cape, and the Rough Rider charging up Tea Kettle Hill. Thus it was easy during the political battles of the Progressive Era to conceive of the actors in symbolic terms. In one corner stood the reformers: Roosevelt, a policeman, clubbing the opposition with his big stick; or Sinclair, wild-eyed like all political radicals. In the other corner, during the meat inspection fight, stood the Beef Trust—Armour, Swift, and the other packers bloated by their ill-gotten gains.

Yet as we have already noted, such symbolic representations inevitably oversimplify the political process to the point of distortion. As rendered by the cartoonist, shades of gray become black and white, and political conflict becomes a Manichaean struggle between good and evil. Even more subtly, distortion arises because symbols come to personalize complex situations and processes. Inanimate institutions (trusts, political machines, Congress) appear as animate objects (a grasping octopus, predatory tigers, braying donkeys) with human motives and designs.

Consequently we tend to visualize political events as being primarily the result of individuals' actions. The story of the meat inspection law is reduced to the tale of Roosevelt, Sinclair, and their enemies. The progression, as we saw, is quite simple: (1) Sinclair's revelations scandalize the president; (2) Roosevelt determines to reform the law; (3) with his usual energy, he overwhelms the opposition and saves the consumer. Such an explanation masks the crucial truth that the actors, whether individuals, groups, or institutions, often have mixed motives and multiple objectives. The outcome of a situation may bear slight resemblance to the original design of any of the participants. As a result, symbolic explanations do not adequately portray the labyrinth of negotiations and institutional hurdles that shape the political process, sometimes to the point of determining the outcome.

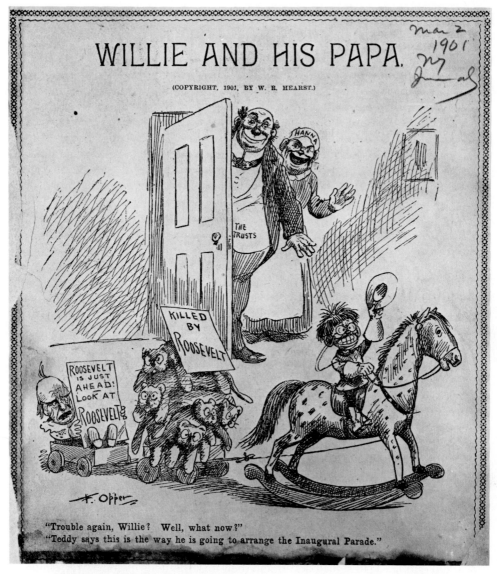

Caricaturists had a field day with Roosevelt's energetic and good-natured self-aggrandizement. In this cartoon by Frederick Opper, Vice-President-elect Roosevelt has rearranged the Inaugural Parade of 1901 so that President William McKinley is forced to bring up the rear. Teddy, of course, displays his teeth as well as a load of hunting trophies from western exploits, while the characteristic Trust figure looms in the background as "Willie's Papa."

Political historians, then, must handle symbolic language and explanations with caution. They cannot simply dismiss or debunk the symbolism, for it can, by influencing opinion, affect the political process. At the same time, historians cannot allow symbols to obscure the information necessary to narrate and explain political events. Granted that Roosevelt played the reformer in seeking to curb the packers' worst abuses; how successfully did he translate his intentions into an effective political instrument? Senator Beveridge, it is true, praised both the new law and the president's role in securing its passage. Yet other supporters of inspection reform did not share Beveridge's enthusiasm. "The American consumer and the ordinary American farmer have been left out of the question," Senator Knute Nelson complained shortly after the act passed. "I must say I feel disappointed. . . . When I go home I will go home like a licked dog."

In fact, prominent Republicans in the Senate led by Beveridge himself and Roosevelt's good friend, Henry Cabot Lodge of Massachusetts, had fought to defeat the law only a few days before Roosevelt signed it. They believed, as Nelson had argued, that the bill was intended "to placate the packers; next to placate the men who raise cattle; and, third to get a good market for the packers abroad." In short, many senators viewed the Meat Inspection Act as a victory for the packers and a defeat for reform. In that light Beveridge's praise has a symbolic meaning that our story thus far cannot explain.

So the historian must seek to set aside the mythic story and its symbols in order to reconstruct the institutional setting in which the real story unfolded. Individual actions must be made to square with motives. The outcome must be treated not as the inevitable triumph of good over evil but as just one of the many possible outcomes, and not necessarily the best at that. It is also the political historian's task to determine how the complex procedural tangle by which a bill becomes law limits the impact of individual actors no matter how lofty or base their motives.

The Tangle behind The Jungle

The mythic tale of the Meat Inspection Act begins with the publication of *The Jungle* in February 1906. That, so the story goes, was the catalytic event that sparked outrage against the packers and their unscrupulous methods. Yet, while *The Jungle* certainly provoked a public outcry, we may legitimately wonder whether a single dramatic story could by itself generate such widespread controversy. For better or worse, we have no Gallup polls from 1906 to measure public response to Sinclair's lurid exposé. But if we poke around in earlier stories about the meat industry, we find that *The Jungle* was merely a final straw, albeit a weighty one, in a long train of unfavorable publicity directed against the packers.

As early as the 1870s some European governments had begun to bar importation of what they had found were unhealthy American meat products. Over the years American exports declined as the Europeans tightened their restrictions. In 1891 the worried packers persuaded Congress to pass a federal meat inspection act in order to win back their foreign customers. The federal stamp would show that all meats in interstate and foreign sales had been subjected to antemortem (preslaughter) inspection. That measure succeeded until 1897, when the "embalmed meat" scandals once again tarnished the industry's reputation. The packers who supplied American soldiers fighting in Cuba had sold the army quantities of rotten and chemically adulterated meats. As the commander of the Rough Riders, Colonel Teddy Roosevelt had seen troops die from poisonous meats as well as Spanish bullets.

Roosevelt had not forgotten what he interpreted as treachery. In 1905 he found an opportunity to punish the packers. He ordered his attorney general to bring suit against the packing house trust under the Sherman Antitrust Act. The President was particularly offended by the packers' brazen disregard for public

Roosevelt with his Rough Riders. *TR's distrust of the packers reached as far back as the Spanish-American War, when packers had sold the American army quantities of rotten and chemically adulterated meats. Humorist Finley Peter Dunne took note of the situation—as well as the disorganized state of the regular army—when he had his fictional Irish bartender, Mr. Dooley, remark on the invincible American army of "injineers, miners, plumbers, an' lawn tinnis experts, numberin' in all four hundhred an' eighty thousand men," sent to do battle against the Spanish "ar-rmed with death-dealin' canned goods."*

safety. In building their industry into one of the nation's ten largest, Armour, Swift, and others boasted openly that they used every bit of the pig "except the squeal." Roosevelt was therefore beside himself when he heard that the judge had dismissed the government's suit on narrow procedural grounds. Suspicious that the packers had bribed the judge, he instructed his attorney general to release a confidential report revealing perjury in the beef trust case. Roosevelt scarcely needed to read *The Jungle* to believe that with their "public be damned" attitude the meat barons might be guilty of any manner of irresponsible behavior. *The Jungle* merely provided a new weapon for his ongoing fight.

Furthermore, the president recognized that the existing meat inspection law left much to be desired. Under it, Congress allocated money for an inspection force, but those appropriations were usually inadequate. Given the limited funds, most inspectors worked only during the day, leaving the packers free to commit their worst abuses at night. Even if inspectors did find diseased cattle at antemortem inspection, they had no power to have the animals destroyed. In fact, the packers made considerable profit selling those tainted animals to other plants not under federal supervision.

The federal government actually had almost no authority over the packers. Nothing under the system forced compliance with government standards. The inspectors could only threaten to leave the premises (and take their stamps with them) if the packers ignored their rulings. And though the law did prevent the industry from exporting meat without the federal stamp of approval, there was no similar provision to protect American consumers. Once a carcass passed the inspector, the government had no further power to impose sanitary standards anywhere in the plants. Roosevelt was aware of these deficiencies and eager to see them corrected.

The public, too, had grounds for suspicion even before *The Jungle* hit the bookstores. Sinclair's accusations had already been published in a popular socialist journal. In doing his research, Sinclair had received information from *The Lancet,* a distinguished British medical journal which had investigated earlier meat industry scandals. In 1905, *The Lancet* renewed its investigation of packing house filth which jeopardized both workers and consumers. At the same time, Samuel Merwyn, a well-known muckraking journalist, had written articles charging the packers with deliberately selling diseased meats.

To understand the impact of *The Jungle,* the historian must place it in the context of the popular muckraking style of journalism. Having discovered that the public possessed an almost insatiable appetite for sensational stories, leading journalists had set out to investigate corruption wherever they could find it. They had exposed the boss-dominated urban political machines, graft in government, greedy senators, Wall Street stock frauds, prostitution, quack doctors, patent medicines, women's inequality, child labor abuses, dangerous factory conditions, and a host of other social ills.

The muckrakers had much in common with the political cartoonists. Their villains made convenient, easily recognizable symbols. Evil could be personified as the Monster Trust, the Self-serving Politician, or the Avaricious Capitalist. Such an approach, while gratifying readers' love of lurid details, seldom got to the heart of social problems. In their indignant style muckrakers told Americans

"An Alphabet of Joyous Trusts" *was Frederick Opper's subject in a 1902 series of cartoons. Predictably "B" stood for the Beef Trusts. The same Trust figure is back (compare it with the one in Opper's Roosevelt cartoon), although here Opper plays on the monopolist's traditional control over market prices rather than on the unsanitary practices of the packing industry.*

what was wrong with their society, but not how the problems arose or what could be done. Somehow the exposure of the symptoms of evil was supposed to motivate reformers and an aroused public to cure the disease. In keeping with the popular style of muckraking, Sinclair had pointed an accusing finger at the packers without offering any specific suggestions for cleaning up the industry.

But just as *The Jungle* can be understood only within the context of the larger muckraking style, so too the Meat Inspection Act stood within the context of progressive reform. Despite Sinclair's lack of analysis, there were many Americans who had identified the sources of such corporate arrogance and who had prepared an agenda for politics. Theodore Roosevelt embodied much of the temperament of those progressive reformers. He shared their hostility to excessive concentrations of power in private hands, their approval of executive regulatory agencies, their faith in democratic forms of government, their humanitarian sensibilities, and their overriding confidence in the people's capacity to shape their future intelligently.

The progressives were actually a diverse group seeking to turn government into a weapon for social justice. They included rural reformers, good government and moral uplift advocates, economic regulators, antitrusters, and political liberals and conservatives. Roosevelt's conservative faith in traditional institutions might easily have led him to oppose the reformers, but he was never a diehard who railed against change in any form. "The only true conservative is the man who resolutely sets his face to the future," he once told a progressive supporter.

It was preoccupation with morality that brought the reform movement together and which attracted Roosevelt to progressivism. "His life, he felt, was a quest for the moral," wrote one biographer, John Blum. The reformers of the early twentieth century saw themselves rooting out evil, which more often than not they defined as "corporate arrogance." Thus, when Roosevelt set out to bust a trust, he did not always pick the biggest corporations. Rather, he picked the more notorious companies like the Northern Securities railroad combination, whose reputation for stock manipulation and rate gouging against farmers and small shippers had outraged popular opinion.

Corporate misconduct would not have spurred moral outrage had the misconduct not frequently resulted in tragedy. Seeking to maximize profits, a railroad might leave a road crossing unguarded; a water company might eliminate safeguards against typhoid fever. "Such incidents made the corporation look like a killer," wrote historian David Thelen. "These specific threats united all classes; anyone's child might be careless at a railroad crossing; and typhoid fever was no respecter of social origins."

The campaign for improved meat inspection had all the ingredients that aroused progressive ire. The packing industry fit Roosevelt's definition of a "bad" trust, since its disregard for even minimum health standards threatened all classes of Americans. The problem was particularly acute because the explosive growth of cities had created a huge demand for processed foods. Other food industries had better sanitary standards than the meat packers. Milk dealers, for example, regularly increased their profits by diluting their product, using chalk, plaster, and molasses to fortify the color and taste. A popular ditty of the day expressed the widespread skepticism with processed foods:

> Things are seldom what they seem;
> Skim milk masquerades as cream;
> Lard and soap we eat for cheese;
> Butter is but axle grease.

As a result, the public was prepared to think the worst of the meat industry.

Reeling from the impact of the Sinclair scandal, the packers agreed that improved federal inspection was the best way to restore public confidence in their products. J. Ogden Armour, head of the packing house that bore his name, defended the industry in a *Saturday Evening Post* article published soon after *The Jungle* appeared. Armour confidently invited the public to visit local packing plants "to see for yourself how the hated packer takes care of your meat supply." But he frankly admitted that "no packer can do an interstate or export business without government inspection." A serious decline in both domestic and foreign meat sales confirmed Armour's estimate of the need for improved inspection. Under the shadow Sinclair had cast, millions of Americans had altered their eating habits. Many foreign countries banned American meats. An industry representative confessed that the loss of public confidence was "hurting us very, very materially."

Thus the historical context surrounding the strident confrontation between reformers and packers reveals that the dramatic appearance of *The Jungle* was only the most conspicuous—and therefore the most obviously symbolic—event among a whole series of developments. All the necessary ingredients were on hand to produce legislation for more stringent federal inspection. And on hand was Theodore Roosevelt, the master political chef who would whip all the ingredients into a dish consumers could taste with confidence.

The Legislative Jungle

In order for public outrage to find a constructive outlet, politicians must translate that anger into law. And historians, for their part, must retrace the same path through the congressional maze in order to see what compromises and deals shaped the final bill. The legislative process is so constituted that willful minorities can sometimes thwart the will of determined majorities. Skillful manipulation of parliamentary rules, the committee system, the party caucus, nuisance amendments, filibuster and other legislative procedures—all these allow senators and representatives to protect special interests, promote their own causes, or delay the legislative process until support for a bill dissolves.

It is during the legislative phase that the historian discovers that support for improved inspection was not so universal as it seemed immediately after the publication of *The Jungle*. Meat inspection, like many reforms of the progressive era, raised issues more consequential than the sanitary standards of a single industry. Many of the larger issues affected the attitudes of the individual actors. President Roosevelt, for example, had on many occasions expressed his determination "to assert the sovereignty of the National Government by affirmative action" against unchecked corporate wealth and power. When added to the Hepburn bill allowing the government to set railroad shipping rates and the Pure Food and Drug Act, a new meat inspection bill would mark a major extension of public regulatory authority over private corporations.

Many people who favored improved inspection had given no indication that they would accept Roosevelt's sweeping definition of executive authority. The popular doctrine of *caveat emptor* (let the buyer beware) placed the burden for policing the marketplace on the consumer, not the government. As recently as 1895 in the case of *E. C. Knight,* the Supreme Court had severely restricted the possible area of government regulation over commerce. The packers, for their part, had given no indication that in agreeing to inspection reform they would accept a bill that in any way impinged on their control of the meat industry. So behind a mask of general agreement many actors entered the legislative process with conflicting motives and objectives. Much of that conflict would be expressed, not as disagreement on major legal or philosophical issues, but as seemingly petty bickering over procedural questions and minutiae of the proposed law.

From the outset Roosevelt indicated that he did not expect to achieve a satisfactory bill without a struggle. He knew that Sinclair's socialist writings would not persuade conservatives in Congress to support the tough bill he wanted. Nor had the government yet taken adequate steps to investigate its own misconduct. Immediately after the furor over *The Jungle,* Agriculture Secretary James Wilson had ordered an internal investigation of the Bureau of Animal Industry (BAI), which ran the inspection system. But Wilson and Roosevelt both suspected that the investigation would not "get to the bottom of this matter." Therefore, they asked Commissioner of Labor Charles P. Neill and New York attorney James Reynolds to undertake an independent investigation. Both men had been active in "good government" causes, though neither had any familiarity with the meat industry. Once they reported back, Roosevelt would have the evidence he needed to discredit either Sinclair as a sensationalist or the meatpackers as "malefactors of wealth."

Agriculture Department investigators confirmed the president's cynicism by whitewashing the BAI. They charged Sinclair with grossly exaggerating conditions in the plants, and treating "the worst . . . which could be found in any establishment as typical of the general conditions." Although they conceded that the system could stand reforming, they argued that Sinclair's accusations against federal inspectors were "willful and deliberate misrepresentations of fact."

Neill and Reynolds suggested that, if anything, Sinclair had understated the abominable conditions. Their official report rivaled his exposé in lurid details. Slime and manure covered the walks leading into the plants. The buildings lacked adequate ventilation and lighting. All the equipment—the conveyors, meat racks, cutting tables, and tubs—rotted under a blanket of filth and blood. Meat scraps for canning or sausages sat in piles on the grimy floors. Large portions of ground rope and pigskin went into the potted ham. Just as Sinclair had charged, foul conditions in the plant proved harmful to the health of both the workers and the consumers of the products they prepared.

The Neill-Reynolds report gave Roosevelt the big stick he liked to carry into any political fight. Should the packers prove recalcitrant he could threaten to make the secret report public. "It is absolutely necessary that we shall have legislation which will prevent the recurrence of these wrongs," he warned. In Senator Albert Beveridge of Indiana he found a willing ally, already at work on a new inspection bill. Beveridge, like Roosevelt, had caught the rising tide of progressive discontent over corporate misconduct. He sensed, too, that leadership on this issue would win him the popular acclaim he craved. Assisted by Agriculture Department experts, Beveridge had a bill drafted by the middle of May 1906. He urged Roosevelt to pave the way for Senate approval by releasing the damning Neill-Reynolds report.

For the moment, the politically adept Roosevelt heeded his own admonition to speak softly. Despite his customary bluster and pugnacious temperament, the president was actually a cautious man. An unnecessary confrontation with the powerful beef trust offended his sense of political expedience. Why waste his political ammunition if he could have his way without a fight? "The matter is of such far-reaching importance," he confided to Neill, "that it is out of the question to act hastily." Besides, having once been a rancher himself, he was reluctant to injure the livestock raisers, who bore no responsibility for the packers' scandalous behavior.

The packers had indicated that they would resist efforts to regulate their business. While Neill and Reynolds were in Chicago, packing house representatives had privately admitted that all was not well in their plants. One had begged Neill to withhold his report, promising in return that the packers would carry out any "reasonable, rational, and just recommendations" within thirty days. After that Neill and Reynolds would be free to reexamine the plants. When Neill refused, packer Louis Swift rushed off to confront the president. He found Roosevelt equally unsympathetic to any scheme involving voluntary compliance. The president assured Swift that he would settle for no less than legislation to "prevent the recurrence of these wrongs."

Beveridge was now ready with his bill. On May 21, he introduced it as a Senate amendment to the House Agricultural Appropriations bill. Why, one might well ask, did such a major reform make its debut in the form of a tacked-on amendment to a House bill? Here, we begin to see how the legislative process affects political outcomes. Beveridge recognized that effective inspection required adequate funds. Previous Congresses had undermined the system by refusing to vote the money needed. Many smaller plants had no inspection at all, and the largest ones had no inspectors at night. Beveridge, therefore, had proposed to shift the funding from the small amount allotted in the House Appropriations bill to a head fee charged for each animal inspected. As the industry grew, so would the funds for the Bureau of Animal Industry. But since the Constitution requires the House to initiate all money bills, Beveridge had to amend a House bill pending before the Senate rather than introduce a separate measure.

Beveridge included two other important changes. The old law did nothing to force the packers to indicate on the label of canned meats either the date on which they were processed or the actual contents. (Neill and Reynolds, for example, confirmed that the product called "potted chicken" contained no chicken at all.) The new law required dating and accurate labeling of the contents. It also invested the secretary of agriculture with broad authority to establish regulations for sanitary standards in the plants. Inspectors could then enforce those conditions as well as ensure the health of animals prior to and after slaughtering. If the owners challenged an inspector's ruling, the secretary had authority to make a "final and conclusive" ruling.

Yet this comprehensive bill, which Beveridge confidently introduced in May, was hardly the same bill Roosevelt signed on June 30, 1906. The small head fee had been replaced by an annual $3 million appropriation. The secretary of agriculture no longer had "final and conclusive" authority, for the federal courts were given the right to review his rulings. And the final measure said nothing about dating canned meats. In those discrepancies undoubtedly lies the source of Senator Nelson's dismay with the outcome of the meat inspection battle. What the historian must now explain is why the reformers who entered the fray holding most of the cards in their hands had given in on so many crucial points.

The battle actually began well enough for Roosevelt and Senate reformers. When the packers first tried to stall Beveridge with promises to make voluntary improvements, the senator threatened them with more damaging disclosures. To show he meant business, he had Neill brief lobbyists for livestock raisers and senators from western cattle states on the contents of his report. The packers had counted on them as allies in their fight against overly stringent federal regulation. But faced with the prospect of more adverse publicity, the meat and cattle interests beat a hot retreat. The Beveridge Amendment passed in the Senate without a single negative vote. Never known for his modesty, Beveridge touted his measure as "the most perfect inspection bill in the world. . . ."

Roosevelt hoped that the smashing Senate victory would lead to equally swift action by the House. The packers, however, had no intention of giving up without a fight. In the House, they had far more substantial support, particularly on the critical Agriculture Committee. Its chairman, James Wadsworth, a Republican from New York, was himself a cattle breeder. He regarded *The Jungle* as a "horrid, untruthful book" which, he claimed, had temporarily unhinged the president. To orchestrate the opposition, Wadsworth could count on the unflagging support of "Blond Billy" Lorimer, a senior committee member, a notorious grafter, and the Republican representative from Chicago's packing house district. The Beveridge bill aroused Lorimer like a red flag waved before a bull: "This bill will never be reported by my committee—not if little Willie can help it."

The packers had another, even more powerful, ally—time. Summer adjournment for Congress was only six weeks away. In the days before air conditioning, most public officials left Washington to escape the oppressive summer heat. While Congress vacationed, the public would most likely forget all about *The Jungle,* and as popular outrage dissipated, so would much of the pressure for reform. Only new and more damaging disclosures could rekindle the fervor that had swept Beveridge's amendment through the Senate.

As long as the Neill-Reynolds report remained secret, Roosevelt could save it as the ultimate disclosure to arouse the public. But by the time the Beveridge bill reached the House, the impatient Upton Sinclair had reneged on an earlier promise to Roosevelt that he would remain silent until his accusations had been proven. To goad the president, he published new charges embellished with even more lurid details. Finally, unable to contain his frustration, he leaked the details of the Neill-Reynolds report to *The New York Times,* and newspapers across the country had picked up the story. Having lost its shock value, Roosevelt's big stick appeared more like a little twig.

The packing-house forces sensed that the worst had passed, and set out to delay a vote on the Beveridge bill until they had forced the reformers to make three concessions they viewed as crucial to their interests. The requirement for stringent labeling, they argued, would force the industry to abandon many well-known brand names, and dates would prejudice consumers against perfectly healthy canned meats. Nor could the packers abide investing such broad discretionary powers in the secretary of agriculture. Such a step, one spokesperson claimed, would in effect "put our business in the hands of theorists, chemists, and sociologists, etc., and the management and control taken away from men who devoted their lives to the upbuilding and perfecting of this great American industry. . . ." In short, the packers argued that the secretary's arbitrary authority could deprive them of their property without the constitutional safeguard of due process in the courts.

Although likely to gain materially from more effective inspection, the packers called the head fees the most unfair aspect of the bill. Condemned animals, they claimed, already cost them millions each year. Now, the government proposed to saddle them with the additional burden of paying inspectors' salaries. That argument artfully concealed the packers' real opposition to a self-financing system. As many reformers quickly pointed out, the small head fee (no more than 3 to 5 cents per animal) could easily be passed on to consumers. But a more effective inspection service might force the packers to abandon some of their most profitable, if unhealthy, practices, such as rerouting cattle rejected at antemortem inspection to other parts of their plants. Furthermore, the old law allowed the packers to undermine the inspection system whenever it hurt profits, simply by arranging for their congressional allies, Lorimer and Wadsworth, to cut the BAI budget in the name of government economy. Forced to lay off inspectors, the BAI could not effectively supervise the plants. The Beveridge head-fee system eliminated that possibility.

When the packers waged their lobbying campaign, they shrewdly pitched their arguments to congressional interests as well as their own. Control over annual appropriations gives the House and its members much of their political clout. By making his system self-financing, Beveridge would have weakened the House's jealously guarded grip on federal purse strings, depriving some congressmen of potential influence. Other representatives who were traditional champions of private enterprise agreed that restrictions on labels and dates, combined with the secretary of agriculture's discretionary authority, constituted unwarranted government interference in private enterprise. Beveridge had unwittingly reinforced his opponents' claims when he boasted that his bill was "THE MOST PRONOUNCED EXTENSION OF FEDERAL POWER IN EVERY DIRECTION EVER ENACTED." Representative E. D. Crumpacker of Indiana warned House members, "The passage of the meat inspection bill as it came from the Senate would mean the ultimate federalization of every industry in the United States."

With substantial support in the House and the sting removed from the damning Neill-Reynolds report, the packers sponsored a substitute bill, which Wadsworth and Lorimer introduced in the House in late May. Their draft eliminated each feature the packers opposed. They authorized the continued use of misleading brand names and preservatives. Dates on the cans were not required. In place of the head fee they had restored the annual appropriation. And in two other sweeping revisions, they removed the Beveridge bill's proposed ban on interstate transportation of uninspected meats and gave packing firms the right to appeal any agriculture department ruling to the federal courts. That last provision promised to be the most destructive of all, for private business had no more sympathetic audience than the champions of laissez-faire who sat on the federal judiciary. By appealing each unfavorable decision to the courts, the packers could paralyze the inspection system.

The Wadsworth-Lorimer substitute outraged President Roosevelt. "It seems to me," he wrote Wadsworth, "that each change is for the worse and in the aggregate they are ruinous, taking every particle of good from the suggested Beveridge amendment." He then made good on his threat to expose the packers. On June 4 he sent the Neill-Reynolds report to Congress along with a sharply worded message calling for a stringent inspection bill.

As might have been expected, Roosevelt's message in no way routed the packing-house forces in the House. Lorimer returned from a hasty trip to Chicago in time to denounce the Neill-Reynolds report as a "gross exaggeration of conditions." Armour accused the president of doing "everything in his power to discredit them and their business." The packers even produced two University of Illinois professors to rebut the Neill-Reynolds report.

All that rhetoric, of course, is a part of the symbolic language that so often monopolizes the public stage of politics. Each side adopts an uncompromising posture and accuses the opposition of all manner of villainy. The combatants strike heroic postures as champions of a larger public or national interest. They use such "disinterested" allies as Neill and Reynolds or university professors to legitimize their position. But at this point, when no accommodation seems possible, the negotiation and compromise begin.

Faced with Roosevelt's demand for quick action on the Beveridge bill and the Wadsworth-Lorimer substitute, the House voted to send both measures to the Agriculture Committee. In doing so, it followed a well-established procedure for reviewing legislation through its committee system. No handbook exists that explains how the committee system works; nor does the Constitution make any mention of it. Congress first established committees to streamline its functioning. Rather than have the entire body deliberate every bill, these smaller groups consider measures relevant to their areas of special interest before making recommendations to the entire House or Senate. A trade bill may go to the Commerce or Foreign Relations Committees, a pork barrel water project to the Rivers and Harbors Committee, and a farm bill to the Agriculture Committee. Those bills encompassing a variety of features have to go through several committees. All bills must eventually pass through the Rules Committee, which establishes parliamentary rules, such as the time allotted for floor debate or the conditions for amendment.

Yet if the committee system promotes efficiency, it also can become an undemocratic process used by a handful of representatives or senators to defeat a popular bill, either by eliminating or amending its central provisions or by refusing to return it to the floor for a vote. In sending the Beveridge bill to the Agriculture Committee, the House had routed it through an enemy stronghold. Wadsworth and Lorimer were both members of the committee; they had only to gain ten of eighteen votes from their colleagues in order to replace the Beveridge bill with their substitute. Other members of the House might never have a chance to vote on the original bill, even if a majority favored it.

Diligently, Wadsworth and Lorimer set out to undermine the Beveridge bill. They opened their attack by holding committee hearings to which they invited only witnesses sympathetic to the packers. Hearings are ostensibly a means to collect information that guides Congress as it formulates legislation. But they can be used for many other purposes—to delay, to discredit opponents, or to gain publicity for committee members. So for four days the Agriculture Committee heard a parade of witnesses defend the packers. The testimony of Thomas Wilson, a leading packer lobbyist, set the tone. Fed leading questions by Lorimer and Wadsworth, he attacked the Neill-Reynolds report as a "compendium of inaccuracies of fact," impugned the two men's competence, and stressed the "non-practical nature" of their background. And though under oath, Wilson swore that no condemned meat ever entered the market! The packers, he explained, were reasonable, public-spirited men. They would support a fair measure, such as Wadsworth and Lorimer had proposed, but not the government interference Beveridge called for.

More moderate committee members finally insisted that the committee hear opposing witnesses as well. That suited Wadsworth and Lorimer, for the longer the hearings lasted, the closer Congress came to adjourning. They also gained an opportunity to confront Neill and Reynolds directly. Neill attempted to refute criticism of his impracticality by stating that "we only reported what we could see, hear, and smell." He soon withered, however, under an unending barrage of hostile questions from the chairman and his crony. Reynolds, the Washington lawyer, was more accustomed to such abusive tactics. He coolly pointed out that, while he had based his conclusions on direct observation, Wilson had relied solely on hearsay gathered from packing-house employees.

As the hearings closed on June 9, Wadsworth eked out a narrow margin of victory, his substitute bill passing by only eleven to seven. Four Republicans had been so disgusted by the "bullyragging" aimed at Neill and Reynolds, they had voted against the substitute. The president exploded when he saw Wadsworth's handiwork. The provisions in the new bill struck him as "so bad that . . . if they had been deliberately designed to prevent remedying of the evils complained of, they could not have been worse."

Historians recognize that parties to a negotiation often inflate their initial demands to allow room for compromise. Still, Wadsworth and Lorimer had been unusually brazen in attacking the heart of Beveridge's inspection system. In their substitute, they made no provision for night inspection. Lorimer had also included a clause that waived for one year the civil service requirements for new inspectors. In that year, he could personally control the list of new appointments. The BAI would be saddled with political hacks loyal only to Lorimer and the packers.

Two provisions particularly infuriated Roosevelt. The agriculture department had suggested as a compromise that Congress authorize an annual appropriation, but also grant the secretary standby power to levy a head fee if the appropriation proved inadequate. Lorimer and Wadsworth insisted on an annual sum of $1 million, scarcely enough to meet current costs. And once again, they had shifted final authority under the act from the secretary of agriculture to the federal courts.

The president did not deny that the packers, like anyone else, were entitled to "due process." But he also believed that court review should be restricted to a narrow procedural question: Had the secretary been fair in reaching a decision? The committee granted the courts power to rule on substantive questions of fact. "You would have the functions of the Secretary of Agriculture narrowly limited so as to be purely ministerial," Roosevelt told Wadsworth, "and when he declared a given slaughterhouse unsanitary, or a given product unwholesome, acting upon the judgment of government experts, you would put on a judge, who had no knowledge of conditions, the burden of stating whether the Secretary was right."

Wadsworth refused to be cowed by the president's angry outburst. "You are wrong, very, very wrong in your estimate of the committee's bill," he responded. He even criticized the president for "impugning the sincerity and competency of a Committee of the House of Representatives" and called his substitute measure "as perfect a piece of legislation to carry into effect your own views on this question as was ever prepared by a committee of Congress." Lorimer, too, vowed to continue his defiance of the president.

All that sniping would not deserve so much notice except for one important factor—all of the antagonists belonged to the same party. The meat inspection battle had pitted a popular and powerful Republican president and his Senate friends against the Republican majority in the House. Senator Henry Cabot Lodge of Massachusetts, perhaps the president's closest political friend, had made the intraparty schism that much more public when he denounced the "greedy" packers for their attempt to derail the reform bill. Sensing the growing embarrassment among Republicans, House Democrats sought to deepen the rift. They insisted that the Beveridge bill be given a full vote on the House floor, even though it had not been voted out of the Agriculture Committee. "Czar" Joseph Cannon, the dictatorial Republican speaker, temporarily retrieved the situation for his party by ruling the motion out of order.

Cannon was now the man on the hot seat. The fight among Republican factions threatened to become a donnybrook that might destroy the political empire he had so ruthlessly built and ruled. His personal and political sympathies lay with the packers and conservatives who opposed government regulation of the free enterprise system. His power came, however, not from leading any particular faction, but from bringing together all the elements of his party into a unified machine. As speaker and chairman of the powerful Rules Committee, he had the means to keep unruly congressmen in line because he handed out all committee assignments. Members of Congress prefer to sit on those committees that deal with issues important to their constituents. Industrial state representatives may want Labor or Commerce, while a representative from a mining state like Nevada might prefer Interior. To earn Cannon's favor, many representatives found themselves forced to vote with the speaker and against their consciences.

With his power base shaken, Cannon sought some way to break the impasse between Republican reformers and conservatives. Since Roosevelt, too, had an interest in party unity, the speaker went to see him at the White House. The president proved amenable to a suitable compromise. They agreed that Wisconsin Representative Henry Adams, a moderate and a member of the Agriculture Committee, was the best person to work out the details. Adams had endorsed earlier compromises and, as a former food commissioner and champion of pure foods legislation, he was free of the taint that clung to Wadsworth and Lorimer. Adams, Reynolds, and Agriculture Department lawyers had soon produced a new bill. From the Wadsworth-Lorimer measure, they dropped the civil service waiver, added a provision for dating canned meats, gave the secretary standby fee authority, and eliminated the section on broad court review. Roosevelt declared their measure "as good as the Beveridge amendment."

All those negotiations took place while Wadsworth and Lorimer were away from Washington, but when they returned, they vowed to reverse the president's apparent victory. Cannon, however, had no appetite for further infighting. He urged the Agriculture Committee to work out yet another compromise. Wadsworth and Lorimer immediately deleted the secretary's standby fee authority from the Adams bill, though they did raise the appropriation to $3 million, more than enough to meet current costs. Their axe next fell on the dating requirement and, in return, they kept out the civil service waiver, while explicitly authorizing inspectors to visit plants "day or night."

One crucial issue remained. What would be the scope of court review? Wadsworth was willing to drop his demand for broad review if the president took out the Senate's phrase giving the secretary "final and conclusive" authority. Roosevelt agreed to that horse trade, which one historian aptly described as "purposeful obscurity." To achieve his larger goal of improved inspection, Roosevelt was willing to let the courts decide the actual scope of judicial review. He regretted the absence of mandatory dating, but did not consider the issue sufficiently important to upset the hard-won compromise. Roosevelt often criticized those diehards who would go down fighting for a "whole loaf," when "half a loaf" was the best they could expect. With the president behind the final committee bill, the entire House passed it on June 19.

The battle was not yet won, however, for Beveridge and the reformers in the Senate continued their fight, threatening to keep the two Houses deadlocked until recess. The Indiana senator had strong support from Redfield Proctor, chairman of the Senate Agriculture Committee. Though nearly crippled by rheumatism, Proctor had stayed on in Washington to assure passage of an effective meat bill. Like Beveridge, he believed a consumer had the right to know whether canned meats were five days or five years old. And if the government stamp would be worth millions in free advertising for the packers, Proctor thought the industry, not the taxpayer, should bear the cost. The Senate, therefore, voted to reject the House bill in favor of its own.

Once again, process more than substance determined the outcome. When the two houses pass different versions of the same bill, they create a conference committee to iron out the discrepancies. With time too short for long wrangling over each point, Roosevelt intervened. He first urged the House members to reconsider their position on dating and fees. They refused so vehemently that Roosevelt turned to the Senate conferees instead. Proctor and Beveridge recognized that further resistance meant total defeat. On June 29, the day before adjournment, they raised the white flag "to make sure of the greater good," and the Senate passed the House bill. The next day, after Roosevelt signed, the Meat Inspection Act of 1906 became the law of the land.

Out of the Jungle?

We might think that the passage of the new act was cause to uncork the champagne for a celebration. Despite their opposition to certain compromises, Roosevelt and Beveridge had endorsed the final measure as a triumph for reform. If historians let the case rest here, however, they would not know whether to accept Roosevelt and Beveridge's enthusiasm or Knute Nelson's despair. Who, after all, had won this legislative battle? Certainly, reformers would be heartened to see that the old toothless law had been replaced by a system that requried "day and night" inspection; banned uninspected meats from interstate commerce; gave the secretary authority to establish sanitary standards; and provided ample funding for the immediate future at least. Yet the final bill contained no provisions for head fees or dating and still left the courts as the final judge of the secretary of agriculture's rulings.

In determining who could claim victory, Roosevelt, Beveridge, and Nelson had to base their judgment only on the provisions of the final act. Yet the real significance of legislation cannot be determined until its effectiveness in practice has been measured. A law must be applied by the executive branch and tested in the courts. In the case of the Meat Inspection Act, future presidents might appoint agriculture secretaries sympathetic to the packers. The standards established might be either too vague or too lax to enforce proper sanitation. More important, the courts might yet call Roosevelt's bluff and interpret their prerogative for review broadly. Only after observing the operation of the new system over time can the historian decide whether the compromises vindicated Roosevelt or proved "half a loaf" worse than none at all.

As it happens, the subsequent history of meat inspection confirms the wisdom of the president's compromise strategy. The $3 million appropriation more than adequately funded the "beefed up" inspection system. By the end of 1907, Secretary Wilson reported that new and more efficient procedures had substantially reduced operating costs. The BAI spent only $2 million the first year, and costs dropped even though the industry grew.

Roosevelt had been shrewdest in his resort to "purposeful obscurity." The packers made no attempt to dismantle the inspection system in the courts—the first important case did not arise for over ten yers. Then in 1917, in *United States v. Cudahy Packing Co., et al.,* a federal judge affirmed the secretary's authority. Congress, he ruled, could "delegate authority to the proper administrative officer to make effective rules. . . ." Two years later the Supreme Court adopted "narrow" rather than "broad" review. In an opinion for a unanimous court in the case of *Houston v. St. Louis Independent Packing Company,* Justice John

Following the public outcry, *meat packers tried to create a better image of conditions in their plants and the thoroughness of government inspection. In fact, when this picture was taken in 1906, postmortem inspection as shown here had not been at all common.*

Clarke wrote that a decision over proper labeling of meat "is a question of fact, the determination of which is committed to the Secretary of Agriculture . . . , and the law is that the conclusion of the head of an executive depart- ment . . . will not be reviewed by the Courts, where it is fairly arrived at with substantial support." After thirteen years, the reformers could finally claim victory, though the outcome by then was scarcely in doubt. Not until 1968 did another generation of reformers, spurred by Ralph Nader, find it necessary to launch a campaign to strengthen the inspection system. Then, they sought higher standards for meats subject only to state inspection.

The controversy over meat inspection reminds the historian that when a legislative issue involves the disposition of economic and political power, all three branches of government influence the outcome. That does not mean, however, that their roles are equal. In this case a politically shrewd and popular executive had shown greater capacity to affect the political process at critical moments. Roosevelt used the power of his office, his control over the Re- publican party, and his ability to generate publicity to overcome opposition on both sides. Beveridge admitted that even in the face of widespread public outrage Congress would not have acted "if the President had not picked up his big stick and smashed the packers and their agents in the House and Senate over the head with it." Yet Roosevelt prevailed in the end only because he recognized compromise as an essential feature of the political process. He had yielded on points he considered less consequential in order to achieve his larger objective.

Just as historians must expand their field of vision to weigh the effects on a law of all three branches of government, so too they must establish the historical context of a bill over time. As we discovered, the meat scandal had a long history before the publication of *The Jungle*. We discovered, too, near-unanimous support for stricter inspection, though little understanding of what form a new bill might take. Only when the bill made its way through the legislative process did we find that the widespread cry for reform masked a deep conflict over the roles of private and public agencies in determining satisfactory standards. The packers wanted the benefits of a new bill without having to relinquish control over any aspect of their business. In addition to chastening the packers, the reformers sought to assert the authority of the federal government to police "corporate arrogance." The success of their efforts remained in doubt until well after the bill's enactment, when the Supreme Court adopted "narrow review."

It becomes clear, then, why the Meat Inspection Act could generate both Beveridge's enthusiasm and Nelson's dismay. All the interested parties had gained some, though not all, of their objectives. With public confidence re- stored, the packers could anticipate renewed growth for their industry. Reform- ers could, however, hold them to higher standards of accountability. The Republicans had averted a destructive intraparty battle and had emerged as defenders of the public interest, despite Wadsworth and Lorimer. Roosevelt had strengthened his control over the party, while extending the scope of his executive authority. Above all, he had demonstrated a capacity for effective leadership. The public gained, too, for they could sit down to dinner having to worry less what their canned foods contained besides meat.

The Meat Inspection Act of 1906 had been a total victory for neither reformers nor packers. As is so often the case, the political system achieved results only after the visible symbols and myths of public discourse had been negotiated, debated, and compromised in the procedural tangle at the heart of the legislative process. Gone from our analysis are those wonderful symbols of corporate villainy and presidential heroism. But in their place we have a more complex story revealing the political processes that shape our history.

ADDITIONAL READING

This chapter grew out of an Early Concentration History Seminar at Yale. To give students their own experience at reconstructing history from primary sources, Mark Lytle put together a package of documents on the Meat Inspection Act of 1906. Many of those students showed remarkable initiative in locating additional materials. In particular, they discovered the section in John Braeman, "The Square Deal in Action: A Case Study in the Growth of the 'National Police Power,'" that discusses the constitutional questions the new meat inspection law raised. That essay appears in Braeman, et al., *Change and Continuity in Twentieth Century America,* vol. I (Columbus, Ohio, 1964), 34–80.

Any reader interested in a similar exploration of secondary and primary materials might begin with Upton Sinclair, *The Jungle* (New York 1906), and *The Brass Check* (Pasadena, Calif., 1919), often autobiographical. On Theodore Roosevelt and the politics of progressivism see George Mowry, *The Era of Theodore Roosevelt* (New York, 1958), John Blum, *The Republican Roosevelt* (Cambridge, Mass., 1958), and Gabriel Kolko, *The Triumph of Conservatism* (New York, 1964). After going through the documents for themselves our students concluded that Mowry's cursory treatment missed much of the significant political maneuvering and that Kolko misused documents and misinterpreted the meaning of the act. Another helpful secondary work is Joel Tarr, *Boss Politics* (Chicago, 1964), which examines the career of "Blond Billy" Lorimer. David Thelen, "Not Classes, But Issues," which first appeared in *The Journal of American History,* vol. LVI (September 1969), 323–334, offers a stimulating review of the many explanations of progressivism, as well as a substantial interpretation of his own. Robert Crunden, *Ministers of Reform: The Progressives' Achievements in Modern America, 1889-1920* (Urbana, Ill., 1982) and Arthur Link and Richard McCormick, *Progressivism* (Arlington Heights, Ill., 1983) give additional insights into the reform impulse that swept the nation.

The documents in this case study are available in good research libraries and can be readily assembled. Such newspapers as *The New York Times, Chicago Tribune, Chicago Record-Herald,* and the *Chicago Inter-Ocean* covered the entire controversy, though the Chicago papers did so in greater depth. Much of Roosevelt's thinking can be found in Elting Morison, et al., *The Letters of Theodore Roosevelt,* vol. 5 (Cambridge, Mass., 1953). Access to some contemporary magazines including *Everybody's Magazine, The Lancet, Cosmopolitan,* and specifically J. Ogden Armour, "The Packers and the People," *Saturday Evening Post,* CLXXVII, no. 37 (March 10, 1906)—a key document in Kolko's interpretation—will provide a picture of the debate over meat packing and other muckraking issues.

This chapter drew most heavily on government documents. Readers should see *Congressional Record,* 59th Congress, 1st Session; House Committee on Agriculture, 59th Congress, 1st Session, *Hearings . . . on the So-called "Bev-*

eridge Amendment" to the *Agriculture Appropriation Bill—H.R. 18537* (Washington, D.C., 1906); Bureau of Animal Industry, *Twenty-third Annual Report* (Washington, D.C., 1906); *House Document 873,* 59th Congress, 1st Session (June 1906)—the Neill-Reynolds Report and Theodore Roosevelt's cover letter; and the Agriculture Committee's minority and majority reports in *House Report* 4935, pts. I and 2, 59th Congress, 1st Session (June 14 & 15, 1906) and *House Report,* 3468, pt. 2, 59th Congress, 1st Session (June 15, 1906). Additional materials can be found in the Roosevelt Papers (Harvard University) and Beveridge Papers (University of Indiana).

Two readable biographies help us understand Theodore Roosevelt: John Milton Cooper, Jr., *The Warrior and the Priest* (Cambridge, Mass., 1983), and Edmund Morris, *The Rise of Theodore Roosevelt* (New York, 1981).

Finally, thanks go to Stuart Drake, Boris Feldman, William Garfinkel, and other Early Concentration students whose research helped locate relevant documents used in this chapter. Professor Lewis Gould of the University of Texas at Austin generously offered some important revisions. Students interested in the interpretations of progressive reform could profitably read Lewis Gould, ed., *The Progressive Era* (1973).

CHAPTER TEN

Sacco and Vanzetti

In the years after World War I, crime statistics curved sharply upward. Armed robberies rose at an alarming rate, and anyone handling large sums of money had reason to exercise caution. On most paydays Frederick Parmenter, paymaster for the Slater and Morrill Shoe Company of South Braintree, Massachusetts, would have used a truck to deliver his money boxes to the lower factory building. Only a few months earlier, in December 1919, a brazen gang of bandits had attempted a daylight payroll heist in nearby Bridgewater. The bandits had fled empty-handed and no one was hurt in the gunfight; still, area businesses were uneasy. On the morning of April 15, 1920, however, the robbery attempt must have been far from Parmenter's mind. It was a mild spring day and he set out on foot for the lower factory building with his assistant, Alessandro Berardelli, walking ahead.

Halfway to their destination, a man approached Berardelli from the side of the road, spoke to him briefly, and then suddenly shot him dead. As Parmenter turned to flee, the bandits fired again, mortally wounding him. A blue Buick pulled from its parking place. The two assailants and their lookout jumped into the car and fled toward Bridgewater. To discourage pursuers, the bandits threw tacks onto the streets. Two miles from Braintree they abandoned the Buick and escaped in another car.

Bridgewater Police Chief Michael Stewart thought he recognized a familiar pattern in the Braintree crime. The same foreigners who bungled the December heist, he guessed, had probably pulled off the Braintree job. Stewart's investigation put him on the trail of Mike Boda, an Italian anarchist. Unable to locate Boda, Stewart kept watch on a car Boda had left at Simon Johnson's garage for repairs. Whoever came to get the car would, according to Stewart's theory, become a prime suspect in both crimes.

His expectations were soon rewarded. On May 5, 1920, Boda and three other Italians called for the car. Mrs. Johnson immediately slipped next door to alert the police, but the four men did not wait for her return. Boda and one friend, Riccardo Orciani, left on a motorcycle, while their companions walked to a nearby streetcar stop. Apparently nervous, they moved on to another stop a half mile away. There they boarded the trolley for Brockton. As the car moved down Main Street, Police Officer Michael Connolly climbed on. Having spotted the two foreigners, he arrested them. When they asked why, he replied curtly, "suspicious characters."

Thus began the epic story of Nicola Sacco and Bartolomeo Vanzetti, two obscure Italian aliens who became the focal point of one of the most controversial episodes in American history. Within little more than a year after their arrest a jury deliberated for just five hours before convicting both men of robbery and murder. Such a quick decision came as a surprise, particularly in a trial that had lasted seven weeks, heard over 160 witnesses, and gained national attention.

Nor did the controversy end with the jury's decision. Six years of appeals turned a small-town incident of robbery and murder into a major international uproar. The Italian government indicated that it was following the case with interest. Thousands of liberals, criminal lawyers, legal scholars, civil libertarians, radicals, labor leaders, prominent socialites, and spokespersons for immigrant groups rallied to Sacco and Vanzetti's cause. Arrayed against them was an equally imposing collection of the nation's legal, social, academic, and political elite.

Nicola Sacco and Bartolomeo Vanzetti, *accused of committing a payroll robbery of the Slater and Morrill Shoe Company in South Braintree, Massachusetts. When police asked witnesses to identify the two men, instead of using a line-up, officers made Sacco and Vanzetti stand alone in the middle of a room and pose as bandits.*

The case climaxed on April 9, 1927. Having denied some eight appeals, trial judge Webster Thayer sentenced Sacco and Vanzetti to die in the electric chair. His action triggered months of protests and political activities. Around Charleston Prison (where the two men were held) and the State House in Boston Sacco and Vanzetti's supporters marched, collected petitions, and walked picket lines. Occasionally violence erupted between protestors and authorities, as mounted police attacked crowds in Boston, clubbed them off the streets in New York. On August 22, the morning before Sacco and Vanzetti were scheduled to die, Charleston Prison appeared like an embattled fortress. Ropes circled the prison grounds to keep protestors at bay as eight hundred armed guards walked the walls. In New York's Union Square, 15,000 people gathered to stand in silent vigil. Similar crowds congregated in major European cities. All awaited the news of the fate of "a good shoemaker and a poor fish peddler."

The historian confronting that extraordinary event faces some perplexing questions. How did a case of robbery and murder become an international *cause célèbre*? How was it that two Italian immigrants living on the fringe of American society had become the focus of a debate that brought the nation's cherished legal institutions under attack? Or as one eminent law professor rhetorically posed the question:

> Why all this fuss over a couple of "wops", who after years in this country had not even made application to become citizens; who had not learned to use our language even modestly well; who did not believe in our form of government; . . . who were confessed slackers and claimed to be pacifists but went armed with deadly weapons for the professed purpose of defending their individual personal property in violation of all the principles they preached?

The Question of Legal Evidence

Lawyers reviewing events might answer those questions by arguing that the Sacco and Vanzetti case raised serious doubts about the tradition of Anglo-Saxon justice so venerated in the United States. More specifically, many legal scholars then and since have asserted that the trial and appeals process failed to meet minimum standards of fairness, particularly for a criminal case in which the defendants' lives hung in the balance.

In the first flush of Sacco and Vanzetti's arrest, prosecutors seemed to have good reason to label the two men "suspicious characters." Both Sacco and Vanzetti were carrying loaded revolvers. Not only that, Sacco had 23 extra cartridges in his pockets, while Vanzetti carried several shotgun shells. When questioned, both men lied about their activities. They claimed not to know Mike Boda or to have been at the garage to pick up Boda's car. But suspicious behavior was one matter; proof that Sacco and Vanzetti had committed the Braintree murders was another. As the police and prosecutors went about making their case, they followed distinctly irregular procedures.

To be sure, in 1920 the police were allowed to conduct an investigation with far greater latitude than the law permits today. The Supreme Court decisions in

Miranda (1966) and *Escobedo* (1964) established that criminal suspects have the right to remain silent, to be informed of their rights, and to stand in an impartial lineup for identification. None of those guarantees existed in 1920. Even so, Katzmann and Stewart showed unusual zeal in constructing a case against Sacco and Vanzetti. At no time during the first two days of questioning did they tell either suspect why they had been arrested. Chief Stewart repeatedly asked them not about the robbery, but about their political beliefs and associates. The district attorney did obliquely inquire about their activities on April 15, though he never mentioned the Braintree crimes. Furthermore, when the police asked witnesses to identify the suspects, they did not use a lineup. Instead, they forced Sacco and Vanzetti to stand alone in the middle of a room posing as bandits.

As the investigation continued, the case came close to collapsing for lack of evidence. Of the five suspected gang members, all but Vanzetti could prove they had not been in Bridgewater during the December holdup attempt. Despite an intensive search of the suspects' belongings, including a trunk sent to Italy, Katzmann was never able to trace the money, even among radical political groups with whom they were associated. Fingerprint experts found no matches between prints lifted from the abandoned Buick and those taken from the suspects.

Faced with those gaps in the evidence, Katzmann still decided, first, to prosecute Vanzetti for the December Bridgewater holdup and, second, to charge both Sacco and Vanzetti with the Braintree murders in April. Arguing the Bridgewater case in June 1920 before Judge Webster Thayer, Katzmann presented a weak case against Vanzetti on the charge of assault with intent to rob. Still, he did manage to make the jury aware of Vanzetti's anarchist views and persuade them to convict. Judge Thayer then meted out an unusually severe sentence (twelve to fifteen years) to a defendant with no criminal record for a crime in which no one was hurt and nothing was stolen.

That conviction allowed Katzmann to proceed with the second trial, to be held in the suburban town of Dedham. Since this would be a special session of the superior court, a judge had to be appointed to hear the case. Judge Thayer asked his old college friend, Chief Justice John Aiken, for the assignment, even though he had presided over Vanzetti's earlier trial and could scarcely consider himself impartial. Thus, the second trial opened with a judge who already believed unequivocally in the defendants' guilt.

At Dedham, District Attorney Katzmann built his case around three major categories of evidence: (1) eyewitness identification of Sacco and Vanzetti at the scene; (2) expert ballistics testimony establishing Sacco's gun as the weapon that fired the fatal shot at Berardelli and Vanzetti's gun as one taken from Berardelli during the robbery; (3) the defendants' evasive behavior both before and after arrest as evidence of what is legally termed "consciousness of guilt."

The prosecution, however, had a difficult time making its case. Of the "eyewitnesses" claiming to place Sacco and Vanzetti at the scene, one, Mary Splaine, claimed to have observed the shooting from a window in the Slater and Morrill factory for no longer than 3 seconds at a distance of about 60 feet. In that time she watched an unknown man in a car traveling about 18 miles an hour.

Immediately after the crime Splaine had difficulty describing any of the bandits, but one year later she picked out Sacco, vividly recalling such details as his "good-sized" left hand. She refused to recant her testimony even after the defense demonstrated that Sacco had relatively small hands.

Louis Pelzer testified for the prosecution that upon hearing shots he had observed the crime from a window for at least a minute. He pointed to Sacco as the "dead image" of the man who shot Berardelli. Two defense witnesses, however, controverted Pelzer's story. Upon hearing the shots, they recalled, the intrepid Pelzer had immediately hidden under his workbench—hardly a vantage point from which to make a clear identification.

Lola Andrews, a third witness, claimed that on the morning of the crime she had stopped near the factory to ask directions from a dark-haired man working under a car. She later identified Sacco as that man. But a companion, Mrs. Julia Campbell, denied that Andrews had ever spoken to the man under the car. Instead, Campbell testified, Andrews had approached a pale, sickly young man who was standing nearby. Other witnesses had recalled the same pale person. A second friend swore that he had heard Andrews say after she returned from police headquarters that "the government took me down and wanted me to recognize those men and I don't know a thing about them." Nor did Andrews's reputation as a streetwalker enhance her credibility. Yet in his summation prosecutor Katzmann told the jury that in eleven years as district attorney he had not "ever before . . . laid eye or given ear to so convincing a witness as Lola Andrews."

Against Katzmann's dubious cast the defense produced seventeen witnesses who provided the defendants with alibis for the day or who had seen the crime, but not Sacco or Vanzetti. One, an official of the Italian Consulate in Boston, confirmed Sacco's claim that he had been in Boston on April 15 acquiring a passport. The official remembered Sacco because he had tried to use a picture over ten inches square for his passport photo. "Since such a large photograph had never been presented before . . . ," the official recalled, "I took it in and showed it to the Secretary of the Consulate. We laughed and talked over the incident. I remember observing the date . . . on a large pad calendar." Others said they had met Sacco at a luncheon banquet that day. Witnesses for Vanzetti claimed to have bought fish from him. Katzmann could only try to persuade the jury that the witnesses had little reason to connect such a mundane event with a specific date.

In the face of contradictory eyewitness testimony, the ballistics evidence might have decided the case. To prove murder, Katzmann wished to show that the fatal shot striking Berardelli had come from Sacco's gun. Ballistics specialists can often identify the gun that fired a bullet by characteristic marks, as distinct as fingerprints, that the barrel and hammer make on the projectile and casing. Two experts, Captains William Proctor and Charles Van Amburgh, connected the fatal bullet to a Colt pistol similar to and possibly the same as Sacco's. But neither of Katzmann's witnesses made a definitive link. "It is consistent with being fired by that pistol," Proctor replied to Katzmann. Van Amburgh also indicated some ambiguity: "I am inclined to believe that it was fired . . . from this pistol."

For unknown reasons defense attorneys never pursued the equivocation of those testimonies. Instead, they called their own ballistics specialists who stated with absolute certainty that the fatal bullet could not have come from Sacco's gun. In addition they controverted the prosecutor's claim that Vanzetti had taken Berardelli's gun during the holdup. Shortly before his murder Berardelli had left his pistol at a repair shop to have the hammer fixed. Shop records, though imprecise, indicated that the gun was .32 caliber, not a .38 such as Vanzetti was carrying. The records also supported Mrs. Berardelli's sworn testimony that her husband had never reclaimed his pistol. The defense then argued that the hammer on Vanzetti's gun had never been repaired.

Since the defense had weakened the ballistics evidence, Katzmann based his case primarily on "consciousness of guilt." To convict on those grounds, he had to convince the jury that Sacco and Vanzetti had behaved like men guilty of the crime, both before and after arrest. Here, Katzmann made his case with telling effect. Why had the defendants been carrying guns when they were arrested? They had gone hunting that morning, they claimed. But if that were the case, why were they still carrying hunting weapons and extra ammunition at night, when they set out to pick up Mike Boda's car? They were in such a hurry, Sacco and Vanzetti replied, that they forgot to leave their revolvers at home. But Katzmann continued his onslaught. Why did the two men lie at first about knowing Mike Boda or having visited the garage? Surely this indicated a clear consciousness of guilt.

To explain such evasive behavior, defense lawyers were forced to introduce the inflammatory issue of Sacco and Vanzetti's political beliefs. For indeed, both men proudly proclaimed themselves to be anarchists, rejecting the authority of any government. Capitalism, they believed, was little more than an organized system of banditry under which the rich and powerful extorted the poor. Sacco and Vanzetti had both been active in the strikes and labor unrest of the era. As a result, they had been alarmed by the government crackdown on radicals that began in 1919. When Officer Connolly arrested them, the two men assumed that they, too, had been snared in the government's dragnet. They acted evasively, defense lawyers argued, not because they were criminals but because radicals were being persecuted and deported. Once arrested, Sacco and Vanzetti's fears were only confirmed by the police's constant questions about their political beliefs.

Similar worries accounted for their peculiar actions at Johnson's garage, the defense argued. Shortly before his arrest, Vanzetti had conferred with the Italian Defense Committee of New York, then inquiring into the fate of a fellow anarchist, Andrea Salsedo. The committee knew only that Salsedo was being held by Justice Department agents; members warned Vanzetti that he and his friends might be in danger of being jailed or deported. Only a week later, newspapers across the nation reported that Salsedo had fallen to his death from a twelfth-floor window. The police insisted the case had been a suicide, but many anarchists thought Salsedo had been pushed. Before he died, had he provided the government with the names of other anarchists? If so, Vanzetti and Sacco were at risk. Anyone found with anarchist literature could be arrested and deported. It was for that reason, Sacco and Vanzetti told the court, that they had gone to retrieve Mike Boda's car: they needed it to carry away the radical pamphlets stored in their homes—something they hardly wished to admit to police questioning them about radical activities.

The revelations of the defendants' radical politics could hardly have raised the jury's opinion of the two men. And their explanations did not stop Katzmann from focusing on consciousness of guilt in his final summation. So too did Judge Thayer in his charge to jury. In theory, a judge's charge guides the jury as it interprets conflicting evidence: in separating the relevant from the irrelevant and in establishing the grounds for an objective verdict. But Thayer made his sympathies all too clear. In discussing the ballistics testimony, he wrongly assumed that Katzmann's expert witnesses had unequivocally identified Sacco's gun as having fired the fatal shot. And he spent no time weighing the defense's argument that prosecution eyewitnesses had been unreliable. Only when he discussed consciousness of guilt did the judge become expansive and specific. He lingered over the evidence offered by the police and the garage owner, while ignoring Sacco and Vanzetti's explanations.

Lawyers and legal historians have raised other telling criticisms—excesses in the trial procedures, prejudice on the part of both judge and prosecutor, bungling by the defense lawyer. Inevitably, these criticisms have influenced the way historians have approached the controversy. Most of them have centered on the issue of *proof* of guilt. Contrary to popular opinion, the courts do not determine whether a person is guilty or innocent of a crime. They decide merely whether the prosecutor has assembled sufficient evidence to establish guilt. The judge may even suspect a defendant is guilty, but if the evidence does not meet minimum standards of legal proof, the court must set the accused free. As one court concluded, "the commonwealth demands no victims . . . and it is as much the duty of the district attorney to see that no innocent man suffers, as it is to see that no guilty man escapes."

Thus lawyers tend to focus on narrow, yet admittedly important, questions. They are all the more crucial when human lives are at stake, as was the case with Sacco and Vanzetti. Believing that the legal system maintains vital safeguards of individual rights, lawyers in general seek to ensure that proper legal procedures have been followed, that evidence is submitted according to established rules, and, in accordance with those procedures, that guilt has been adequately determined. A lawyer answering the question, "Why all the fuss?" over the Sacco and Vanzetti case would most likely reply, "Because the trial, by failing to prove guilt beyond reasonable doubt, perpetrated a serious miscarriage of justice."

Beyond Guilt or Innocence

So far in these essays we have considered enough historical methods to understand that history affords far more latitude in weighing and collecting evidence than the legal system. The law attempts to limit the flow of evidence in a trial to what can reasonably be construed as fact. A judge will generally exclude hearsay testimony, speculation about states of mind or motives, conjecture, and vague questions leading witnesses to conclusions. But those are sources of information upon which historians can and do draw in their research. They can afford to speculate more freely, because their conclusions will not send innocent people to jail or let the guilty go free. In one instance, for example, appeals judges refused to act upon defense claims that Judge Thayer had allowed his prejudices against Sacco and Vanzetti to influence his conduct of the trial. They ruled that remarks made outside the courtroom, no matter how inappropriate, had no bearing on what occurred inside. By contrast, the historian can accept the fact of Judge Thayer's prejudice regardless of where he revealed it.

Given their broader canons of evidence, historians might be tempted to go the lawyers one step further by establishing whether Sacco and Vanzetti actually did commit the robbery and murders at Braintree. To succeed in such an investigation would at least lay the controversy to its final rest. Yet that approach does not take us beyond the lawyers' questions. We are still dealing with only two men—Sacco and Vanzetti—and one central question—guilty or innocent?

We must remember, however, that when historians confront such "either/or" questions, their overriding obligation is to construct an interpretation that gives full play to *all* aspects of the subject being investigated, not just the question of guilt or innocence. They must look beyond Sacco and Vanzetti at the actions of the people and society around them. What political currents led the prosecutor to bring those two men to trial? How much were Judge Thayer, District Attorney Katzmann, and the men in the jury box representative of Massachusetts or of American society in general? Of just what crime did the jury actually convict the defendants? In answering those questions, historians must lift their drama out of the Dedham courtroom and into a larger theater of action. In short, we cannot answer our original question, "Why all the fuss?" merely by proving the defendants guilty or innocent. Historians want to know why this case provoked such sharp controversy for so many years.

Any historian who studies the climate of opinion in the early 1920s cannot help suspecting that those who persecuted Sacco and Vanzetti were far more concerned with who the defendants were and what they believed than with what they might have done. Throughout the nation's history, Americans have periodically expressed hostility toward immigrants and foreign political ideas which were perceived as a threat to the "American way of life." Nativism, as such defensive nationalism has been called, has been a problem at least since the first waves of Irish immigrants came ashore in the first half of the nineteenth century. Until then, the United States had been a society dominated by white Protestants with a common English heritage. The influx of the Catholic Irish and then political refugees from the 1848 German revolution diversified the nation's population. Native-born Americans became alarmed that immigration threatened their cherished institutions. Successive waves of newcomers from Asia, Mediterranean countries, and eastern Europe deepened their fears.

In analyzing nativist ideology, historian John Higham has identified three major attitudes: anti-Catholicism, antiradicalism, and Anglo-Saxon nationalism. Anti-Catholicism reflected northern European Protestants' distrust of the Catho-

Going to Join the Indian and Buffalo?

The sturdy old American breed that wrested this country from the wilderness might now try a hard, quick shove toward the middle of the bench

Many "old stock" Americans from northern Europe feared that *the new flood of immigrants from southeastern Europe would, by sheer force of numbers, displace them from their dominant place in society. Even a progressive like George Creel, who had been sympathetic to immigrants during World War I, turned hostile and referred to the newcomers as "so much slag in the melting pot." Respected academics published research which purported to prove "the intellectual superiority of our Nordic groups over the Alpine, Mediterranean, and negro groups."*

lic Church, rejection of its hierarchical and undemocratic structure, and its fear of the pope as a religious despot. Nativists often viewed Catholic immigrants as papal agents sent to bring the United States under the tyranny of Rome. Antiradicalism stemmed in part from an increasing rejection of America's own revolutionary tradition and in part from the American tendency to associate violence and criminal subversion with Europe's radical political creeds such as Marxism, socialism, and anarchism. Anglo-Saxon nationalism was a more amorphous blend of notions about the racial superiority of the northern European people and pride in the Anglo-Saxon heritage of legal, political, and economic institutions. One of the most cherished has always been the Anglo-Saxon tradition of justice.

The tides of nativism tend to rise and fall with the fortunes of the nation. During periods of prosperity, Americans often welcome immigrants as a vital source of new labor. In the 1860s, for example, many Californians cheered the arrival of the strange Chinese coolies without whom the transcontinental railroad could not have been so quickly completed. In the 1870s, as the nation

The rabid patriotism of the war *led to widespread abuses of civil liberties. Here, angry servicemen on the Boston Commons destroy a Socialist party flag seized during a 1918 peace march. The same spirit of intolerance was also reflected in the Red Scare, during which an Indiana jury deliberated only two minutes before acquitting a defendant who had shot and killed a radical for yelling, "To hell with the United States!"*

struggled through a severe industrial depression, nativism became a virulent social disease. The same Californians who once welcomed the Chinese now organized vigilante groups to harass them and clamored for laws to restrict the number of Asian immigrants.

The period following World War I, which Higham labeled the "Tribal Twenties," marked the high tide of nativism. No group more fully embodied the nativist impulse than the reborn Ku Klux Klan. By 1924 it claimed large chapters not only in its traditional southern strongholds but also in major cities, in Oregon, and in the states of the upper middle west—Indiana, Ohio, and Illinois in particular. The Klan's constitution unabashedly advertised the organization's commitment to all three nativist traditions:

> to unite white, male persons, native born gentile citizens of the United States of America, who owe no allegiance of any nature to any foreign government, nation, institution, sect, ruler, person or people; whose morals are good, whose reputations and vocations are exemplary . . . ; to shield the sanctity of white womanhood; to maintain forever white supremacy. . . .

Loyalty to the Church, the pope, a motherland, old world culture, or any other tie outside the United States eliminated almost all immigrants from possible Klan membership.

Several factors accounted for the resurgence of nativism in the 1920s. World War I had temporarily interrupted the flow of immigrants who, since the 1880s, had increasingly included a preponderance of Catholics and Jews from countries with strong radical traditions. In 1914 alone, over 1.2 million Jews came to the United States. By 1918 the number fell to just 110,000 but then rose to 805,000 in 1921, the last year of unrestricted immigration. A similar pattern occurred among Italians. In the entire decade of the 1870s only 50,000 Italians came to the United States. In the first fifteen years of the twentieth century almost 2.5 million made the crossing. That torrent, which slowed to a trickle during the war years, swelled again with the return of peace. More than ever, nativists protested that foreigners threatened to destroy cherished institutions, weaken the genetic pool, or in other ways undermine the American way of life.

The rocky transition to a peacetime economy only aggravated resentment toward immigrants. Returning veterans expected jobs from a grateful nation; instead, they found crowds of unemployed workers around factory gates. The army had discharged millions of soldiers almost overnight. The government dismissed hundreds of thousands of temporary wartime employees and canceled millions of dollars' worth of contracts with private businesses. As the economy plunged downward, native-born Americans once again looked on new immigrants as a threat to their livelihoods. Organized labor joined other traditional nativist groups in demanding new restriction laws.

Union leaders called for relief on another front. During the war they had cooperated with the government to control inflation by minimizing wage increases. At the same time, high wartime employment had attracted millions of new recruits to the union movement. The government had orchestrated labor-management harmony to ensure uninterrupted production schedules. Once the war ended, labor set out to consolidate its gains. Union leaders asked for higher wages, improved working conditions, and the recognition of collective bargaining.

Most business leaders were in no mood to compromise. They resented the assistance the government had given organized labor during the war. Now, they not only rejected even the mildest union demands but also sought to cripple the labor movement. Conservatives launched a national campaign to brand all organized labor as Bolsheviks, reds, and anarchists. They called strikes "crimes against society," "conspiracies against the government," and "plots to establish communism." As the market for manufactures declined, employers had little reason to avoid a showdown. Strikes saved them the problem of laying off unneeded workers.

In 1919 American industry lost more labor hours to strikes than ever before in history. March brought 175 significant strikes, followed by 248 in April, 388 in May, 303 in June, 360 in July, and 373 in August. By September, strikes in the coal and steel industries alone had idled over 700,000 workers and led to repeated violence. The average strike lasted thirty-four days, while some exceeded four months. Even employers who made minor concessions on wages or hours refused to yield on the question of collective bargaining.

Radicals played a minor role in the postwar labor unrest. Most union leaders were as archly conservative as the employers they confronted. Still, the constant barrage of anti-red propaganda turned public opinion against the unions. And American radicals fed that hostility by adopting highly visible tactics. The success of a small band of Bolsheviks in capturing Russia's tottering government in October 1917 had rekindled their waning hopes, at the same time startling most Americans. Two years later, the Bolsheviks boldly organized the Third Communist International to carry the revolution to other countries. Communist-led worker uprisings in Hungary and Germany increased conservative anxiety that a similar revolutionary fever might infect American workers, especially when a Comintern official bragged that the money spent in Germany "was as nothing compared to the funds transmitted to New York for the purpose of spreading Bolshevism in the United States."

Only a few shocks were needed to inflame the fears of Americans caught in the midst of this economic distress, labor unrest, and renewed immigration from southern and eastern Europe. They were provided by a series of anarchist bombings inspired by Luigi Galleani, an Italian immigrant who had settled in New England. Although authorities at the time did not know it, members of Galleani's circle were the source of a series of thirty parcels mailed in April 1919 to eminent officials, including Attorney General A. Mitchell Palmer, Supreme Court Justice Oliver Wendell Holmes, members of Congress, mayors, as well as the industrial magnates John D. Rockefeller and J. P. Morgan. Only one of the deadly packages detonated (blowing off the hands of the unsuspecting servant who opened it), but in June a series of even more lethal explosions rocked seven cities. The most spectacular demolished the entire front wall of Attorney General Palmer's home. The device exploded prematurely, blowing to bits the man who was crouching by the front steps.

The American public had already learned to associate such deeds with anarchists: the Haymarket Square explosion of 1886, as well as the assassination of President William McKinley in 1901 by radical Leon Czolgosz. ("The anarchist is the enemy of humanity, the enemy of all mankind," proclaimed McKinley's successor, Teddy Roosevelt.) Following the bombings of 1919 Attorney General Palmer reacted swiftly, launching a roundup of as many radicals as he could find, branding each "a potential murderer or a potential thief." That the majority were only philosophical anarchists, who had never undertaken any violent acts toward the government, did not deter Palmer. That the majority were foreign-born served only to raise his patriotic bile: "Out of the sly and crafty eyes of many of them leap cupidity, cruelty, insanity, and crime; from their lopsided faces, sloping brows, and misshapen features may be recognized the unmistakable criminal types."

For over a year, Palmer and his young red-hunting assistant J. Edgar Hoover organized government raids on homes, offices, union halls, and alien organizations. Seldom did the raiders pay even passing attention to civil liberties or constitutional prohibitions against illegal search and seizure. One particularly spectacular outing netted over 4,000 alleged subversives in some thirty-three cities. Most of those arrested, though innocent of any crime, were detained illegally by state authorities either for trial or Labor Department deportation hearings. Police jammed suspects in cramped rooms with inadequate food and sanitation. They refused to honor the suspects' rights to post bail or obtain a writ of habeas corpus.

The public quickly wearied of Palmer and the exaggerated stories of grand revolutionary conspiracies. Not one incident had produced any evidence of a serious plot. Palmer predicted that on May 1, 1920, radicals would launch a massive attempt to overthrow the government. Alerted by the Justice Department, local police and militia girded for the assault. But May Day passed without incident. The heightened surveillance did, however, have profound consequences for Nicola Sacco and Bartolomeo Vanzetti. Both men were on a list of suspects the Justice Department had sent to District Attorney Katzmann and Chief Stewart. Just four days after the May Day scare, Officer Connolly arrested the two aliens.

Sacco and Vanzetti fit the stereotypes nativists held of foreigners. Sacco arrived in the United States in 1908 at the age of seventeen. Like so many other Italians he had fled the oppressive poverty of his homeland with no intention of making a permanent home in America. Most of the young men planned to stay only until they had saved enough money to return home and improve their family fortunes. Though born into a modestly well-to-do family, Sacco was no stranger to hard labor. Shortly after his arrival he found steady work in the shoe factories around Milford, Massachusetts.

Sacco's resourcefulness and industry marked him as the kind of foreign worker whose competition American labor feared. Though he lacked formal schooling, Sacco understood that skilled labor commanded steadier work and higher wages and he paid $50 out of his earnings to learn the specialized trade of edge trimming. His wages soon reached as high as $80 per week. By 1917 he had a wife and child, his own home, and $1,500 in savings. His employer at the "3 K" shoe factory described him as an excellent worker and recalled that Sacco often found time, despite his long work days, to put in a few hours each morning and evening in his vegetable garden.

Vanzetti conformed more to the nativist stereotype of shiftless foreigners who drifted from one job to the next. Born in 1888 in the northern Italian village of Villafalletto, he had come to America in 1908 where, like many other immigrants, he found a limited range of jobs open to him. He took a job as a dishwasher in hot, stinking kitchens. "We worked twelve hours one day and fourteen the next, with five hours off every other Sunday," he recalled. "Damp food hardly fit for a dog and five or six dollars a week was the pay." Fearing an attack of consumption, Vanzetti migrated to the countryside in search of open air work. "I worked on farms, cut trees, made bricks, dug ditches, and quarried rocks. I worked in a fruit, candy and ice cream store and for a telephone company," he wrote his sister in Italy. By 1914 he had wandered to Plymouth where he took a job in a cordage factory.

If that sketch captured the essence of Sacco and Vanzetti's lives, they would most likely never have come to the attention of Justice Department agents. But because they were aliens and anarchists, they embodied the kind of foreign menace American nativists most feared. Though not a student of politics like Vanzetti, Sacco was a rebel. He identified closely with the workers' struggle for better wages and the right to organize. In 1912 he and Vanzetti had independently participated in a violent textile strike at Lawrence, Massachusetts. Three years later plant owners around Plymouth had blacklisted Vanzetti for his role in a local strike. Sacco had walked off his job to express sympathy for the cordage workers. Soon after a local labor leader organized a sympathy strike to support workers in Minnesota, authorities arrested Sacco and convicted him of disturbing the peace. All this time, he and his wife regularly joined street theater productions performed to raise money for labor and radical groups.

American entry into World War I created a crisis for both men. Their anarchist beliefs led them to oppose any war that did not work to overthrow capitalism. Sacco even refused the patriotic pressures to buy war bonds. He quit his job rather than compromise his principles. Both began to dread the law requiring them to register (though in fact as aliens they were ineligible for military service). They decided to join a group of pacifists who in May 1917 fled to Mexico, where the two first became personal friends. The hard life and absence from his family finally drove Sacco to return home under an alias, though he did resume his name and former job after the war. Vanzetti returned to Plymouth and soon outfitted himself as a fish peddler.

So in the eyes of many Americans, Sacco and Vanzetti were guilty in at least one important sense. As self-proclaimed enemies of the capitalist system, they had opposed "the American way of life" that nativists cherished. Their suspicious behavior, which Katzmann successfully portrayed as consciousness of guilt, was all too real, for they knew that their radical beliefs might subject them to arrest and deportation, the fate hundreds of other friends and political associates had already faced.

Certainly, the trial record shows that nativism influenced the way judge and jury viewed the defendants. Almost all the eyewitnesses who identified Sacco and Vanzetti were native-born Americans. That they saw a resemblance between the Italian suspects and the foreign-looking criminals proved only, as Harvard law professor Felix Frankfurter remarked, that there was much truth in the popular racist song, "All Coons Look Alike to Me." On the other hand, almost all the witnesses substantiating the defendants' alibis were Italians who answered through an interpreter. The jury, also all native-born Americans, would likely accept Katzmann's imputation that foreigners stuck together to protect each other from the authorities.

The choice of Fred Moore as chief defense counsel guaranteed that radicalism would become a central issue in the trial. In his earlier trial, Vanzetti had been defended by a conservative criminal lawyer, George Vahey. His conviction persuaded Vanzetti that Vahey had not done all he could, especially when Vahey entered into a law partnership with Katzmann shortly after the trial. For the

Dedham trial, friends, local labor leaders, and anarchists created a defense fund to see that no similar betrayal by counsel occurred. From Elizabeth Gurley Flynn, an Industrial Workers of the World agitator and wife of anarchist publisher Carlo Tresca, the committee learned of Moore, who had participated in the trials of numerous radicals, including two Italian anarchists charged with murder during the Lawrence strike. Only later did the committee learn that Moore had contributed little to the acquittal of the Lawrence defendants.

Moore's participation must have reinforced the impression that Sacco and Vanzetti were dangerous radicals. He spent the bulk of defense funds to orchestrate a propaganda campaign dramatizing the plight of his clients and the persecution of radicals. He gave far less attention to planning defense strategy, left largely in the hands of two local co-counsels, Thomas and Jeremiah McAnarney.

Yet in the courtroom Moore insisted on playing the major role. The McAnarneys soon despaired of making a favorable impression on the jury. An outsider from California, Moore wore his hair long and sometimes shocked the court by parading around in his shirtsleeves and socks. Rumors abounded about his unorthodox sex life. And at critical moments he sometimes disappeared for several days. Judge Thayer once became so outraged at Moore that he told a friend, "I'll show them that no long-haired anarchist from California can run this court." Not until 1924 did Moore finally withdraw in favor of William Thompson, a respected Massachusetts criminal lawyer.

Nativism, particularly antiradicalism, obviously prejudiced Judge Thayer and District Attorney Katzmann. We have already seen how Thayer used his charge to the jury to underscore Katzmann's construction of the evidence in the trial. Outside the courtroom, Thayer consistently violated the canons of judicial discretion by discussing his views of the case. George Crocker, who sometimes lunched with Thayer, testified that on many occasions the judge "conveyed to me by his words and manner that he was bound to convict these men because they were 'reds.'" Veteran court reporter Frank Silbey had been forced to stop lunching at the Dedham Inn to avoid Thayer and his indiscreet remarks. Silbey later recalled, "In my thirty-five years I never saw anything like it. . . . His whole attitude seemed to be that the jurors were there to convict these men."

From the moment the trial opened, Thayer and Katzmann missed few opportunities to strike a patriotic pose or to remind the jury that both defendants were draft dodgers. Thayer told the prospective jurors at the outset, "I call upon you to render this service . . . with the same patriotism as was exhibited by our soldier boys across the sea." Katzmann opened his cross-examination of Vanzetti with a cutting statement dressed up as a question: "So you left Plymouth, Mr. Vanzetti, in May 1917 to dodge the draft did you?" Since Vanzetti was charged with murder, not draft evasion, the question served to arouse the jury's patriotic indignation.

Katzmann struck hardest in his questioning of Sacco, whose poor command of English often left him confused or under a misapprehension. Judge Thayer never intervened to restrain the overzealous prosecutor even when it became clear that Sacco could neither follow a question nor express his thoughts clearly.

Playing again upon the residual patriotic war fervor, Katzmann hammered away at the defendant's evident disloyalty:

> KATZMANN: And in order to show your love for this United States of America when she was about to call upon you to become a soldier you ran away to Mexico. Did you run away to Mexico to avoid being a soldier for the country that you loved?
>
> SACCO: Yes.
>
> KATZMANN: And would it be your idea of showing love for your wife that when she needed you, you ran away from her?
>
> SACCO: I did not run away from her.

When the defense objected, Thayer ruled that this line of questioning would help establish Sacco's character. But instead of showing Sacco's philosophical opposition to war, Katzmann made the defendant appear, as one critic expressed it, "an ingrate and a slacker" who invited the jury's contempt. With such skillful cross-examination Katzmann twisted Sacco's professed love of "a free country" into a preference for high wages, pleasant work, and good food.

The prosecutor summed up his strategy in his final appeal to the jury: "Men of Norfolk do your duty. Do it like men. Stand together you men of Norfolk." There was the case in a nutshell—native American solidarity against alien people and their values. Whether he had proved Sacco and Vanzetti guilty of murder mattered little, for he had revealed their disloyalty. In case the point was lost, Judge Thayer reiterated it in his charge:

> Although you knew such service would be arduous, painful, and tiresome, yet you, like the true soldier, responded to the call in the spirit of supreme American loyalty. There is no better word in the English language than "loyalty."

And just who were those "men of Norfolk" to whom the judge and prosecutor appealed? Could they put aside inflammatory rhetoric and render a just verdict? Not a single foreign name, much less an Italian one, appeared on the juror's list. Because Fred Moore had rejected any "capitalists" during jury selection, a few prospective jurors whom the McAnarneys knew to be fairminded were kept off the jury. Those jurors selected were drawn from the tradespeople and other respectable Protestants of the town. None would share the defendants' antipathy to capitalism; few would have had any compassion for the plight of Italian immigrants or union members. Even worse, the jury foreman, Harry Ripley, was a former police chief who outdid himself in persuading his fellow jurors to convict. He violated basic rules of evidence in a capital case by bringing into the juryroom cartridges similar to those placed in evidence. A short time before, he had told his friend William Daly that he would be on the jury in "the case of the two 'ginneys' charged with murder at South Braintree." When Daly suggested that they might be innocent, Ripley replied, "Damn them, they ought to hang anyway."

By using the concept of nativism to gain a broader perspective, the historian has come to understand the answer to a question lawyers need not even ask: What factors accounted for the conviction of Sacco and Vanzetti where legitimate evidence was so clearly lacking? Nativism explains many prejudices exhibited in the trial record. It also explains why those attitudes were so widespread in 1920-1921. We must accept the truth of law professor Edmund M. Morgan's assertion that it was "almost impossible to secure a verdict which runs counter to the settled convictions of the community." Sacco and Vanzetti symbolized for a majority of Americans and the "men of Norfolk" alien forces that threatened their way of life.

Yet, having answered one important question, the historian still faces another. Granted that a jury convicted two alien radicals of robbery and murder in 1921; "why all the fuss," as we asked earlier, in the years that followed? After all, Sacco and Vanzetti were not sentenced until 1927, long after the virulent nativist mood had passed. Corruption and scandal had by then killed the Klan. Prohibition had closed that infernal den of immigrant iniquity, the saloon. The Immigra-

Seeking to screen out those immigrants who were "undesirable," many nativists urged Congress to adopt a literacy test. Although campaigns for such a law had been mounted since the 1890s, only in 1917 did a literacy requirement pass Congress. The cartoon shown here disparages such exclusionist policies, but in the 1920s the pressure for even tighter restrictions mounted, to be embodied (as one Minnesota representative put it) in a "genuine 100 per cent American immigration law."

THE AMERICANESE WALL, AS CONGRESSMAN
BURNETT WOULD BUILD IT.
UNCLE SAM: You're welcome in — if you can climb it!

tion Acts of 1921 and 1924 had severely curbed the flow of newcomers from Italy and eastern Europe. The damage from unsuccessful strikes, management opposition, and government hostility had sent organized labor into a decline from which it would not recover until the New Deal years. The historian must still explain how a local case extended its impact beyond Norfolk County to the nation and even the international community.

No single answer, even one so broad as nativism, can account for the notoriety. Certainly, from the beginning the case had sent ripples across the nation. Socially prominent individuals, intellectuals, the American Federation of Labor, immigrant groups, and radicals had all contributed to the defense fund for the Dedham trial. Those people represented a small minority without great political influence. But by tracing out the appeals process, the historian discovers a series of events that enlarged the significance of the case, heightened the public's awareness of the crucial issues involved, and raised the stakes many groups risked on the judicial outcome.

A Nation Stirred

In the American legal system, the right of appeal is designed to protect defendants against any miscarriage of justice rising out of the original trial. But in 1920 the appeals process in Massachusetts contained a provision that ultimately proved fatal to Sacco and Vanzetti. Any motion for a retrial based on new evidence had to be granted by the original trial judge. On each of eight motions made by the defense, including substantial evidence of prejudice on the part of the judge, the person who heard that appeal was none other than Webster Thayer! Thayer did not have to determine whether new information proved the men innocent; only if another jury might reasonably reach a different verdict.

The next higher court, the Supreme Judicial Court, had only narrow grounds on which to reverse Thayer's decisions. It could review the law in each case, but not the facts. That meant it could determine only if the procedure conformed to the criteria of a fair trial established under state and federal constitutions. Though it found some irregularities in procedure, the Supreme Judicial Court ruled that they did not prejudice the verdict against the defendants. At no time did that court review the weight of evidence presented at the trial or on appeal. It determined, instead, that a reasonable judge might have acted as Thayer did.

And what of the American Supreme Court, the ultimate safeguard of civil liberties? On three separate occasions the defense attempted to move the case into the federal courts. Defense attorneys argued that Sacco and Vanzetti had been the victims of a sham trial, particularly given Judge Thayer's overwhelming prejudice. Justice Oliver Wendell Holmes, Jr., long a champion of civil liberties, wrote that the court could rule only on the grounds of constitutional defects in Massachusetts law. Since none existed, he refused in 1927 to grant a writ of *certiorari* allowing the Supreme Court to review the weight of evidence. Thus the appeals procedure created a formidable barrier to rectifying the injustice done at Dedham.

Despite such inequities, the defense spent six years in an effort to overturn the conviction. Between July 1921 and October 1924 it presented five motions for a new trial. The first involved the behavior of jury foreman Harry Ripley. In response, Thayer completely ignored the affidavit from Ripley's friend William Daly and ruled that Ripley's tampering with evidence had not materially affected the verdict. Eighteen months later the defense uncovered an important new witness, Roy Gould, who had been nearly shot at point black range by the fleeing bandits. Gould had told his story to police immediately afterward, but Katzmann never called him to testify. Eventually defense lawyers uncovered Gould and realized why he had been kept off the stand. Gould had been so close to the escape car that one shot passed through his overcoat; yet he swore that Sacco was not one of the men. Judge Thayer rejected that appeal on the grounds that since Gould's testimony did no more than add to the cumulative weight of evidence, it did not justify a new trial.

Later appeals attempted to show that the prosecutor had tampered with the testimony of two key witnesses. Both witnesses had recanted their courtroom statements and then later recanted their recantations. Rather than find Katzmann guilty of impropriety, Thayer condemned Moore for his "bold and cruel attempt to sandbag" witnesses. Yet another motion came after the prosecution's ballistics expert, Captain Proctor, signed an affidavit in which he swore that on many occasions he had told Katzmann that there was no evidence proving Sacco's gun had fired the fatal shot. He warned that if the prosecutor asked a direct question on that point, Proctor would answer "no." Katzmann had, therefore, carefully tailored his questions during the trial. By the time Thayer heard this motion, Proctor had died. The judge ruled that the jury had understood perfectly what Proctor meant and that Katzmann had not been unfairly evasive.

After that setback, Fred Moore finally withdrew from the case in favor of William Thompson, a distinguished trial lawyer who devoted the rest of his career to Sacco and Vanzetti's cause. Thompson made the first appeal to the Supreme Judicial Court. He argued that the accumulated weight of new evidence and the repeated rejection of appeals demonstrated that Thayer had abused his authority out of hostility to the defendants. Unlike historians, who would render judgment on the basis of the totality of evidence, the appeals judges turned down the defense arguments case by case, point by point. In each separate instance, they ruled that Judge Thayer had acted within his proper authority.

Throughout this drawn-out process, public interest in the case had steadily dwindled. But after November 18, 1925, controversy exploded once again. Sacco received a note from a fellow inmate which read, "I hear by [sic] confess to being in the South Braintree shoe company crime and Sacco and Vanzetti was not in said crime. Celestino F. Medeiros." Medeiros was a young prisoner facing execution for a murder conviction.

The defense soon connected Medeiros to the Morelli gang of Providence, Rhode Island. In the spring of 1921, the Morellis badly needed money to fight a pending indictment, and so had ample reason to commit a payroll robbery. Joe Morelli carried a .32 Colt pistol and bore a striking resemblance to Sacco. Another gang member carried an automatic pistol, which could have accounted for spent cartridges found at the scene. Mike Morelli had been driving a new Buick, which disappeared after April 15. Another member fit the description of the pale, sickly driver. A number of defense and prosecution witnesses identified Joe Morelli when shown his picture. The New Bedford police had even suspected the Morellis of the Braintree crime.

Once again, the District Attorney's office refused to reopen the case. The defense then appealed to Thayer to order a new trial. In reviewing the evidence, Thayer did not have to determine if it conclusively demonstrated Medeiro's guilt or Sacco and Vanzetti's innocence. He had only to decide that a new jury might now reach a different verdict. It took Thayer some 25,000 words to deny this motion.

That decision, more than any other, unleashed the torrent of outrage that surrounded the last months of the Sacco and Vanzetti case. Felix Frankfurter, an eminent Harvard Law School professor and later Supreme Court Justice, published a lengthy article in the *Atlantic Monthly* in which he questioned the conduct of Thayer and Katzmann, and the state appeals court's refusal to grant either clemency or a new trial. "I assert with deep regret but without the slightest fear of disproof," he wrote, "that certainly in modern times Judge Thayer's opinion [on the Medeiros motion] stands unmatched, happily, for discrepancies between what the record discloses and what the opinion conveys." Frankfurter described the document as "a farrago of misquotations, misrepresentations, suppressions, and mutilations." The *Boston Herald* rebuked Thayer for adopting "the tone of the advocate rather than the arbiter." Once a staunch supporter of the prosecution, the *Herald* now called on the Supreme Judicial Court to overturn this ruling. Once again, the court refused to weigh the evidence. It ruled in rejecting the appeal that the defense motion involved questions of fact lying totally within the purview of the trial judge.

That decision, in combination with Frankfurter's blistering attack, shifted public sympathy to Sacco and Vanzetti. A mounting body of evidence seemed to indicate that the two men were innocent. Yet, as the courts remained deaf to the defense appeals, more and more reasonable people came to suspect that, indeed, powerful men and institutions were conspiring to destroy two people perceived as a threat to the social order. Thayer's sentence of death by electrocution seemed but a final thread in a web of legal intrigue to commit an injustice.

Sacco and Vanzetti played an important part in winning broad popular support for their cause. Steadfastly, in the face of repeated disappointments, they maintained their innocence. Sacco, the more simple and direct of the two, suffered deeply as a result of separation from his family. During the first trying years, he went on a hunger strike and suffered a nervous breakdown. From that point on, he stoically awaited the end, more preoccupied with saving his wife further anguish than with saving himself. To assist the defense effort, however, he had begun in 1923 to study English, though with little success. A letter written to his teacher in 1926 conveys his energetic, simple idealism. Sacco had wanted to explain to his teacher why he had been unable to master the language:

No, it isn't, because I have try with all my passion for the success of this beautiful language, not only for the sake of my family and the promise I have made to you—

Many artists, intellectuals, and literary figures *sympathized with Sacco and Vanzetti. Maxwell Anderson wrote a play,* Gods of the Lightning; *Upton Sinclair, the novel* Boston; *and Edna St. Vincent Millay, a series of sonnets. Artist Ben Shahn, himself an immigrant from Lithuania, received recognition during the 1930s for his series of twenty-three paintings on Sacco and Vanzetti. When the painting shown here is compared with the photograph of the two men (page 229), Shahn's source becomes evident. But the artist transformed the photograph in subtle ways. Given our earlier discussion of photographic evidence, how do the changes lend more force to his painting? (Ben Shahn,* Bartolomeo Vanzetti and Nicola Sacco, *1931-32.)*

but for my own individual satisfaction, to know and to be able to read and write correct English. But woe is me! It wasn't so; no, because the sadness of these close and cold walls, the idea to be away from my dear family, for all the beauty and joy of liberty—had more than once exhaust my passion.

Vanzetti's articulate, often eloquent speeches and letters won him the respect of fellow prisoners, defenders, and literary figures drawn to the case, including Upton Sinclair, whose reformist instincts had not deserted him since writing *The Jungle* twenty years earlier. (Vanzetti was "one of the wisest and kindest persons I ever knew," Sinclair wrote, "and I thought him as incapable of murder as I was.") When at last Vanzetti stood before Judge Thayer on the day of his sentencing, he spoke passionately of the first principles that moved him:

Now, I should say that I am not only innocent of all these things, not only have I never committed a real crime in my life—though some sins but not crimes—not only have I struggled all my life to eliminate crimes, the crimes official law and official moral condemns, but also the crime that the official moral and official law sanctions and sanctifies,—the exploitation and the oppression of man by man, and if there is reason why you in a few minutes can doom me, it is this reason and nothing else. . . . I would not wish to a dog or to a snake, to the most low and misfortunate creature of the earth—I would not wish to any of them what I have had to suffer for things that I am not guilty of. But my conviction is that I have suffered for things I am guilty of. I am suffering because I am a radical and indeed I am a radical; I have suffered because I was an Italian, and indeed I am an Italian; I have suffered more for my family and beloved than for myself; but I am so convinced to be right that if you could execute me two times, and if I could be reborn two other times, I would live again to do what I have done already.

The question of guilt or innocence, Vanzetti seemed to suggest, involved more than courtroom evidence. Despite the safeguards of the rule of law, society had judged Vanzetti guilty as judged by a broad constellation of attitudes, beliefs, and prejudices embedded in American culture. And, a historian might add, from out of Vanzetti's own constellation of beliefs, attitudes, and prejudices, he continued to condemn all governments as oppressive, all institutions as evil. This was the anarchist philosophy he lived by—*the Idea*, as he and fellow believers termed it. Vanzetti reaffirmed his right to war against American society and against "the crime that the official law sanctions and sanctifies."

As the debate and protests continued, public support for the execution began to erode. Yet an equally vocal element of the populace hailed Thayer's conduct as a message to "reds" that they could not subvert the Commonwealth of Massachusetts. Thus Governor Alvan Fuller faced a difficult decision when he received a plea from Vanzetti for executive clemency.[1] To ease the political pressure on him, Fuller appointed a blue-ribbon panel to review the entire trial and appeals process. The three men he chose were symbols of the commonwealth's social and educational elite. Unfortunately, retired Judge Robert Grant was a socialite more often preoccupied with black-tie parties than public affairs. Samuel Stratton, president of Massachusetts Institute of Technology, was clearly overshadowed by the committee chair, A. Lawrence Lowell—a pillar of Boston society, a lawyer by training, and the president of Harvard. Lowell had already demonstrated his capacity for ethnocentrism, having introduced quotas to limit the number of Jewish students admitted to Harvard. As the liberal *New Republic* remarked of the committee, "the life of an Italian anarchist was as foreign to them as life on Mars."

For over ten days the three men heard testimony on the evidence, much of it new. The defense also submitted a lengthy brief. But the committee's deliberations were short: on July 27, it filed its final report, upholding both the verdict

---

[1] Sacco refused to sign. Though he agreed with Vanzetti's arguments, he did not want to violate his anarchist principles by appealing to government authorities—or to give his wife further vain hopes.

and sentence against Sacco and Vanzetti. Sympathizers reacted with a mixture of despair and disgust. "What more can immigrants from Italy expect?" asked editorial writer Haywood Broun. "It's not every prisoner who has the President of Harvard throw the switch for him."

By the time all appeals were exhausted, the Sacco and Vanzetti case had brought to public attention not only issues of guilt and innocence, but more fundamental tensions in American society. On one side were arrayed immigrants, workers, and the poor for whom Sacco and Vanzetti stood as powerful symbols. On the other stood Thayer, the "men of Norfolk," the Protestant establishment, and those who believed that America should tolerate only certain peoples and ideas.

On the night of August 22, 1927, John Dos Passos, a young writer, stood with the crowd outside Charleston Prison waiting for news of Sacco and Vanzetti's fate. Shortly after midnight word came—the "good shoemaker and poor fish peddler" were dead. Grief and anger raked the crowd. Some wept, others cried out in the name of justice, and many tore their clothes in anguish. The scene outside the prison was repeated in New York and other cities around the world. Years later, Dos Passos expressed the outrage he felt against those who had persecuted Sacco and Vanzetti:

> they have clubbed us off the streets they are stronger they are rich they hire and fire the politicians the newspapereditors the old judges the small men with reputations the collegepresidents the ward heelers (listen collegepresidentsjudges America will not forget her betrayers). . . .
>
> all right you have won you will kill the brave men our friends tonight
> there is nothing left to do we are beaten. . . .
>
> America our nation has been beaten by strangers who have turned our language inside out who have taken the clean words our Fathers spoke and made them slimy and foul. . . .
>
> they have built the electricchair and hired the executioner to throw the switch
> all right we are two nations

Two nations—that was the reason for "all the fuss."

Will the real truth of the case ever be known? Perhaps not—at least "beyond a reasonable doubt," to borrow the language of the courts. Yet historians have unearthed enough additional information to provide, if not the certainties of fact, at least a few ironies of probability. After Sacco and Vanzetti's execution, Upton Sinclair began to collect material for a novel about the case. As a socialist who had staunchly defended the two men during their years in prison, he was able to interview scores of friends and associates. While Sinclair remained convinced that Sacco and Vanzetti were innocent of the Bridgewater and Braintree robberies, he became less sure whether the two men were merely "philosophical" anarchists. Both had "believed in and taught violence," he discovered. "I became convinced from many different sources that Vanzetti was not the pacifist he was reported to be under the necessity of defense propaganda. He was, like many fanatics, a dual personality, and when he was roused by the social conflict he was a very dangerous man."

Historian Paul Avrich, investigating the anarchist community of which the two men were a part, noted that Vanzetti was indeed a close friend of Luigi Galleani, the firebrand whose associates had launched the letter bombs of 1919 and dynamited Attorney General Palmer's home. "We mean to speak for [the proletariat through] the voice of dynamite, through the mouth of guns," announced the anarchist leaflet found nearby. Carlo Valdinoci, the man who was blown up carrying out his mission, had been a good friend of both Sacco and Vanzetti. Indeed, after Valdinoci's death, his sister Assunta moved in with Sacco and his family. Then, too, rumors within the anarchist community suggested that Vanzetti himself had assembled the bomb that demolished a judge's home in Boston the night Valdinoci had done his work in Washington.

"But my conviction is that I have suffered for things I *am* guilty of," Vanzetti told Thayer at the end. Perhaps there was pride as well as indignation in this response. What, in the end, was the guilt of which Sacco and Vanzetti were so conscious during the trial? Was it merely the knowledge that their radical pamphlets, if found, would get them deported? But both men had been preparing to flee the country anyway, before being arrested. (Recall Sacco's outsized passport photo.) Could their evasive behavior have resulted from the fact that they had more to conceal at home than a few pamphlets?

Upton Sinclair came to believe so. After the execution, Fred Moore confided to him that Sacco and Vanzetti had admitted "they were hiding dynamite on the night of their arrest, and that that was the real reason why they told lies and stuck to them." If true, Sacco and Vanzetti, like Valdinoci, had been willing to commit acts of anarchism which, by the laws of American society, would have been punishable by death. Sacco made clear his own distinction between being tried for his beliefs and being arrested for mere bank robbery. "If I was arrested because of the Idea I am glad to suffer. If I must I will die for it. But they have arrested me for a gunman job."

Is the final irony that Sacco and Vanzetti were willing to die—perhaps even to kill others—for their Idea? Just as the "men of Norfolk" and the officials of Massachusetts were willing to execute Sacco and Vanzetti on behalf of *their* Idea of what America should be? ("Damn them, they ought to hang anyway," remarked juror Ripley.) The historian must suspect that on that August night in 1927, citizens were not merely fighting over a matter of guilt or innocence, but (as Dos Passos put it) over the meaning of those "clean words our Fathers spoke." Sacco and Vanzetti had forced the nation to ask who in their own times best embodied the principles of freedom and equality inherited from 1776. Perhaps neither historians nor lawyers can resolve that question to the satisfaction of a divided nation.

ADDITIONAL READING

Novelists often make excellent historians. Though they may play hob with facts or freely mingle real and fictitious characters, they just as often have a keen sense of the temper of the times and the issues facing a society. Thus, someone interested in the Sacco and Vanzetti case in the context of the 1920s might begin by reading the trilogy by John Dos Passos, *U.S.A.* In volume three, *The Big Money* (New York, 1930), Mary French, an idealistic young liberal, becomes deeply involved in the fight to save Sacco and Vanzetti. More important, Dos Passos writes about the tensions besetting American society and particularly the sense among liberals and radicals that the ruling class had betrayed the nation. This work made Dos Passos a hero to many radicals of the 1930s, though he gravitated steadily to the right.

There are several general histories of the 1920s that make good reading. Among the best are Geoffrey Perrett, *America in the Twenties* (New York, 1987), William Leuchtenberg, *The Perils of Prosperity* (Chicago, 1958), Frederick Lewis Allen, *Only Yesterday* (New York, 1931), and Arthur Schlesinger, Jr., *The Crisis of the Old Order* (New York, 1957). All those works treat Sacco and Vanzetti briefly in the context of the time. Richard Pells, *Radical Visions and American Dreams* (New York, 1973), places the case in its intellectual context and explains how reactions among those involved set much of the radical tone of the depression era. John Higham, *Strangers in the Land* (New Brunswick, N.J., 1955), remains not only the outstanding work on nativism but also one of the best monographic treatments of modern American history. On the political repression of labor and radicals, Robert Murray, *Red Scare* (New York, 1955), is a colorful, though not deeply analytical, account. Athan Theoharis and John Stuart Cox, *Boss: J. Edgar Hoover and the American Inquisition* (Philadelphia, 1988), offers insight into the government's star red hunter.

Like so many controversial episodes in American history, the Sacco and Vanzetti case has become something of a cottage industry for devotees, polemicists, scholars, and writers seeking a provocative subject. To read all the works might take a dedicated person much of a lifetime. Among those works which have sought to establish the guilt of Sacco, Vanzetti, or both, the most forceful presentation is made by Francis Russell, *Tragedy in Dedham* (New York, 1971). To our minds, the following works have made a far stronger case. Readers might best start with Felix Frankfurter, *The Case of Sacco and Vanzetti* (New York, 1962), a reprint of his famous *Atlantic Monthly* critique of the case. It reveals why the establishment reacted so violently—to the extent that the Justice Department tapped his phone until after the execution. The trial transcripts, though available in some libraries in five volumes, may be found in adequate length in Robert Weeks, ed., *The Sacco-Vanzetti Case* (Englewood Cliffs, N.J., 1959), though unfortunately this edition is recently out of print.

One work which recognized that this case had a social as well as legal side is Edmund M. Morgan and Louis Joughlin, *The Legacy of Sacco and Vanzetti* (New York, 1948). Morgan, like Frankfurter a Harvard law professor, used his expertise on rules of evidence to analyze the legal issues, while Joughlin, an English professor, traced the strong effects of the case on intellectuals and writers. Another compelling treatment of the evidence, trial, and appeals procedure is Herbert Ehrmann, *The Case That Will Not Die* (Boston, 1969). Erhmann entered the case as an assistant to William Thompson. His first assignment was to research the Medeiros confession. From that experience he developed a lifelong commitment to establish Sacco and Vanzetti's innocence. Any reader who wishes to encounter Sacco and Vanzetti through their own words can read Marion Frankfurter and Gardner Means, eds., *The Letters of Sacco and Vanzetti* (New York, 1960).

After seventy years in which many people have spent nearly a lifetime of digging, it might seem that historians would be hard-pressed to produce any new evidence about this case. But William Young and David Kaiser, *Postmortem: New Evidence in the Case of Sacco and Vanzetti* (Amherst, Mass. 1985), have uncovered startling evidence of police improprieties, including extensive wiretaps of the defense and its friends and tampering with the ballistics evidence. Young and Kaiser make a powerful case that Sacco and Vanzetti were innocent of robbery and murder. More recently, Paul Avrich, *Sacco and Vanzetti: The Anarchist Background* (Princeton, 1991), has focused attention on the anarchist movement itself, including many previously untapped sources in Italian, that help clarify Sacco and Vanzetti's involvement with "the Idea" and with a philosophy of violence. Among the book's most startling revelations: Mike Boda, apparently outraged by the arrest of Sacco and Vanzetti, drove a wagon full of dynamite to Wall Street. The ensuing blast, notorious in American history, killed thirty-three people in September 1920.

CHAPTER ELEVEN

❦

Huey Generis

Franklin Roosevelt called him one of the two most dangerous men in America. Other contemporaries casting a troubled eye toward Hitler's Nazi Germany and Mussolini's Italy feared he might lead an American fascist movement. Folks back home in Winnfield, Louisiana, remembered him more simply as a smart aleck kid always butting into someone else's business. Many political foes hated him as the political boss who had overwhelmed their entrenched machine only to replace it with a more powerful one of his own. Southerners recognized him as one of those colorful demagogues like Cole Blease, James K. Vardemann, or Theodore Bilbo, who periodically played upon the deep-seated economic grievances and racial hatreds of poor whites. His supporters cheered him as a statesman—a politician who made promises, then delivered. To millions of poor Americans he appeared as a potential savior in the darkest days of the depression.

Whatever people called him, Huey Long took second place to no one. In school, he challenged his teachers. In the courtroom he swung judge and jury to his view of a case. When he first appeared before a committee of the Louisiana legislature, the members heaped abuse on the unknown twenty-two-year-old attorney. Then suddenly, they found themselves charged as the "henchmen and attorneys for the interests." Soon, with a mixture of vituperation and skillful argument, the upstart backed them into a political corner. They had little choice but to pass Huey's amendments to strengthen the state's worker's compensation laws.

Even routine affairs of state afforded the "Kingfish," as he liked to be called, an opportunity to capture headlines. He once turned a visit from the commander of a German warship into an international incident. Eager to meet the political phenomenon from Louisiana, the stiff officer was jolted to find the Kingfish casually attired in lime green pajamas. The chagrin of Germany proved the delight of backwoods Louisiana. Even Franklin Roosevelt found himself occasionally overshadowed by Huey. In 1933 H. G. Wells, the noted British historian and writer, came to Washington to observe the new political rage—

Huey Long, not the president. Gertrude Stein, who earlier had "discovered" the lost generation in Paris, found Huey as well. To her, he was "not boring the way Harding, President Roosevelt, and Al Smith have been boring."

As much as the president, Long mastered the new art of media and mass communications. Millions of Americans would gather eagerly around their radios when they heard, "Hello friends, this is Huey Long speaking." Suddenly the mood would brighten in anticipation of some political fun: Huey was off and running, regaling his audience with funny stories and playing upon their fears, prejudices, and anger. His enemies were their enemies—the lying newspapers, the selfish rich, and the greedy corporations with their corrupt political allies. At least for two enjoyable hours, Huey's millions could dream of striking back at those who left them poor and desperate.

Physical presence could hardly explain Long's power. His unkempt red hair fell loosely across his broad forehead. His pug nose and dimpled chin emphasized his round, fleshy face. Over the years, rich food and late-night carousing

"Hello, friends, this is Huey Long speaking." Thus commenced the refrain of Long's popular radio show. Huey knew how to build his audience, too. "Before I begin," he would inform his curious listeners, "I want you to do me a favor. I am going to talk about four or five minutes. While I am doing that I want you to go to the telephone and call up five of your friends and tell them Huey Long is on the air, and he has some very important revelations to make." After the interlude, Huey would be off and running with more political fun and mayhem.

settled a noticeable paunch on his otherwise average frame. It was the eyes that revealed the difference. Sharp and intense, they sparked with the demonic energy of the man. They were a hater's eyes. Huey never forgave an insult or a political treachery. Unlike his brother Earl, who hated with an unbridled fury that often led to loss of control and physical violence, Huey hated with a cold, calculating intensity that warned friend or foe that he might destroy them when it served his purpose. His fear of physical confrontation, advertised by the constant presence of burly state policemen, led many people to call him a coward, but in politics he never ran from a fight: "Once disappointed over a political undertaking, I could never cast it from my mind. I awaited the opportunity of a political contest."

Personal style set Long apart from other politicians. He had the common touch without ever appearing common. One minute he could play the "good ol' boy" full of easy-going down-home charm; the next minute he would rage with fury at his enemies. As with most mass leaders and celebrities, his mere presence could excite a crowd. Plain folks loved his flair. New York sophisticates might laugh at the lavender shirts, pink ties, shiny suits, and jaunty straw hat, but to Huey and millions of small farmers, workers, and downtrodden Americans, his outlandish garb seemed the height of elegance.

Whether flailing the ruling classes or chiding the president for refusing to redistribute wealth, Long never lost touch with his audience. He would try out a series of ideas or themes until he evoked the right response. He talked the people's language, but with an eloquence that gave their hopes and fears special meaning. Once when asked to compare the Hoover and Roosevelt administrations, Huey likened Hoover to a hoot owl and Roosevelt to a scrootch owl. To catch a hen, he explained, a hoot owl knocked her off the roost and grabbed her as she fell. The scrootch owl was much smoother. He "scrootches up to the hen and talks softly to her, and the hen just falls in love with him, and the next thing you know, there ain't no hen."

Anyone who met Long recognized immediately that he had an extraordinary mind and almost inhuman energy. His near-photographic memory enabled him to recall an infinite number of names, faces, and details of even the most mundane matters. As a lawyer, Huey won the praise of Chief Justice William Howard Taft, who described him as one of the best legal minds to appear before the United States Supreme Court. One writer recalled a typical political conference held in Huey's hotel bedroom. There was Huey lounging drowsily in the notorious lime green pajamas. Then suddenly, an issue fired his imagination. He exploded from bed waving his arms in windmill fashion, shouting at his henchmen, while pointing a finger and pounding them with his fist for emphasis. No matter what the topic—whether to build a drainage ditch at a parish hospital or how to run the next campaign—Huey knew as much or more about it than anyone in the room. Raymond Moley, a member of FDR's braintrust, admitted, "I have never known a mind that moved with more clarity, decisiveness or force." But as one of Long's many critics, Moley regretted the way in which he thought Long "misused his fine mind, battered it, as a child mistreats a toy the value of which he could not understand."

꜒   Like Long's contemporaries, historians have been divided in their judgments on the Kingfish. Arthur Schlesinger, Jr., a fervent champion of the liberalism of Franklin Roosevelt and John Kennedy, recognized Long's talents, but portrayed him as a vicious and dangerous man. Finding Long devoid of any larger social or political vision, Schlesinger banished him from the ranks of both liberal reformers and fascist dictators. "The Messiah of the Rednecks," as Schlesinger condescendingly labeled Long, belonged in the company of such petty politicians as the corrupt dictators of South American "banana republics." "Like them," Schlesinger concluded, "he stood in some muddled way for economic modernization and social justice; like them, he was most threatened by his own arrogance and cupidity, his weakness for soft living and his rage for personal power."

Less doctrinaire in his liberalism, William Leuchtenberg, another leading New Deal historian, treated Long with a bit more sympathy and respect. He recognized that the backwoods buffoon which Long displayed in public was a cleverly conceived act. "A shrewd, intelligent lawyer," Leuchtenberg noted, "Huey cultivated the impression he was an ignoramus. Yet at the same time he lampooned the serious social thinkers of the day." In the end, though, Leuchtenberg dismissed Long as an overblown phenomenon, seriously threatening neither to FDR's reelection in 1936 nor the survival of liberal democracy. His pledge to "Share Our Wealth" linked Long to the "Pied Piper" as he led the poor masses on a futile quest.

In contrast to both Leuchtenberg and Schlesinger, Long's chief biographer, T. Harry Williams, found much to admire in the Kingfish and his legacy. That Williams studied Long from an office at Louisiana State University might cause cynics to doubt his impartiality. Yet even the most hostile of Long's detractors must agree with Williams that Huey Long was no ordinary man. Whatever the label—dictator, demagogue, fascist, populist, liberal reformer, political boss, or revolutionary—Williams concluded that Long "was undeniably a great leader, one of those breed who has to move and drive ordinary men, one of those who break the pattern of their time and shape it anew."

"Great Man" Theory

Over the centuries, historians and philosophers have debated the influence of "great men"[1] in shaping the course of human history. At one extreme stands the nineteenth-century romantic philosopher Thomas Carlyle, who argued that the actions of great leaders have determined history. "Universal history," he wrote, "the history of what man has accomplished in this world, is at bottom the history of the Great Men who have worked here." At the other extreme stand the social determinists, followers of Hegel, Marx, and Darwin, who argued that great

---

[1] The term unfortunately displays its male bias. Since the historians and others we quote have traditionally used it, we make grudging acknowledgment of the tradition. But hereafter we will prefer the more impartial phrase "great leaders."

leaders do not make history. They are products of the times, a reflection of spiritual or material forces, that call forth the heroes demanded by the unfolding of historical laws. As Marx's collaborator Frederick Engels argued, "That Napoleon . . . should have been the military dictator made necessary by the exhausting wars of the French Revolution—that was a matter of chance. But in default of Napoleon, another would have filled his place, that is established by the fact that whenever a great man was necessary, he has always been found: Caesar, Augustus, Cromwell."

Between those extremes—heroes who stand above and direct the social forces of the day and heroes who act as instruments of historical laws—there are, of course, other points of view. Many social Darwinists, for example, saw great leaders as the product of chance brought forth through the process of natural variation. Once these "mutants" arrived, the social environment acted as a selective mechanism by providing the opportunities for those actions that demonstrated their heroic nature. William James, the father of American pragmatist philosophy, suggested, "The mutations of society from generation to generation are in the main due directly or indirectly to the acts or examples of individuals whose genius was so adapted to the receptivities of the moment, or whose accidental position of authority was so critical that they became ferments, initiators of movement, setters of precedent or fashion, centers of corruption, or destroyers of persons whose gifts, had they had free play, would have led society in another direction." In short, James concluded that the "receptivities of the moment" mediate between genius and society. Many potentially great leaders may have died in obscurity because the times or the presence of another dominant figure did not permit them to realize their talents.

T. Harry Williams's sense of Huey Long as a great leader is reflective of the position defined by philosopher Sidney Hook. As a liberal and disillusioned Marxist, Hook took pains to reject the social determinists' view that individuals had little impact on history. "The hero in history," he wrote, "is the individual to whom we can attribute preponderant influence in determining an issue or event whose consequences would have been profoundly different if he had not acted as he did." Hook's heroes are limited neither to the world of public affairs nor to the world of politics. They may be men or women of science, the arts, literature, or any other field. Nor must they be people whose actions history approves. Hitler, Rasputin, and Napoleon have been as crucial as Joan of Arc, George Washington, or Einstein.

Heroes appear for Hook at the "forking point of history." Antecedent events have prepared the stage for their entrances and decisive acts, choices, or discoveries. Such a conception forces Hook to distinguish between what he calls the "eventful" hero and the "event-making" hero. Paul Revere exemplifies the "eventful" man, a person who commits a critical act, but through chance, rather than personal achievement. Anybody who could ride a horse, tell the difference between one or two lanterns, find the road to Concord and Lexington, and yell, "The Redcoats are coming!" could have filled Revere's heroic shoes. Still, his actions were of grave importance, for history might have taken a different course had he fallen off along the way.

By contrast, the "event-making" person is a hero for who and what he or she is as well as does. This person not only leads people at the "fork in the road"; he or she also helps create that fork. The quality of leadership will then sweep aside potential opposition to assure that people accept the alternate road chosen. Surely George Washington's imposing presence as the first president helped assure the survival of republican government when others sought a monarch or benevolent dictator. Another measure of his greatness is his significant "imprint" still visible long after his death. Americans for almost two hundred years have treated the "Farewell Address" as historical verity carved in stone. His character has served as a model for generations of schoolchildren and national leaders. Who else has sanctified as many inns and bedrooms by his choice of accommodations? Washington clearly exemplifies the event-making hero.

Was Huey Long another event-making hero? Is T. Harry Williams correct when he asserts that Long fulfilled the definition of such persons offered by historian Jacob Burckhardt? "He appears complete in every situation," Burkhardt wrote, "but every situation seems to cramp him. He does not merely fill it. He may shatter it. . . . Confronted with parliaments, senates, assemblies, press, public opinion, he knows at any moment how far they are real or only imaginary, and makes frank use of them. . . ."

Modern historians have moved steadily away from Carlyle's romantic view toward the social determinists' opinion of great leaders. It becomes increasingly attractive to dismiss the notion of "heroes" and "heroic" abilities as irrelevant or of little consequence in directing the course of history. Certainly the worldwide magnitude of the Great Depression and its devasting impact on industrial nations underscores the large impersonal forces that affect modern society and that mock the efforts of individuals to understand, much less control them. Around the world factories stood idle and food rotted in the fields while millions of unemployed workers faced growing poverty and even starvation. The political and business leadership that took so much credit for American prosperity in the 1920s now stood impotent in the face of spiraling disaster. President Herbert Hoover symbolized the bankruptcy of leaders and ideas with his much-heralded "no business" conferences. Business leaders paraded to the White House for talks that led to further inaction. The subsequent history of the 1930s would seem to confirm the social determinists' view that perilous times evoke great leaders. That single decade brought forth an almost unprecedented generation of political giants, among them Franklin D. Roosevelt, Winston Churchill, Adolf Hitler, Joseph Stalin, and Mao Zedong.

Long's Louisiana

Louisiana, too, seemed fertile ground for the emergence of a leader who would attack the corrupt political alliance that had held the people in the thralls of poverty, ignorance, debt, and disease. In the 1920s, the state had only 331 miles of paved roads. Among the forty-eight states it had one of the lowest expenditures for education and ranked forty-seven out of forty-eight in literacy. A good

16 percent of the population could neither read nor write. A state as poor as Louisiana could scarcely afford the health, educational, and other social services the poor so desperately needed.

But Louisiana was poor by choice as well as circumstances. Through corruption, police intimidation, and fraud, the Old Regulars and their allies in the Choctaw Club, the political machine that ran New Orleans, assured victory for their chosen candidates. Across the state the conservative business and planter classes and their henchmen used the political system to preserve their special privileges. Louisiana had the same combination of cotton planters, merchants, and professional politicians who feasted regularly at the public trough all across the South. Together they thwarted any efforts to raise taxes or divert state resources to programs for the poor. "We were secure. We were the old families," one prominent society matron recalled. "We had what we wanted. We didn't bother anybody. All we wanted was to keep it."

One corporation in particular, Standard Oil of Louisiana, dominated the economic and political life of the state. It paid almost nothing for the right to drain Louisianas's oil riches. Standard joined with the conservative hierarchy to ensure a favorable climate for business at great expense to the workers and the poor. Citizens of New Orleans, for example, paid among the highest utility rates in the nation, while business taxes were among the lowest. From the Civil War to the 1920s such self-serving greed and class interest kept Louisiana in a condition comparable to feudalism.

Several peculiarities explain the plight of Louisiana's lower classes. Besides cotton planters, the state had a powerful block of sugar planters to reinforce the conservative hierarchy. The Old Regulars and Choctaws constituted the only powerful urban machine in southern politics. That combination of planters and urban bosses had long managed to rule the state without serious challenge. Briefly during the populist uprising of the 1890s poor black and white citizens had joined to demand redress for their manifold economic grievances. But the conservatives had an issue along with race-baiting to keep the poor divided. Most of southern Louisiana was Catholic, while the poor northern hill farmers were largely Protestant. No one outside the conservative hierarchy had ever found a way to unite the two groups.

Mired in poverty, exploited by the wealthy few, and without a political voice, the masses of Louisiana were indeed ripe for a popular leader. Yet, since the Civil War, the conservatives had crushed or absorbed anyone who sought to upset the state's balance. A "good ol' boy" might come around preaching the politics of discontent to farmers along the creek forks, upland hills, or bayous, but sooner or later he would lose his fire and sell out to the interests.

Huey Long was different. His claim to greatness as an event-making leader rests largely on the capacity he demonstrated to redefine the rules and goals of politics at almost every stage of his career. Even a brief summary of that career suggests why T. Harry Williams could claim Long as an example of the great leaders who redirect the course of history. Huey was born in 1893 at the beginning of a severe national depression and died forty-two years later in the middle of an even worse economic disaster. Those who seek the roots of character in childhood will find potential confirmation of Long's greatness in his early years. Even before walking at just nine months, Long showed signs of the electric energy and devilish curiosity that set him apart. His sisters recalled that if left alone, he might roll off the porch, crawl to the fence, and unlatch the gate, so that he could sit by the road and watch the people passing.

 By the age of twenty-five, Long had accomplished more than many people achieve in a lifetime. He moved with the sense of urgency and destiny historians often discover in the lives of great leaders. After turning the local Winnfield schools upside down with his irrepressible antics, he embarked at age seventeen on a brief career as a salesman. Though he earned little, he gained valuable experience dealing with the public and learning to survive by his wits. Five years after high school, he had been through several jobs, a brief stint at the University of Oklahoma, marriage, a year at Tulane University Law School, and the Louisiana bar exam. Over the next three years, he established a successful law practice, became the father of two children (one a future senator), and won his first election to public office.

Such a fast-moving, ambitious young man was bound to experience frustration and a few failures along his way. At the age of thirty-one, he lost his first race for the governorship. Four years later, in 1928, he came back to beat the odds and the conservative hierarchy to become one of the youngest governors ever elected. He still had to withstand an impeachment effort before he could count on keeping his office out of the clutches of his enemies. That unsuccessful effort to destroy his political career seemed to have hardened his ambition to smash anyone who stood in his way. He allowed the shattered remnants of the Standard Oil, cotton and sugar planter, and urban Choctaw machine alliance to survive because he understood that in politics such enemies make useful scapegoats. Whenever he needed to arouse his followers or justify the ruthlessness of his politics he could flail the conservative oligarchy. Under Long, Louisiana became the one southern state that had something resembling a two-party system, though his dictatorial power made political opposition virtually meaningless.

Preoccupied with the state's economic and social injustice, Long avoided the traditional southern demagogues' passion for race baiting and religious bigotry. Instead, he made Louisianans face up to the real sources of their poverty: inequitable income distribution, regressive taxation, poor education, paucity of social services, and the domination of corporate interests. As one critic of his dictatorship conceded, "Huey Pierce Long has the distinction of having injected more realism into southern politics than any man of his generation."

In 1930, while still governor, Long began his ascent into national politics. He was just thirty-seven when elected senator from Louisiana. For one year he refused to leave the state to assume his seat until he had found a successor he could trust to mind the store in his absence. It was that same year that the notorious "green pajamas" episode with the German naval commander helped project him into the national limelight. In the Senate, he associated himself with a small band of hopelessly outnumbered progressives, centered around George Norris of Nebraska. He soon broke with the stodgy and conservative Democratic leadership of Arkansas's Joe Robinson. In 1932 he began his troubled association with Franklin Roosevelt, when at Norris's urging, he helped the New York governor win the 1932 Democratic presidential nomination. Long then stumped effectively for Roosevelt and, one suspects, for himself in the few midwestern states where Roosevelt's wary campaign managers dared to send him. The raves from enthusiastic local party leaders astounded Roosevelt's advisors. "We never again underrated him," recalled campaign chief Jim Farley.

Before Roosevelt had completed the spectacular first "hundred days," the Kingfish had bolted from the New Deal. Long charged that Roosevelt was too much the captive of the special interests to confront the real issue facing the United States—maldistribution of wealth. "When one man decided he must have more goods to wear for himself and his family than any other ninety-nine people," Long explained, "then the condition results that instead of one hundred people sharing the things on earth for one hundred people, that one man through his greed, takes over ninety-nine parts for himself and leaves one part

*A **buoyant Kingfish** celebrates the 1934 election-night victory of one of his allies, James P. O'Connor (**left**), along with Governor O. K. Allen (**right**). Less than a year later, Long was gunned down in the Louisiana state capitol building by an irate physician. Reeling down the corridor, Long slumped into the arms of O'Connor, who had come running to investigate the commotion. "Jimmy, my boy, I've been shot," gasped Long. Governor Allen, also present, reportedly seized a pistol and dashed down the corridor toward the assassin shouting, "If there's shooting I want to be in on it!"*

for ninety-nine." While Frank-lin De-La-No-Roo-Se-Velt, as Long twittingly pronounced the president's name, catered to bankers and took money from veterans to plant trees, the hard-working middle class of America was disappearing into poverty.

Long countered the president's reformism with a grandiose scheme for sharing wealth. He proposed to tax away income over $1 million and inheritance over $5 million. With little regard for economic realities, Long began to promise his followers some remarkable benefits. Every family would receive a $5,000 homestead allowance and a guaranteed income of $2,000 a year. He offered additional support for labor, farmers, the elderly, and the young. If someone suggested that Long's plan sounded like Hitler's or Lenin's, he referred the heckler to his true source—the Bible. "It's all in the scriptures," he would claim and then cite Leviticus, Deuteronomy, or Isaiah.

The real cause of Long's dissatisfaction, most historians would agree, was that Franklin Roosevelt's success blocked his own road to national power. The Kingfish had grown too accustomed to solo performances to play second violin to Roosevelt. By 1934 he had begun organizing his own political base outside the Democratic Party. With his slogan "every man a king, but no man wears a crown," he attracted perhaps as many as seven million members to his Share Our Wealth Clubs. But whether Long could have translated membership into enough votes to mount a serious threat to Roosevelt's reelection in either 1936 or 1940 can never be known. On a whirlwind trip to tend to business in Louisiana, his career ended tragically. Carl Weiss, a brilliant surgeon and son-in-law of a disappointed officeholder, mortally wounded the Kingfish in the corridor of the state capitol building. Weiss died immediately in a hail of gunfire.

Death at an early age left Long's promise unfulfilled. "God don't let me die," friends around his deathbed heard him whisper. "I have so much to do." The circumstance of his death evokes an eerie resemblance to Hegel's description of great leaders as instruments of history to be discarded when their work is done. "Their whole life is labor and trouble . . . ," Hegel wrote, "They die early like Alexander; they are murdered like Caesar. . . ."

The Greatness of Huey Long

Long's tragic death has made it impossible for historians to measure his potential for national leadership. When he died, he was on the verge of greatness, but he had held office only as the governor and senator from a relatively backward southern state. He demonstrated a capacity for dynamic leadership at the state level and for using his flamboyant personality to attract a national audience of uncertain political persuasion. In that light he would stand in the second tier of political leaders and invite comparison to such regional aspirants for national office as Dixiecrat Strom Thurmond of South Carolina or former Governor George Wallace of Alabama. Wallace, like Long, dramatized working- and lower-middle-class discontent without proving that he could establish the broad-based national coalition needed to win the presidency. It is impossible to determine if

Long could have lured many followers away from Franklin Roosevelt and his popular New Deal programs. At the time of Long's death, federal investigations into the corruption in Louisiana threatened to weaken or destroy the machine that served as his political base.

Since actual events cannot sufficiently measure Long's potential as a great national and international leader, historians must search for alternatives to the standard biographical practice of chronicling a subject's many achievements. One method that appealed to many of Long's contemporaries was to draw comparisons between the Kingfish and other great political leaders. The ruthlessness with which Long dominated Louisiana in the 1930s inevitably suggested parallels with Nazi dictator Adolf Hitler. Many of the conditions that accompanied Hitler's rise to power existed in the United States: an increasingly impoverished middle class, growing radical political groups, a leadership that often failed to respond to popular fears and suffering, and huge inequities of power and wealth created by capitalism. Some people predicted that if Roosevelt faltered in his efforts to bring the country out of the Depression or to provide a measure of security, Long stood lurking in the wings to "Hitlerize America."

Upon closer analysis the comparison breaks down. In at least two important particulars, Long rejected Hitler's program. He was not anti-intellectual nor was he a religious or racial bigot. The growth in size and quality of Louisiana State University remained one of his proudest accomplishments. And when a reporter once tried to compare him to Hitler, Long shot back, "Don't liken me to that sonofabitch. Anybody that lets his public policies be mixed up with his religious prejudices is a plain goddamned fool." As a hard-bitten political realist, Long never indulged in Hitler's sometimes dreamy forays into romantic fantasy. Both Hitler and Mussolini dabbled in social thought and evolved theories of the state as the endpoint of politics. Beyond his scheme to redistribute wealth, Long generated few political ideas.

Still, Long's potential appeal to mass discontent gave special cause for concern. Raymond Graham Swing, the commentator who most fully explored the parallels to Hitler, worried over the remark of a young Louisiana State University professor. "There are many things Huey does I don't approve of," the professor admitted. "But on the whole he has done a great deal of good. And if I had to choose between him without democracy and going back to the old crowd . . . I should choose Huey. After all, democracy isn't any good if it doesn't work. Do you really think freedom is so important?"

More fruitful comparisons can be drawn between Long and politicians of a homegrown variety. Among other senators in the twentieth century who built a national following, Robert LaFollette and Joseph McCarthy, both from Wisconsin, offer the historian some interesting parallels. Comparison to LaFollette brings out Long's capacity for constructive and innovative politics, while the link to McCarthy illuminates his disruptive tactics and his facility for exploiting institutional and human weaknesses. All three careers provide insight into the nature of national leadership below the presidential level.

Though not as politically precocious as Long, "Battle Bob" turned early in his life from law to politics. At age twenty-five, just seven months out of college and recently admitted to the bar, LaFollette defied the local machine boss to win election as district attorney. Soon, like Long, he had built a reputation as a champion of the little guy and foe of the interests. In 1885, he began the first of his three terms in Congress and by 1900 after two unsuccessful bids he was elected governor of Wisconsin. He brought to public office the same burning ambition that set Long apart from ordinary politicians. His enemies were Long's enemies: corrupt political machines, large corporations, greedy bankers, and concentrated wealth. His first electoral defeat at the hands of the entrenched interests led him, like Long, to declare war on the machine. In its place he constructed an equally powerful organization loyal to himself, but one which for forty years earned a well-deserved reputation for efficient, honest, and progressive government.

It was not just progressive zeal that differentiated LaFollette from Long. "Battle Bob" possessed little of the common touch. His stern Calvinist soul, intense convictions, and unbending nature led him to champion minority causes and to set his eye on what was right rather than expedient. Where Long used his barbed wit, biting invective, and homespun ebullience to win an audience, LaFollette preferred the power of truth and moral rectitude to persuade his followers. Such political asceticism could never achieve the broad mass appeal that attracted millions to Long. And LaFollette, too, had his Roosevelt—in this case the popular Teddy Roosevelt—who for a season blocked any aspirations he might have had for national leadership.

A comparison to Senator Joseph McCarthy must dwell on the dark side of Long's political nature—his capacity for hate, his wanton destructiveness, and his disregard for rules of fair play or responsible politics. What Euripedes said of the demagogue in *Orestes* might apply equally well at times to either McCarthy or Long: "A man of loose tongue, intemperate, trusting in tumult, leading the population to mischief with empty words." Long drew his followers from the millions suffering the fear and deprivations of the Depression. McCarthy exploited the cold war fear of communism to wreak havoc on the apparatus of American foreign policy-making. His goal, as far as historians can judge, was neither a safer America nor the eradication of domestic communism, but a prominent place in the public limelight. He relished his ability to generate headlines and confusion among his political foes.

Like Long, McCarthy was something of a political innovator. While Long perfected the devices of the state political machine, McCarthy mastered the "multiple untruth," a falsehood so large, hyperbolic, and complex that it defied refutation. "The Multiple Untruth," observed McCarthy's biographer Richard Rovere, "places an unbearable burden of disproof on the challenger. The work of refutation is always inconclusive, confusing, and—most important of all, perhaps—boring to the public." No one, either friend or foe, ever found Long or McCarthy boring. Still, McCarthy relied even more than Long on the measure of public gullibility. Americans love facts and McCarthy seemed weighted down with them. His briefcase, bulging with documents, photostats, and transcripts, lent an air of credibility to his extravagant accusations. Close examination usually proved that his documents had little relevance to the charges he raised. McCarthy, too, matched his public excesses with a private passion for voluptuous living. Boozing, womanizing, and late nights (possibly drug addiction as well) took their toll just as they did for Long.

For all the parallels, "Tail-gunner Joe" differed from Long in at least one critical aspect. McCarthy never tried to direct his popularity into a political organization. Rovere described him as a leader with a following but no movement. He did not employ the demagogue's practice of tempting his audience with a vision of a better tomorrow but dwelt, instead, on their darkest fears and insecurities. When the Senate censured him for his misconduct, he did not whip his followers into frenzied outrage, as Long surely would have. McCarthy had no program, and possibly no ambition other than to sustain his capacity to dominate the headlines.

Since Long built a stronger national political organization than either LaFollette or McCarthy, it might be more productive to compare him to the popular presidents rather than senators. Abraham Lincoln, Lyndon Johnson, and Harry Truman, among others, followed Long's path from modest beginnings and political obscurity in remote rural communities to the top and center of American politics. But none of those men who achieved more in politics moved so far outside traditional channels or advanced as rapidly at such a young age. The presidents who did achieve their ambitions early, Theodore Roosevelt and John Kennedy, both started with the advantages of wealth and prominence. Their road to the White House was shorter than that of any president save, perhaps, John Quincy Adams. Each faced obstacles, nonetheless, as formidable as any Long encountered. Roosevelt had to overcome the prejudice of patricians against politics and of professional politicians against patricians. Kennedy surmounted the deep-seated American prejudice against Catholics. It is improbable, though certainly not impossible, that Long could have conquered the national bias that kept southerners out of the White House until Lyndon Johnson's victory in 1964.

 ## Instances of Greatness?

The attempt to find adequate parallels in the lives of other national leaders proves ultimately as unsatisfactory as contemporaries' efforts to fix Long with an accurate political label. Just as his program defied precise definition, his brand of politics was unique. He had elements of the demagogue, populist, liberal reformer, radical, and native fascist, but he conformed to no particular type. Once again, historians are forced to accept the label Long pinned on himself; he was indeed *sui generis*. To measure his potential as a great leader, historians must look closely at some of the critical moments in his career. We can then better judge whether Long brought circumstances to a "forking point" and then, through the force of his character, determined the path history followed. Or we might conclude that Long was little more than an instrument of larger political forces at work in that turbulent era in the history of Louisiana and the United States.

One of the first key episodes in Long's public life occurred before he formally embarked on his career in politics. As a struggling young lawyer, he had come under the benevolent wing of a successful Winnfield politician, State Senator S. J. Harper. True to the dissenting heritage of Winnfield County politics, Harper adopted a body of unorthodox, even eccentric ideas. He opposed war, Wall Street bankers, liquor, the microbe theory, and high heels for women. It was in support of Harper's worker's compensation amendments that Long first spoke before the Louisiana legislature. When the United States entered World War I in 1917, Harper demanded that Congress finance the war effort by conscripting wealth. He later elaborated his views in a pamphlet denouncing war profiteers, bankers, and Wall Street. His outburst incurred the wrath of state officials who, along with most Americans caught in the contagion of war fever, had lost all tolerance for dissent. A federal grand jury indicted Harper for violating the Espionage Act.

Despite the popular furor, Long made the risky decision to serve as Harper's attorney. He understood that the government's case amounted to a political vendetta and, therefore, politicized the defense by denouncing the indictment at a press conference. By defusing some of the hostility, Long shifted opinion in favor of his client and thereby reduced the personal risk of committing political suicide prematurely. As the case came to trial, Huey was unwilling merely to stand by and let the law take its course. While his brother Julius prepared the legal side of the defense, Huey worked behind the scenes to shift the odds in Harper's favor. He soon learned that government agents were shadowing all the prospective jurors. As openly as possible, he contacted all those who might be hostile to Harper and engaged them in drinks and conversation. The agents duly reported those friendly encounters, though Huey, in fact, had never mentioned the case. When each of those compromised jurors was called, suspicious government attorneys excused them. Huey had virtually cleared the jury of potentially unsympathetic elements.

T. Harry Williams has persuasively argued that Long's antics had little to do with Harper's acquittal. The government's weak case simply fell apart in the courtroom. But what does impress the student of "great leaders" is a certain characteristic behavior that recurs throughout Long's career. First, Long perceived in an apparently damaging case an opportunity to advance his own political fortunes and earn the gratitude of an ally as well. Second, he showed his cleverness at redefining the rules to suit his own purpose. Tampering with the jury violated the spirit, if not the letter, of the law. Third, his decision to attack the prosecution involved a cardinal rule of American politics, later perfected in California by campaign strategist Murray Chotiner and his apt student, Richard Nixon. Do not defend yourself, and let the public know where you stand. Attack your opponents, and let the public know where they stand, while revealing as little about yourself as possible. Once attention is focused on what voters resent in your opponents, they will be on the defensive. Americans, Long understood, are as likely to decide *against* candidates and issues as they are *for* them. Long would use those tactics—projecting himself to the public, redefining the rules of the game, and mastering the attack—to win victories even when defeat seemed virtually inevitable.

The most dramatic instance of Long's talent for improvisation and survival came during his 1929 impeachment case. Conservative leaders, outraged by his attempt to tax Standard Oil; by his progressive textbook, road, and welfare programs; and by his high-handed political methods, formed the "Dynamite Squad" to impeach the governor before he became too popular with the masses. The most serious charge leveled against him was that he had tried to bribe his former bodyguard, "Battling" Harry Bozeman, to murder J. Y. Sanders, Jr., leader of the conservative anti-Long faction in the state senate. Other charges referred to Long misusing state funds, abusing the powers of his office, and attempting to influence judges, legislators, and other officials through bribery, political pressures, and intimidation. Beginning in April 1929, the Dynamite Squad met daily in Sanders's office to mastermind impeachment strategy. They started with all the advantages on their side—initiative, an eager staff, and ample volunteer legal assistance.

Momentarily stunned by the strength and organization of the opposition, Long realized he had reached the crossroads of his political career. Out of habit, he did what he knew best—attacked. For two months he flooded the state with almost a million copies of circulars he composed himself (and had delivered by off-duty state police and other state workers). He laid the impeachment fight on the doorstep of his favorite villain, Standard Oil. The real contest, he charged repeatedly, pitted Huey Long, champion of the people, against a corporation and its henchmen determined to keep Louisiana in bondage.

Once on the offensive, Long defeated his enemies by using his infinite energy, his organizational skills, and his political and legal shrewdness. Since the Dynamite Squad needed a two-thirds majority in the senate to impeach, Long required support from just fourteen senators to block them. He and his allies crossed and recrossed the state rounding up support and rousing the voters to bring pressure to bear on reluctant legislators. Where those pressures failed, both sides resorted to all manner of argument, including bribery and promises of patronage.

Long's masterstroke came when he adopted a tactic used in 1919 by senate Republicans to frustrate Woodrow Wilson's attempt to offer them a "Democratic" Versailles peace treaty. During the negotiations, thirty-nine, or more than enough to prevent a two-thirds majority, had signed a round robin letter expressing their opposition to the treaty as then written. Huey or some member of his inner circle had proposed the same strategy to win the impeachment fight. As the Louisiana Senate met to hear the evidence against the governor, a pro-Long senator rose to announce that he and fourteen others, in light of the "unconstitutionality and invalidity" of the charges, had signed a round robin in which they pledged to vote against all articles of impeachment. No matter what evidence the Dynamite Squad hoped to present, no matter how they villified the fifteen pro-Long senators, they had already lost. In stunned silence the legislature agreed to adjourn.

Whenever Huey Long rallied support *in a campaign or a debate over legislative issues, he flooded Louisiana with circulars and posters. He often prepared them himself and then used his army of political supporters and government employees to spread the materials around the state. This photograph was taken by Ben Shahn, who painted the portrait of Sacco and Vanzetti on page 248. From 1933 through 1938 Shahn was one of about a dozen photographers who created a pictorial record of rural life during the Depression on behalf of the Farm Security Administration.*

Over the years many of Long's opponents reaped the whirlwind of failure, for Huey always revenged himself against his enemies. Some he drove from office; some he denied patronage; and a few he simply ruined. And just as he never forgave his enemies, he never forgot his supporters. Once five years later, when his successor O. K. Allen claimed he had no position to give an old Long loyalist, Huey shouted at him, "That's one of my old friends who signed the 'Round Robin' to keep them from impeaching me. What do you mean, you haven't got a job?" On such reciprocal loyalties, Long understood, successful organizations were built.

Among his many political skills none surpassed Long's genius as a campaigner. Few politicians have ever had his capacity to organize and conduct a successful race. One of his greatest electoral achievements did not even come on his own behalf, but in the incredible upset he engineered for Hattie Caraway of Arkansas, the first woman elected to the United States Senate. Mrs. Caraway had originally filled her husband's seat after he died in office. Arkansas Democrats apparently expected her to retire gracefully at the end of her term, but Mrs. Caraway had ideas of her own. While in Washington she had met and become friends with the junior senator from Louisiana, Huey Long. Appreciative of the courage she showed in voting regularly with the outnumbered progressives, Long began to act as an informal advisor.

As the new election approached, leading Arkansas Democrats vied to replace Mrs. Caraway. Few noticed, or even cared, when she announced in July that she too would be a candidate in the August 9 election. Not only was she a woman in a region that frowned on women in politics, but she also had no organization, no financial support, and no significant backers. Analysts predicted that at most she would receive 1 percent of the vote. They had not anticipated that Huey would come to campaign for his friend.[2] Even after he announced his intention, Arkansas politicians scoffed, for Long had just six days to salvage the weakest candidate in the race. Without the advantages of mass communications like television, he would be hard-pressed to reach a substantial number of voters in such a rural state.

Huey gave those smug Arkansas politicians a lesson they did not soon forget. With his sound trucks and circulars, he treated the state to what one observer described as a "circus hitched to a tornado." When it was over, he had given thirty-nine speeches, covered over 2,000 miles, and spoken to some 200,000 people. His campaign rhetoric was vintage Long—maldistribution of wealth, politicians under Wall Street's thumb, and the unnecessary suffering from the Depression. At the end of each speech he would praise Hattie Caraway for courageously fighting on behalf of the common people. When the cyclone had subsided, Mrs. Caraway won a smashing victory with more votes than the combined totals of her six opponents. Out of the seventy-five counties in Arkansas, Huey had campaigned in thirty-one and Hattie carried twenty-nine of those.

Once again Long had confounded the political professionals. He showed that he understood the mood of the electorate far better than they. His vote-getting tactics presaged a new era in American politics. Out in California the public relations firm of Whitaker and Baxter was already perfecting the "Madison Avenue" blend of media, image, and packaging that has come to dominate election campaigns. Huey had proved as well that his popular appeal was not confined to his native Louisiana. Once aware of his awesome vote-getting talents, national political leaders could no longer dismiss him as a backwoods buffoon.

No historian would build a case for a great leader around three isolated successes. In Long's case that is not necessary. His political triumphs were legion. He turned a minor office on the moribund state railroad commission into a major public platform. To win the governorship he became the first candidate outside the old machine who gained broad support in both the Protestant north and the Catholic south. He then welded those factions into a

---

[2] T. Harry Williams has argued convincingly that friendship could hardly have been Long's primary motive. Success in Arkansas would enhance his prestige, increase his public exposure, and frighten his arch political enemy, Joe Robinson, leader of the conservative Senate Democrats and the senior senator from Arkansas.

tight organization. As a senator, he showed similar disregard for convention when he attacked one of the most popular and powerful presidents in the nation's history—and from his own party, no less! Many historians agree that his campaign to redistribute wealth forced Roosevelt to propose his own radical tax measure, which led to the Wealth Tax Act of 1935.

At each stage of his career Long had shown that through the force of his charismatic personality and his political savvy he could force others to adopt his agenda for public debate. Whether he could have had that same impact on the U.S. Senate and the national political agenda is open to serious question. During the Depression most politicians or parties with a single issue or a narrow constituency flourished briefly and then disappeared. Roosevelt and the New Deal often coopted their issues, or frustration pushed them further into the extremes of the political spectrum, from which they could not attract a significant following. Corruption, too, whether from wealth or power, took a heavy toll

The Kingfish lives on: a poster tacked to the wall of a Louisiana farmhouse, and caught by another Farm Security Administration photographer, Russell Lee.

among the political aspirants of the era. Long was vulnerable to all those forces—cooptation, frustration, and corruption. Yet repeatedly, he had proved the experts and their conventional wisdom wrong. He was more forceful, dynamic, and charismatic than most of them recognized. No matter what the yardstick, Sidney Hook's event-making hero or Jacob Burkhardt's great leader, Long met their criteria.

What remains uncertain is what role such persons play in determining the course of history. Long seems to offer some confirmation to both the social determinists and the "great man" theorists. Along with Father Coughlin, Hitler, Franklin Roosevelt, and the California media moguls, Long taught Americans what a charismatic leader could accomplish with the aid of modern mass communications. Still, it seems inevitable that politicians would have learned that lesson even without him. In Louisiana, he redefined state politics and threw the bums out. But soon after he died, his followers had equaled the Old Regulars' reputation for venality, inefficiency, and catering to special interests. On the national level, his plan to redistribute wealth died with him. Only World War II led to tax policies that in a small measure shifted wealth from one class to another. Since then, however, the inequities of income and wealth have remained a fixed part of American life.

How then did Huey Long, a great leader, redirect the course of history? While historians might agree that he was far more than "The Messiah of the Rednecks," they could not determine what would have happened if Long had never entered politics or had lived to sixty-five. Such speculation takes them into the realm of seers, metaphysicians, and theologians. Those are grounds on which the modern historian treads lightly, if at all.

ADDITIONAL READING

Writing in the 1940s, when the presence of Hitler, Roosevelt, Churchill, Stalin, and Mussolini naturally focused attention on the topic, Sidney Hook composed *The Hero in History* (New York, 1943), a clear survey of almost 150 years' historical and philosophical debate over great leaders in history. Since Hook is no particular partisan of the Marxist tradition, a reader might want to give Marx his due by reading Karl Marx and Frederick Engels, *The German Ideology* (New York, 1970).

The issue of the great leader in history is the interpretive framework adopted by T. Harry Williams, *Huey Long* (New York, 1969). Williams set out to write the definitive Long biography, but despite the length and rich detail in his book, he fell short. He records and respects Long's achievements as well as some of the blemishes without fully analyzing the consequences of either. Aside from Williams, Long has had few biographers who did not make use of either a hatchet or kid gloves. Probably the most balanced appraisal comes in Hugh Davis Graham, ed., *Huey Long* (Englewood Cliffs, N.J., 1970), a volume in the "Great Lives Observed" series. Graham provides a mix of documents, contemporary views, and historical perspectives, including Arthur Schlesinger, Jr.'s "Messiah of the Rednecks." That selection is from *The Politics of Upheaval* (New York, 1960), 42-69. Graham also includes a selection from Huey Pierce Long, *Every Man a King* (Baton Rouge, La., 1933), Long's autobiography that became the bible of his Share Our Wealth Clubs. Alan Brinkley, *Voices of Protest* (New York, 1982), has produced the most persuasive interpretation of Long (as well as the "Radio Priest," Father Charles Coughlin) yet written. Placing the Kingfish in the mainstream of the American political tradition, Brinkley debunks the idea that Long threatened to bring fascism to the United States. He was, in Brinkley's eyes, if not a "great man," at least a remarkable politician who gave voice to the desire of millions of Americans "to defend the autonomy of the individual and the independence of the community against encroachments from the modern industrial state."

William Leuchtenberg's fine survey, *Franklin D. Roosevelt and the New Deal* (New York, 1963), 96-99, contains a superb brief biographic sketch of Long. For a history of the era sensitive to broad social issues, see Robert McElvaine, *The Great Depression* (New York, 1984). Otherwise, the reader has to turn to scholars who have studied Long's politics more than his personality. One good place to begin is V. O. Key, *Southern Politics in State and Nation* (New York, 1950), or Allan Sindler, *Huey Long's Louisiana* (Baltimore, Md. 1956). Among the best Long biographies produced by his contemporaries are Forrest Davis, *Huey Long: A Candid Biography* (New York, 1935), and Carleton Beals, *The Story of Huey P. Long* (Philadelphia, Pa. 1935).

Many people now know the documentary work of filmmaker Ken Burns because of his widely acclaimed PBS series *The Civil War* (1990). But Burns first came to the attention of historians with his documentary *Huey Long* (1985), one of the best biographic treatments of Long, much enriched by its wealth of historical film and newsreel footage. In the previous chapter we expressed our opinion that novelists are often excellent historians. Robert Penn Warren, *All the King's Men* (New York, 1946), certainly vindicates that judgment. Critic Robert Alter called it the best political novel of the century, and we agree. Warren did not write a novel about Huey Long, but he wrote about the nature of good and evil and the uses and abuses of power. Still, anyone who wants a feeling for Long's Louisiana could find no better source than *All the King's Men*.

CHAPTER TWELVE

The Decision to Drop the Bomb

Just before dawn on July 6, 1945, only a few clouds hung over the still New Mexico desert. The air possessed that lucid clarity which skews all sense of distance and space. Out on the desert stood several large towers, yet from the perspective of the blockhouse, where the observers anxiously waited, they appeared as little more than a few spikes stuck in the sand.

Suddenly, one of the towers erupted into a brilliant fireball, searing the air and instantly replacing the dawn's pastels with a blazing radiance. With the radiance came heat: an incredible, scorching heat that rolled outward in waves. Where seconds before the sand had stretched cool and level in every direction, now it fused into glass pellets. The concussion from the fireball completely vaporized the tower at its center, created a crater a quarter of a mile wide, and obliterated another forty-ton steel tower one-half mile away. Above the fireball an ominous cloud formed, shooting upward, outward, then back upon itself to form the shape of a mushroom, expanding until it had reached eight miles in the air. The effects of the fireball continued outward from its center: the light, followed by the waves of heat, and then the deadening roar of the concussion, sharp enough to break a window over 125 miles away. Light, heat, concussion—but first and foremost, the brilliance of the light. At the edge of the desert a blind woman was facing the explosion. She saw the light.

In the blockhouse at Alamogordo, where scientists watched, feelings of joy and relief were mixed with foreboding. The bomb had worked. Theory had been turned into practice. And devastating as the explosion appeared, the resulting fireball had not ignited the earth's atmosphere, as some scientists had predicted. But the foreboding was impossible to shake. Humankind now had in its hands unprecedented power to destroy.

General Leslie R. Groves, director of the atom bomb project, shared none of the scientists' fears. Groves could barely contain his joy when he wired the news to President Harry Truman, who was meeting allied leaders at Potsdam outside the conquered city of Berlin. "The test was successful beyond the most optimistic expectations of anyone," reported Groves. Buoyed by the message,

Truman returned to the conference a changed man. British Prime Minister Winston Churchill noticed the president's sudden self-confidence. "He stood up to the Russians in a most decisive and emphatic manner," Churchill remarked. "He told the Russians just where they got on and got off and generally bossed the whole meeting." Since the British were partners on the bomb project, Churchill soon learned what had so lifted Truman's spirits.

Less than three weeks later, on August 6, 1945, a second mushroom cloud rose, this time above Hiroshima in Japan. That explosion destroyed an entire city, left almost 100,000 people dead and thousands more dying from radiation poisoning. Three days later another bomb leveled the city of Nagasaki. Only then did World War II come to an end, the bloodiest and most costly war in history. Ever since, the world has lived with the stark prospect that in anger or in error, some person, group, or government might again unleash the horror of atomic war.

The New Mexico test of the first atom bomb marked the successful conclusion of the Manhattan Project, the code name for one of the largest scientific and industrial efforts ever undertaken. Between 1941 and 1945 the United States spent over $2 billion to build three atom bombs. Twenty years earlier that would have equaled the entire federal budget. The project required some thirty-seven factories and laboratories in nineteen states and Canada, employed more than 120,000 people, and monopolized many of the nation's top scientists and engineers during a period when their skills were considered essential to national survival. Leading universities, as well as some of the nation's largest corporations—Du Pont, Eastman Kodak, and General Electric—devoted substantial resources to the undertaking.

Even before the Manhattan Project, physicists and other scientists had experienced the trend in modern industrial society toward ever more human work, creativity, and important decisions to take place from within large organizations. For much of the nineteenth century, scientists, like artists, worked alone or in small groups, using relatively simple equipment. Thomas Edison, however, led the way toward rationalized, business-oriented research and development, establishing his own "scientific" factory at Menlo Park, New Jersey, in 1876. Like a manufacturer, Edison subdivided research tasks among inventors, engineers, and toolmakers. By the first decades of the twentieth century, Westinghouse, Du Pont, U.S. Rubber, and other major corporations had set up their own industrial labs.

Then too, World War I demonstrated that organized, well-funded science could be vital to national security. During the war scientists joined in large research projects to develop new explosives, poison gases, optical glass for lenses, airplane instruments, and submarine detection devices. In less than two years, physicists and electrical engineers had doubled the advances of radio technology over the previous ten years. The government, for the first time, funded research on a large scale. But scientists were as much committed to the notion of laissez-faire as any conservative robber baron. They were suspicious of any "scheme in which any small group of men, appointed as a branch of the government, attempt to dominate and control the research of the country," as one scientist put it.

At 0815 hours August 6, 1945, *the bomber Enola Gay and its flight crew received weather clearance and proceeded toward Hiroshima. An hour later, flying at 328 miles per hour, it dropped its bomb directly over the city, from 31,000 feet. It then turned and dove sharply in order to gain speed. The bomb detonated at about 2,000 feet above Hiroshima in order to increase the effective radius of its blast; the resulting cloud, photographed by a nearby observation plane, reached 50,000 feet into the air and was visible for 390 miles. The final statistic: approximately 100,000 people killed and thousands dying from radiation poisoning.*

The end of the war halted government interference and financial support. Still, like most Americans, scientists shared in the prosperity of the 1920s. Economic boom meant increases in research budgets. Success in the laboratory attracted contributions from private foundations and wealthy individuals. American science began to produce both theoretical and applied results that rivaled the quality of science in Europe.

The Depression of the 1930s forced researchers to tighten their belts and lower their expectations. The government, though seldom an important source of funding, drastically cut the budgets for its scientific bureaus. Even when the New Deal created jobs for scientists, it did so primarily to stimulate employment, not research. But by the late 1930s private foundations had resumed earlier levels of support. One of their most prominent beneficiaries was Ernest Lawrence, a physicist with a flair for showmanship who had established himself as the most famous, most funded, and most bureaucratically organized scientist in the United States. During the 1930s Lawrence built what he called a cyclotron, a machine designed to accelerate atomic particles in a focused beam, in order to penetrate the nucleus's shell and unravel its structure and dynamics. By 1939, his Radiation Lab at the University of California at Berkeley was raising the unprecedented sum of $1.5 million to build an enormous, 100-million-volt cyclotron.

The movement of science toward organization and bureaucracy reflected similar forces at work elsewhere in American society. As Lawrence expanded his laboratory at Berkeley, the New Deal was establishing new regulatory agencies, social welfare programs, and other government organizations that reached into many areas of daily life. Furthermore, much that the New Deal instituted through government and politics in the 1930s, large corporations had accomplished in the preceding era. Centralized slaughterhouses, with their elaborate distribution system involving railroads, refrigerated warehouses, and trucks, replaced the local butcher as the source of meat for many American tables. What Armour and Swift did for meatpacking, Heinz did for the pickle, Henry Ford for the automobile, and other corporations for the multitude of food, clothing, and goods used in American homes and industry. To understand the nature of the modern era, to grasp an undertaking as vast as the making of an atomic bomb or a decision as complex as how to use it, historians must understand how large organizations work.

Models of Decision Making

"Truman dropped the atom bomb in order to win the war as quickly as possible." Historians routinely use such convenient shorthand in their historical narratives. Yet physically, of course, Truman was nowhere near Japan or the bomb when it was dropped. He was halfway around the world, returning from the Potsdam Conference with Stalin and Churchill. The actual sequence of events was rather more complicated. President Truman did give an order. It passed through the Pentagon to an airbase on the island of Tinian in the western Pacific. The base commander ordered a specially trained crew to arm an American airplane with a single atom bomb, designed and built by scientists and technicians, under the authority of the War Department. The pilot of the plane then followed an order, conveyed through the military chain of command, to proceed to a target in Japan, selected by the secretary of war in consultation with his military advisers, in order to destroy a Japanese city and thereby hasten the end of the war.

The difference in meaning between "Truman dropped" and what actually happened encapsulates the dilemma of a historian trying to portray the workings of a systematized, bureaucratic modern society. The first explanation is coherent, clear, and human. It accords with Harry Truman's own well-known maxim, "the buck stops here"—implying that the important, truly difficult decisions were his and his alone. The second explanation is cumbersome and confusing, but more comprehensive and descriptive. It reflects the fact that the president stood at the tip of a pyramid of advisers, agencies, bureaus, offices, and committees, all going about their own business. And such organizations create their own characteristic ways' of gathering information, planning, working, and acting. To a large extent, what Truman decided or did not decide depended on what he learned from those organizations. To that extent also, the shorthand "Truman dropped the bomb . . ." conceals as much as it reveals.

To better analyze the workings of organizations, historians have borrowed a technique from the social sciences. They work with interpretive models. For many people the term "model" might bring to mind an object like a small plastic airplane or an electric train. For social scientists a model, not unlike the small plane, reduces the scale of reality and increases the researchers' capacity to describe the characteristics of what they observe. Models can be applied to systems as basic as individual behavior or as grand as the world's climate. If the average daily temperature goes up, will we have more or less rain? If the amount of carbon dioxide in the atmosphere increases, will temperatures rise? A computer model of weather patterns allows meteorologists to test the relationship between such variables in the climate. Even so, the number of variables is so great, meteorologists are forced to speak of probabilities, not certainties. While their model provides insights into several components of a weather system, it inevitably simplifies as well. In that sense, models too have limits.

The phrase "Truman dropped the bomb . . ." typifies the application of what some social scientists have called a "rational actor" model. This is perhaps the interpretive framework that historians most often adopt without even thinking about models. Rational actor theory treats the actions of governments and large organizations as the acts of individuals. Further, it assumes that the individual actor, like Adam Smith's capitalist, behaves rationally, in that he or she uses the most efficient means to pursue ends that are in his or her self-interest. When forced to choose among a range of possible actions, government leaders will select the option that achieves the best result at the lowest cost. One does not use a bat to swat a fly, nor would a government go to war to collect a small debt, unless war served some larger purpose.

The appeal of this model lies in its predictive powers. Often enough, governments do not make clear why they act. On other occasions, they announce their goals but keep their strategies for achieving them secret. By applying standards of rational behavior, an analyst can make inductive leaps about a government's unclear goals or hidden actions. If we know that a government has suddenly ordered highly mobile assault troops to the borders of its nation, but we lack evidence about goals, we might still conclude that a rational actor would not use mobile assault troops merely to defend borders: an invasion is planned. The process works in reverse as well. If analysts know what goals a nation has at hand, they can guess with some confidence what its leaders might do in a situation, given their resources.

Franklin Roosevelt's decision to launch the Manhattan Project presents historians with an example of how rational actor analysis can help reveal motivations and goals. Roosevelt was not an easy person to read—either for his advisers or for historians. Often enough, his orders to different people seemed contradictory. Or he would encourage competing bureaucracies to implement the same policy. In setting in motion the bomb project, Roosevelt left little evidence about why he made his decision. But the rational actor model suggests that Roosevelt recognized the military potential of nuclear fission; calculated that the United States had the financial, industrial, and scientific resources needed; and concluded that the nation's security demanded full-scale research and development.

The available evidence does support that conclusion. The Manhattan Project owed its beginnings to several physicists, primarily refugees from fascist Germany and Italy, who feared that recent atomic research would allow the Nazis to develop a weapon of unparalleled destructive force. In March 1939 Enrico Fermi, a Nobel prize-winning physicist who had fled from Mussolini's Italy, paid his own way to Washington to warn the military. Fermi himself had been on the verge of discovering fission reactions in 1934, but had not then recognized the meaning of his results. If he had, the fascist powers might have appropriated his results and put the process of fission to military use. Though Fermi had become an American citizen and a faculty member at Columbia University, Navy technical experts ignored his warning. Other refugee physicists, led by Leo Szilard, joined the campaign. Szilard persuaded Albert Einstein, the world's most admired scientist, to lend his name to a letter explaining their concern to President Roosevelt. Alexander Sachs, an economic adviser to the president, acted as their emissary. After Roosevelt read the letter and heard Sachs out, he remarked, "Alex, what you are after is to see they don't blow us up."

The president took immediate action, but he did not yet set in motion a massive research project. That would have been irrational, for as Sachs had made clear, the scientists had not yet found a way to harness the power of fission for war. Instead, he merely created a Uranium Committee to promote American research on a fission bomb. The research got under way slowly, for the committee requested only $6,000 for its first year of operations. Other more promising experimental efforts competed for research funds that were particularly scarce since the United States was not yet at war.

In England, however, two German emigrés were making progress in understanding how a "superbomb" might work. When war had broken out in September 1939, British security restrictions barred former German scientists like Otto Frisch and Rudolph Peierls from being involved in sensitive projects. Thus they were free to do their own research. In June 1941 they determined that the fast neutrons needed to set off an explosive chain reaction could be produced using either plutonium or uranium 235, a fissionable isotope that could be separated from uranium 238. They also suggested ways to separate uranium 235 from uranium 238. The amount of fissionable material needed would be small enough to fit into a bomb that existing aircraft could carry. Such a bomb, Frisch and Peierls calculated, could probably be built within two years. What was more frightening, German physicists were known to have made similar discoveries. Their high-quality physics programs might have put them as much as two years ahead of Allied efforts.

The British passed this information along to the American administrators supervising war research, the National Defense Research Committee (NDRC). Its head, Vannevar Bush, wasted no time in bringing the news to Roosevelt in June 1941. "If such an explosive were made," he told the president, "it would be thousands of times more powerful than existing explosives, and its use might be determining." The British research had given the rational actor—in this case President Roosevelt—cause to commit the United States to a larger project. To accelerate the research effort, Roosevelt replaced the ineffective Uranium Committee with a group called S-1. The membership of the committee reflected the new priority of the bomb project. It included Bush, now head of the Office of Scientific Research and Development; his successor at NDRC, James Conant (the president of Harvard University); Vice President Henry Wallace; Secretary of War Henry Stimson; and Chief of Staff General George Marshall. Bush and Conant assumed primary responsibility for overseeing the project and keeping the president informed. In September 1942, they were joined by General Leslie Groves, who had been appointed to command construction and operation of the rapidly expanding facilities that were named the Manhattan Project.

For three years, American, British, and emigré scientists raced against time and what they feared was an insurmountable German lead. At first, research focused on the work of scientists at the Chicago Metallurgical Lab (another code name). There, on a squash court under the old University of Chicago football stadium, Fermi and his associates achieved the first self-sustaining chain reaction. The next goal was the separation of enough pure uranium 235 or sufficient plutonium to build a bomb. That required the construction of huge plants—an expense that now seemed rational, in light of the work at Chicago. Conant authorized Groves to begin building facilities at Oak Ridge, Tennessee, and Hanford, Washington.

Actual design of the bomb took place at a remote mountain site near Los Alamos, New Mexico. Los Alamos was the choice of physicist Robert Oppenheimer. As director of the design laboratory, Oppenheimer sought a place to isolate the most outstanding collection of experimental and theoretical physicists, mathematicians, chemists, and engineers ever assembled. Free from the intrusions of the press and inquisitive colleagues, world-renowned scientists rubbed elbows with brilliant, eager young graduate students, all bringing to bear the abstract theories of physics to the question of how to produce an atomic weapon.

By the summer of 1944, the race with the Nazis had ended. Spies discovered that German physicists had long since given up hope of building a bomb. As Allied forces marched into Berlin in April, 1945, scientists knew that peace would come to Europe before the bomb was ready to be used. Still, the war

J. Robert Oppenheimer *directed the construction, completion, and testing of the first atomic bomb at a remote desert site near Los Alamos, New Mexico. He was an intense, introspective man and a chain smoker early in his career—who confessed he found it nearly impossible to think without a cigarette in his hand. The burden of the Manhattan Project took its toll on him: the chain smoking commenced again and his weight, normally only 130 pounds, dropped to 116.*

against Japan seemed far from over. As Allied troops approached the home islands, Japanese resistance grew more intense. Fearing heavy American casualties during an invasion, President Roosevelt had asked Stalin to enter the war against Japan. Yet as the tide of battle began to favor the Allies, the president became more reluctant to draw the Soviets into Japan. If the bomb could win the war for the United States, all the sacrifices of time, personnel, and materials would not have been in vain. Oppenheimer, Groves, and the Manhattan Project scientists redoubled their efforts to produce a working bomb.

Thus the rational actor model explains adequately the progression of events that brought about the bomb's development: (1) physicists saw the potential of nuclear fission and warned the president; (2) Roosevelt ordered a speed-up in research; (3) scientific breakthroughs led to greater certainty of eventual success, causing the president to give bomb research top priority; (4) the race with

Germany, and then Japanese resistance in the Far East, encouraged scientists to push toward success.

 Although this outline of key decisions proceeds logically enough, there are troubling features to it, suggesting limits to the rational actor model. Certainly Roosevelt could be viewed as the rational actor. But we have already seen that a host of committees and subgroups were involved in the process. And the model becomes murkier when we seek answers to a number of controversial questions surrounding the decision actually to *use* the bomb. Did the military situation in the summer of 1945 justify launching the attacks without warning Japan? Could a nonmilitary demonstration of the bomb's power have persuaded the Japanese to surrender without immense loss of life? Why drop a second bomb on Japan so soon after the first? And finally, who did the United States really want to shock with its atomic might—Japan or the Soviet Union?

To be sure, rational actor analysis provides answers to these questions. The problem is, it provides too many. Historians have offered contradictory answers to the way a rational actor might have been expected to behave under the circumstances.

To begin with, what was the most crucial problem to be solved by a rational actor in that summer of 1945? On the one hand, convincing Japan to surrender was the primary goal of the war—something the use of atomic bombs would be expected to hasten. On the other hand, military and diplomatic planners had already begun to focus on the transition from war to peace. Increasingly, they worried about the postwar conduct of the Soviet Union. Following the surrenders of Italy and Germany, the Russians had begun consolidating control over Eastern Europe. Many British and American officials feared that Stalin saw victory as a way to extend the global reach of communism. The larger the role assumed by the Soviets in the Pacific, the greater their opportunity for expansion there too.

But what if the bomb were used to end the war before Stalin's troops could make any headway in the Far East? Wasn't it likely Stalin would become more cooperative once he saw the awesome power of such a weapon? That "rational" line of reasoning raises an unsettling possibility. Did the United States drop the bomb primarily to send a warning to the Soviet Union? So concluded historian Gar Alperovitz. Alperovitz argued that after Franklin Roosevelt's untimely death in April 1945, President Truman was more concerned with containing the Soviet Union than with defeating Japan.

Alperovitz came to that conclusion by examining the information available to Truman and his advisers in the summer of 1945. That data, he argued, should have convinced Truman (or any rational actor) that the United States had no compelling military reason to drop atomic bombs on Japan. The American navy had already established a tight blockade around Japan, cutting off delivery of raw materials and isolating Japan's army in Manchuria from the home islands. Allied land-based bombers had leveled whole sections of Tokyo without opposition from Japanese fighters. By July 1945, Japan was ready to consider capitulation, except that in 1943, Roosevelt had laid down uncompromising terms of "unconditional surrender." The Japanese feared that the United States would insist that their emperor leave his throne, a humiliation they wished at all costs to avoid. Their only hope was to negotiate terms of surrender, using the Russians as intermediaries, to obtain a guarantee that the institution of the emperor would be preserved.

Truman knew that the Japanese had made overtures to the Soviet Union. "Unconditional surrender is the only obstacle to peace," the Japanese Foreign Minister had cabled his emissary in Moscow, in a coded message intercepted by American intelligence. Still, Truman refused to deviate from Roosevelt's policy of unconditional surrender. At the Potsdam conference, Allied leaders issued a vaguely worded proclamation warning the Japanese that they faced "prompt and utter destruction" if they fought on. Nowhere did the proclamation mention the existence of a new superbomb. Nor did it offer hope that the Allies might permit the Japanese to keep their emperor. When the Japanese ignored the warning, the Americans concluded that Japan had resolved to continue fanatic resistance.

In fact, the emperor himself had taken unprecedented though cautious steps to undermine the war party. He had decided that the military extremists must accept surrender on Allied terms. But the bombing of Hiroshima, on August 6, followed two days later by a Russian declaration of war, threw the Japanese government into confusion. Before it could digest this double shock, Nagasaki was leveled on August 9. Even then, the Japanese surrendered only when the United States made an implicit commitment to retain the emperor. Despite Truman's insistence on an "unconditional" surrender, in the end it had been conditional.

Alperovitz's conclusion is sobering. If ending the war had been Truman's *only* goal, the rational response would have been to give Japan the extra few days or weeks to negotiate a surrender. There would have been no need to drop the bomb. But of course it *was* dropped. Therefore (so the logic goes) the president's primary goal must have been to intimidate the Soviets. This was a possibility that Alperovitz understandably condemned, for it would have meant that Truman had wantonly incinerated hundreds of thousands of Japanese for reasons that had nothing to do with the war itself. Furthermore, if Truman had hoped to intimidate the Russians into cooperating, he seriously erred—for the Soviet Union became, if anything, more intractable after Japan's surrender. Failure to achieve a nuclear arms control agreement with Stalin, while the United States and Britain had a monopoly on atomic weapons, led to a postwar arms race. Possession of the atom bomb resulted finally in a decrease in American security and a loss of moral stature. Those are not the desired results of rational decision making.

Alperovitz's reconstruction of Truman's choices placed most emphasis on the diplomatic effects of dropping the bomb. But were these the factors that weighed most heavily in the minds of Truman and his advisers? Other historians have placed more emphasis on the military factors behind the development of the bomb—not only in 1945 but in the years preceding it. In doing so, they have constructed an alternate set of motivations that might have influenced a rational actor.

Franklin Roosevelt was the first president who had to consider whether the bomb would actually be used. And merely by approving the massive effort to build a weapon, there was an implicit assumption on the president's part that it would be used. "At no time," recalled former Secretary of War Stimson, "did I ever hear it suggested by the President, or by any other responsible member of the government, that atomic energy should not be used in the war." Robert Oppenheimer, whose leadership at Los Alamos played a critical role in the success of the project, confirmed Stimson's point about the bombs: ". . . we always assumed if they were needed, they would be used."

In fact, Roosevelt was proceeding a bit more cautiously. He discussed the delicate subject with British Prime Minister Winston Churchill when the two men met at Roosevelt's home in Hyde Park, in September 1944. At the end of their private interview, with only the two of them present, they signed a memorandum summarizing their attitudes. Both men agreed that the bomb would be kept a secret from the Russians, an action that made it clear (as Alperovitz contended) that they recognized how valuable a lever the weapon might be in postwar negotiations. As for the war itself, Roosevelt and Churchill agreed that the bomb might be used against Japan after "mature consideration," while warning the Japanese "that this bombardment will be repeated until they surrender."

If Roosevelt had lived, conceivably he might have proved more cautious than Truman. But if he had any serious doubts about using the bomb, they died with him. None of his military and diplomatic advisers were aware of the Hyde Park memorandum. After Roosevelt's death, responsibility for atomic policy shifted largely to Secretary of War Stimson, the cabinet officer in charge of the Manhattan Project. The new president, Truman, knew nothing about the bomb or, for that matter, most other critical diplomatic and military matters. Roosevelt had seldom consulted the vice president or even met with him. Once, while acting as chair of a Senate Committee, Truman had stumbled onto information about the vast sums being spent on some unknown project, only to be persuaded by Stimson that secrecy should prevail. As the war approached its end and the new president faced a host of critical decisions, Stimson cautiously introduced him to the bomb. "I mentioned it to you shortly after you took office," the secretary prompted him on April 23, 1945, "but have not urged it since on account of the pressure you have been under. It, however, has such bearing on our present foreign relations . . . I think you ought to know about it without further delay."

To present his case, Stimson prepared a memorandum setting out his two most pressing concerns. He wanted Truman to recognize the monumental importance of the bomb for postwar relations, particularly with the Soviet Union. And he wanted to emphasize the bomb's capacity to shorten the war. Stimson displayed no qualms about using it against Japan and considered no steps to avert a postwar nuclear arms race. But the two men did agree that Stimson should form a committee to formulate further policy options. This, it would seem, was the rational actor at work: If Truman wanted to weigh all his options, the committee would provide him with a full range from which to choose.

The Interim Committee, as the group was known, met three times. It also created a scientific panel including Oppenheimer, Fermi, Lawrence, and Arthur

Compton (head of the Chicago lab) to advise the committee. During its meetings, it scarcely touched the question of whether to drop the bomb on Japan. "It
seemed to be a foregone conclusion that the bomb would be used," Arthur
Compton recalled. "It was regarding only the details of strategy and tactics that
differing views were expressed." When those issues were debated, some members briefly considered a nonmilitary demonstration in place of a surprise
military attack. They asked Oppenheimer how such a demonstration might be
prepared. Since the bomb had yet to be tested, Oppenheimer could only
estimate its power. He replied that he could not conceive any demonstration
that would have the impact of an attack on a real target of factories and buildings.
Furthermore, the committee had to consider what might happen if Japanese
representatives were taken to a test site and the mighty atomic "demonstration"
fizzled. And if the Japanese were given advance warning about a superbomb,
wouldn't that allow them to prepare their defenses or move American prisoners
of war to likely bombing targets?

For all those reasons the Interim Committee decided against giving any
advance warning. In addition, it made several assumptions about Japan that
predetermined its recommendations to the president. First, committee members considered the military leadership of Japan so fanatic that only a profound
shock such as an atomic attack would persuade them to surrender. Kamikaze
attacks by Japanese pilots as well as other resistance continued to claim a heavy
toll in American lives. General Douglas MacArthur, who had led the Western
Pacific campaign against Japan, discounted the effectiveness of either a naval
blockade of the home islands or continued air raids with conventional bombs.
Only a full-scale invasion, MacArthur argued, would compel surrender. The
army continued to organize an invasion for November 1, anticipating as many as
a half million American casualties.[1]

In any case, by 1945 committee members had become somewhat hardened
to the idea of killing enemy soldiers or civilians. Conventional firebombing had
already proved as horrifying as the atom bomb promised to be. In one incendi-
ary raid, American bombers leveled one-quarter of Tokyo, left 83,000 people
dead, and wounded another 40,000. Having lived with the fear that the Germans
might use an atom bomb against the United States, committee members had
ample reason to see it as a potential weapon against the Japanese. Since it
promised to save American lives, the committee sensed that the public would
want, even demand, combat use. And finally, though the members were far from
agreed, the committee decided that a combat demonstration would facilitate
negotiations with the Russians. From those assumptions they reached three
conclusions: (1) the bomb should be used as quickly as possible against Japan;
(2) to maximize the shock value, the target should be a war plant surrounded by
workers' homes; (3) no warning should be given. When Stimson communicated
those views to Truman, he included a recommendation that both bombs sched-

---

[1] This casualty figure has become quite controversial. Martin Sherwin has discovered that a
number of prominent military figures offered a much lower estimate. That would have made an
invasion a more reasonable option.

uled for completion by August should be dropped in separate raids, in order to maximize the shock and convince Japanese leaders that further resistance meant certain destruction.

In only one small but vital way did Truman deviate from the committee's determination of how and why to use the bomb. A group of scientists at the Chicago laboratory, led by Leo Szilard, had become persuaded that combat use of the bomb without warning would lead to a postwar arms race between the Soviets and the Americans. They urged Truman and his advisers to tell the Russians about the bomb and to plan a demonstration before using it in combat. In a concession to Szilard and his colleagues, the Interim Committee recommended that Truman disclose the bomb to Stalin in order to help gain his cooperation after the war. At Potsdam, Truman chose not to discuss the bomb or atomic energy. But he did make an oblique reference to Stalin "that we had a weapon of unusual destructive force." Stalin was equally cryptic in his reply. "He was glad to hear it and hoped we would make 'good use of it' against the Japanese," the president recalled. And so Truman acted.

By retracing the series of decisions made over the entire year preceding the attack on Hiroshima, it becomes clearer that, for Truman, military considerations about how to end the war with a minimum number of casualties remained paramount. Resolution of Soviet-American differences was a secondary goal, though rapidly becoming the administration's chief concern. Using the bomb would also forestall any criticism in Congress for having spent $2 billion on the secret Manhattan Project. Thus the bombing of Hiroshima and Nagasaki appeared to be the optimum way to reach the administration's primary objective, with the additional virtue of promoting secondary goals as well. When applied at the level of presidential decision making, rational actor analysis suggests that the decision to drop the bomb was consistent with perceived American goals.

A Model of Organizational Process

Despite those results, the rational actor model exhibits definite limitations. It leads us to focus attention on the policy-making debates of key actors like Roosevelt and Truman, or even on scientists like Szilard and Oppenheimer. But in truth, our narrative of events has involved numerous committees far from the top of the organizational pyramid: the Uranium Committee, S-1, the National Defense Research Council, the Interim Committee. Roosevelt and Truman relied on the recommendations of those groups in making decisions. Should that make any difference to our explanations?

Imagine, for a moment, the government as a kind of giant clock. Rational actor analysis would define the telling of time as the visible movements of the hands controlled by a closed box. Inside are the gears, springs, and levers that move the clock's hands: the bureaucracy supporting decision makers at the top. In the rational actor model, these gears are seen as neutral cogs in the machine, passing along the energy (or in government, the information) that allows the hands to do their highly visible work. But suppose we look at the decision-making process using a model that focuses on the organizational processes themselves. Is there something about their structure or behavior that influences the outcome of decisions made by supposedly rational actors?

Of course, the actions of bureaucracies and agencies are usually less regimented than the movements of a clock. Often enough, the subgroups that make up a government end up working at cross purposes or pursuing conflicting objectives. While the Surgeon General's office warns that cigarette smoking is "hazardous to your health," the Department of Agriculture produces films on the virtues of American tobacco. Perhaps, then, it would be better to envision not a clock but a football team. If we observe a game from the stands, the players can be seen moving in coordinated patterns, in an effort to control the movement of the ball. Rational actor analysis suggests that the coach, or another centralized decision maker like the quarterback, has selected the strategies best suited to winning the game. That larger strategy, in turn, determines the plays that the offense and defense use.

After closer observation, we begin to sense that the play is not as centrally coordinated as we anticipated. Different groups of players move in patterns determined by their positions as well as the team strategy. We come to understand that the team is made up of subgroups that execute regularly assigned tasks. Linemen block, ends run pass patterns. On each down, the players do not try to think anew of the best imaginable play. Rather, they repeat actions they have been trained to perform. A halfback will generally advance the ball by running and leave the passing to the quarterback. On some plays, we observe that a few players' actions seem inappropriate. A halfback runs when he should be blocking. Where the rational actor model might interpret such a move as a purposeful attempt to deceive the opposing team, a model focusing on organizational processes might recognize it as a breakdown of coordination among subgroups. What one model treats as planned, the other treats as a mistake.

Thus the organizational process model leads the historian to treat government behavior not as centralized acts and choices, but as the actions of bureaucracies functioning in relatively predictable patterns. Organizations begin by breaking problems into parts, which are assigned to the appropriate subgroup to solve. The subgroups do not have to understand the larger problem, only the piece assigned to them. They follow what the military refers to as SOP— standard operating procedure. If the quarterback decides on a sweep to the right, the lineman's SOP is to block left. On a sweep to the left, he blocks right; for a pass, straight ahead. SOPs allow organizations to coordinate the independent activities of many groups and individuals.

While SOPs make coordination possible, they also limit the actions of organizations. The more specialized a subgroup, the fewer tasks it is able to perform. Its training is more narrowly focused, its equipment is more specialized, the information available to it is more limited. All those factors make it more difficult for the group to deviate from regular routines. The weather bureau, for example, would find it impossible to apply its computer programs and specialized knowledge to predicting changes in the economy rather than the weather. Furthermore, where the rational actor is presumed to weigh all available choices to select the best one, in the real lives of organizations, SOPs determine the range and pattern of choices that are considered. Specialized groups are generally content to choose standardized and previously determined policies rather than searching for the optimum one.

Since organizations are generally more concerned with avoiding failure than with gambling on success, they also tend to be more conservative. Where the rational actor might weigh the potential benefits against possible consequences, and then make a bold new departure, organizations tend to change in small, incremental steps. Corporations, for example, like to test-market a product before investing in expensive new plants, distribution networks, and advertising. And we have already seen that the American government moved relatively slowly in producing an atomic bomb. In authorizing the quest for a bomb, Roosevelt was ordering the government to do something it had never done before: conduct nuclear research. He soon discovered that the military and scientific bureaus could not readily execute such an unprecedented decision. They lacked the scientific personnel, equipment, and research routines that made the Manhattan Project possible. In the end, Roosevelt and project managers like Groves, Conant, Bush, and Oppenheimer had to create new organizations and routines.

Reward structures in organizations reinforce their conservatism. Those who do their jobs properly day after day continue to work. Those who make errors lose their jobs or fail to win promotions. Critical decisions are generally made in committees, so that no individual assumes sole responsibility if a venture fails. But committees take much longer to act and often adopt unwieldy compromises. (An old adage defines a camel as a horse designed by a committee.) As a further hedge against failure, goals and responsibilities are set well within the individual or group performance capabilities. Such practices stifle individual initiative and encourage inefficiency. Mountains of paperwork and miles of red tape are the ultimate symbol of organizational caution and conservatism.

By treating the decision to drop the bomb not as a single act but as the outcome of many organizational routines, historians can see more clearly why progress on the bomb came slowly. In fact, the project could not have gotten under way in the first place if emigré scientists had not broken through the bureaucratic chain of command. When Fermi first approached Navy officials, none of them could even comprehend the concept of nuclear power. Only by writing the president directly did scientists attract the support they needed. To get the project under way, Roosevelt was forced to create an ad hoc committee to investigate the military potential of nuclear fission. His decision to appoint Lyman Briggs, a government physicist, as head of the Uranium Committee may have delayed the project by at least a year. As the director of the Bureau of Standards, Briggs knew little about nuclear physics. He was by temperament "slow, conservative, methodical"—ideal bureaucratic qualities totally unsuited to the bold departure Roosevelt sought. Not until the president created the National Defense Research Committee did nuclear physics gain adequate support.

As chairman of NDRC, Vannevar Bush made the farsighted decision to keep his organization independent of the military bureaucracies. He knew generals and admirals would fight against civilian interference and that scientists would balk at military regulation of their research. Under Bush, scientists remained free to pursue the research that they and not the military thought was important. Traditional definitions of missions and military needs would not cut off funds for new research projects. Furthermore, Bush wisely chose to operate under the jurisdiction of the War Department rather than the Navy.[2] The Navy had repeatedly shown either indifference or hostility to advice from civilian scientists. The Army and particularly its Air Corps branch proved far more receptive to new research. Consequently, the atom bomb was developed with the Army's mission and routines in mind. Bush's skillful negotiation of organizational bottlenecks was a crucial factor in shifting the Manhattan Project into high gear.

In other areas, organizational conflicts resulted in delays. President Roosevelt had established two incompatible priorities for Bush: speed and security. The scientists felt speed should come before security; military administrators like Groves opted for security over speed. Military SOP had well-established ways to safeguard classified material. Officers were required to operate strictly within the chain of command and were provided information only on a "need-to-know" basis. Thus, each soldier performed only a portion of a task without knowledge of the larger mission and without talking with anyone beyond his or her immediate circle. In that way, information was "compartmentalized"— securely protected so that only a few people at the top of the chain of command saw the entire picture.

To maximize security, Groves proposed placing the laboratory at Los Alamos under military control. All scientists would don uniforms and receive ranks based on their importance. As a group, however, scientists were among the least likely candidates for military regimentation. Their dress was more informal than most working professionals (*sloppy* might have been the adjective that jumped to the military mind). In their laboratories, they operated with a great deal of autonomy to pursue research as they saw fit. Oppenheimer could not recruit many scientists to come to Los Alamos until he assured them the project would not be militarized.

Compartmentalization, also promoted by Groves, seriously inhibited research. Physicists insisted that their work required access to all relevant information. They thought best when they understood the wider implications of their work. Groves disdained their habit of engaging in creative, freewheeling discussions that regularly drifted far afield of the topic at hand. Scientists should stick to their jobs and receive information only on a need-to-know basis. "Just as outfielders should not think about the manager's job of changing pitchers," Groves said to justify his system, " . . . each scientist had to be made to do his own work." While compartmentalization promoted security, it denied researchers vital information from other areas of the project. Some scientists, like Szilard, simply violated security procedures whenever they chose to. Oppenheimer eased the problem at Los Alamos by conducting seminars where his

---

[2] At that time the Army and Navy had separate organizations. The head of each held a cabinet post. The Marines were a branch of the Navy, the Air Corps a branch of the Army. Congress created a unified defense structure under a single secretary in 1947.

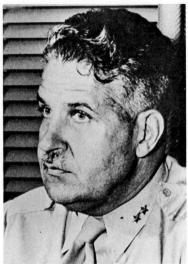

In 1942 General Leslie Groves *was placed in charge of the construction and operation of the Manhattan Project. He got the job in part because he was a good organizer, having supervised the construction of the Pentagon, still unfinished in this 1942 photo. The building became the largest office facility in the world, containing 16 miles of corridors, 600,000 square feet of office space, and a capacity to house 32,000 workers. As historian Warren Susman recognized, it also became a symbol of its era: "For the age it climaxed indeed the triumph of order, science, reason. . . . And yet, for the age being born it was the home of the atom bomb and a frightening bureaucratic structure, the beginning of a brave new world of anxiety."*

staff could exchange ideas and information. But information never flowed freely among the many research and production sites.

Security procedures indicate, too, that long before the war ended many policymakers saw the Soviet Union as their chief enemy. Few precautions were designed against Japanese or even German agents. Military intelligence concentrated its counterespionage against Soviet and communist spies. Known communists or scientists with communist associations were kept under constant surveillance. Had intelligence officers prevailed, they would have barred Oppenheimer from the project because of his previous involvement with communist-front organizations. To his credit, Groves overruled the nearsighted sleuths in Army intelligence and saved the project's most valuable member. In the meantime, security precautions against a wartime ally continued to work to the advantage of the Nazis by delaying the project.

The military was not solely responsible for project bottlenecks. The procedures of organized science caused delays as well. Scientists recruited from private industry did not share their academic colleagues' preoccupation with speed. Work in industry had conditioned them to move cautiously, with an eye toward efficiency, permanence, and low risk. Academic scientists felt such industrial values "led to a considerable retardation of the program." But the traditions of academic science also created problems. The bulk of research money had most often been directed to the celebrities in each field. Ernest Lawrence's reputation made him a magnet for grants and contributions. Manhattan Project administrators automatically turned to him as they sought methods to refine the pure uranium 235 needed for the bomb. Much of the money spent at Oak Ridge, Tennessee, went into Lawrence's electromagnetic process based on the Berkeley cyclotron.

In the end, Lawrence's program proved to be a conspicuous failure. By 1944, Oppenheimer had the design for a uranium bomb, but scarcely any uranium 235. In desperation he looked toward a process of gas diffusion developed four years earlier by Harold Urey and a young, relatively unknown physicist named John Dunning. Lawrence had been so persuaded of the superiority of his own method that Groves gave it priority over the process developed by Urey and Dunning. And compartmentalization prevented other physicists from learning more about gas diffusion. As Dunning recalled, "compartmentalization and security kept news of our program from filtering in to Ernest and his Laboratory [the Radiation Lab at Berkeley]." Physicists soon acknowledged that electromagnetic separation was obsolete, but in the meantime, the completion of the uranium bomb, "Little Boy," was delayed until July 1945.

A Model of Bureaucratic Politics

Clearly, bureaucratic structures and SOPs played major roles in determining how the bomb was developed. Yet the example of an energetic and forceful Vannevar Bush makes clear that within that organizational framework, not all bureaucrats were created equal. Powerful individuals or groups can often override the standard procedures of organizations as well as the carefully thought-out choices of rational actors. It makes sense, then, for historians to be alert to decisions shaped by the politics within government institutions.

It we return to our vantage point in the football stadium, we see linebackers blocking and receivers going short or long—all SOPs being executed as parts of a complex organization. The team's coach—the rational actor—remains prominent, pacing the sidelines, deploying forces. But we notice now that often an assistant sends in a play or the quarterback makes a decision at the line of scrimmage. There is not just one decision maker, but many. And the play finally chosen may not reflect rational choice, but bargaining and compromise among the players and coaches. Although final authority may rest with a coach or the quarterback, other players, such as a star halfback, gain influence and prestige from the skill with which they play their position.

A historian applying those insights, in what might be called a model of bureaucratic politics, recognizes that a person's official position as defined by the organization does not alone determine his or her bargaining power. According to an organizational flowchart, the most influential members of the executive branch, after the president, would be the secretaries of state, defense (war and Navy), and treasury. Yet American history abounds with examples where power has moved outside normal bureaucratic channels. Sometimes a political actor, through astute jockeying, may convert a relatively less influential office into an important command post, as Henry Kissinger did when he was Richard Nixon's national security adviser. Kissinger, through forceful advocacy, shaped foreign policy far more than Secretary of State William Rogers. Colonel Edward M. House, the most influential adviser to Woodrow Wilson, held no formal position at all. House achieved his power by maintaining a low profile and offering the president seemingly objective counsel. For Attorney General Robert Kennedy, it was family ties and political savvy, not the office, that made him a powerful figure in his brother's administration.

In the case of the atom bomb, the lines of political influence were shifted by President Roosevelt's untimely death. When Harry Truman assumed the presidency, all the old institutional and informal arrangements of decision making had to be readjusted. This was especially true in Truman's case, since few members of Roosevelt's administration had less access to information and decision-making channels. Ignorance of Roosevelt's policies forced Truman to rely far more heavily on a wider circle of advisers. Stimson, for one, suddenly found that for several months the need to initiate the president into the secrets of S-1 or the Manhattan Project greatly enhanced his influence.

Thus, during the same months that Truman was trying to set up his own routines for decision making, individuals within various bureaucracies were jockeying for influence within the new order. And amid all this organizational turmoil, key decisions about the bomb had to be made—decisions that were neither clearcut nor easy. Would a Soviet entry into the war force Japan to surrender? Would conventional bombing raids and a blockade prove sufficient to end the war? Did Japan's peace initiatives indicate victory was at hand? Would a compromise on unconditional surrender, specifically a guarantee for the emperor, end the war? Would a demonstration of the bomb shock the Japanese into suing for peace?

As critics of Truman's decision have pointed out, each of those options had significant advocates within government circles. And each presented policymakers with reasons to avoid dropping the bomb—something which, as historian Barton Bernstein pointed out, was "precisely what they were not trying to do." But why not? Why did the decision makers who counseled use of the bomb outweigh those who championed these various alternatives? By applying the bureaucratic politics model, historians can better explain why the alternatives were never seriously considered.

The chief advocates for continued conventional warfare came from the Navy. From the beginning, Navy leaders had been skeptical of nuclear fission's military potential. Admiral William Leahy, the senior Navy representative on the Joint Chiefs of Staff and also an expert on explosives, always doubted the bomb would have anywhere near the force scientists predicted. The Alamogordo test laid his argument to rest. Chief of Naval Operations, Admiral Ernest King, believed a naval blockade would successfully end the war. King had no qualms about developing the bomb, but as a loyal Navy officer, he hated to see the Air Force end a war that his service had dominated for four years. He knew, too, that the bomb might undermine the Navy's defense role after the war. Among military brass, Admirals Leahy and King had somewhat less influence than General George Marshall, Army Chief of Staff. Marshall, along with General Douglas MacArthur, felt that further delay would necessitate an invasion and an unacceptable loss of American lives. Since they favored using the bomb instead, the Navy lost that round.

Some members of the State Department, led by Acting Secretary of State Joseph Grew, believed that diplomacy should end the war. As early as April 1945, Grew had urged administration officials to extend some guarantee that the imperial throne would not be abolished. Without that assurance, he felt, the peace party could never overcome the military's determination to fight on. As former ambassador to Japan, Grew knew more about Japanese politics and culture than any major figure in the Truman administration. On the other hand, he had spent much of his career as a foreign service officer far from Washington. Thus he could exert little personal influence over Truman or key advisers. Even within the State Department, Assistant Secretaries Dean Acheson and Archibald MacLeish, both more influential than Grew, opposed his position. They considered the emperor as the symbol of the feudal military tradition they hoped to see destroyed. By the time of the Potsdam conference, Grew had made just one convert for negotiations—Secretary Stimson—and a partial convert—Harry Truman. "There was [sic] pretty strong feelings," Stimson recalled, "that it would be deplorable if we have to go through the military program with all its stubborn fighting to the finish." Truman showed sufficient interest to arrange talks between Grew and the military chiefs, but he did not feel he could bring congressional and public opinion in line with Grew's position on the emperor.

The ghost of Franklin Roosevelt proved to be Grew's major opponent. Lacking Roosevelt's prestige, popularity, and mastery of government, Truman felt bound to pursue many of FDR's policies. Any move away from "unconditional surrender" posed political risks at home and military risks abroad that Truman did not feel strong enough to take. Acheson and MacLeish reminded their colleagues that Americans despised Emperor Hirohito as much as they did Hitler. The Joint Chiefs of Staff argued that premature compromise might reduce the emperor's incentive to subdue military extremists after the armistice.

James Byrnes emerged as the leading defender of unconditional surrender. In contrast to Grew, Byrnes had little training in foreign affairs. His importance in the government reflected his consummate skill at domestic politics. During the war, many people considered him second in power only to Roosevelt. In fact, Truman himself had risen to prominence as Byrnes's protégé and had repaid his debt by making Byrnes secretary of state. Deep down, Byrnes could not help feeling that he, not Truman, was the man best qualified to be president. He never got over thinking of himself as Truman's mentor.

Byrnes was exceptionally sensitive to the political risks of modifying unconditional surrender. More important, among Truman's advisers he was the most preoccupied with the growing Soviet threat. Using the bomb quickly would minimize Russian demands for territorial and political concessions in Asia, he believed, as well as strengthen the United States in any postwar negotiations. Since Byrnes's chief opponents, Grew and Stimson, were old and near retirement, and since he had strong support in both the military and State Department, his position carried the day. If the Japanese "peace feelers" to Moscow had been followed by more substantive proposals, either to the Russians or the Americans directly, perhaps some compromise might have been reached. But no other proposals were forthcoming. Thus at Potsdam, Byrnes and Truman remained convinced that the peace party in Japan would never marshal enough support against the military unless American attacks made further resistance seem futile. And it was again Byrnes who persuaded Truman to delete a provision in the Allied declaration that would have guaranteed the institution of the emperor.

By now it must be obvious why none of Truman's advisers wanted to rely on Soviet entry into the war as an alternative to dropping the bomb. By the time of the Potsdam conference, Japan's military position had become hopeless. Why encourage Stalin's imperial ambitions, especially when the bomb was available for use?

"Fat Man," also familiarly known to scientists working on the project as "Fat Boy." The graffiti on the tail include the notation, "Chicago is represented in here more than once."

Some Americans proposed that the bomb be demonstrated before a group of international observers instead of being dropped on Japan without warning. But advocates of this alternative were found largely among scientists working at the Chicago Metallurgical Laboratory. This group had been the first to finish its work on the bomb. While the Los Alamos lab rushed to complete the designs for "Little Boy" and "Fat Man," the Chicago lab began discussing the postwar implications of nuclear weapons and the threat of an international arms race. The eminent scientist Niels Bohr had already raised those issues with Roosevelt and Churchill. Yet, as we have seen, Churchill and Roosevelt agreed at their 1944 Hyde Park meeting to keep the bomb secret from Stalin, hoping to use it to advantage in any postwar rivalry with the Russians.

Unaware of the Hyde Park agreement, scientists continued to press their case. Ironically it was Leo Szilard, the physicist who marshaled support for creating the bomb, who six years later led the opposition to its use against Japan. The chain of command required Szilard to make any appeal outside the Chicago lab through its director Arthur Compton. Instead, Sziland violated security rules and tried to reach Truman through his newly appointed secretary of state. After all, it had been an earlier unorthodox appeal that first persuaded Roosevelt of the bomb's importance. But this time, James Byrnes acted as the gatekeeper. A man of shallow mind and deep prejudices, he had little patience with an intellectual like Szilard and almost no understanding of the scientists' concerns about a nuclear arms race. To Byrnes, the bomb was a weapon that would cripple Japan and shock the Russians. He refused to take up Szilard's concerns with Truman. The internal politics of the situation proved determinative.

Nonetheless, scientists at the Chicago lab continued to speak out on bomb policy. Arthur Compton had organized a series of committees to make further recommendations, the most important of which was headed by emigré James Franck. The Franck Committee concluded that a surprise attack against Japan would destroy the trust and good will of other nations for the United States, as well as "precipitate the race for armaments, and prejudice the possibility of reaching an international agreement on the future control of such weapons." When Franck went to present the report to Stimson, the secretary avoided a meeting. The Interim Committee then steered the report to their scientific panel, whose members were Karl Compton, Fermi, Lawrence, and Oppenheimer. Those scientists, all of whom had greater prestige and influence, concluded that they could "propose no technical demonstration likely to bring an end to the war . . . and no acceptable alternative to direct military use."

That conclusion came before the first test of the bomb, and Oppenheimer later regretted the panel's shortsightedness. The explosion over the New Mexico desert so profoundly moved him that its eerie glow recalled an image from the *Bhagavad-Gita*: "I am become death, the shatterer of worlds." Perhaps after Alamogordo, the scientific panel might have concluded that a demonstration would be worthwhile, but by then the time for deciding had passed. The momentum of the bureaucracy proceeded inexorably toward launching the missions over Japan. Scientists lacked the political influence to alter the assumptions of leading policymakers.

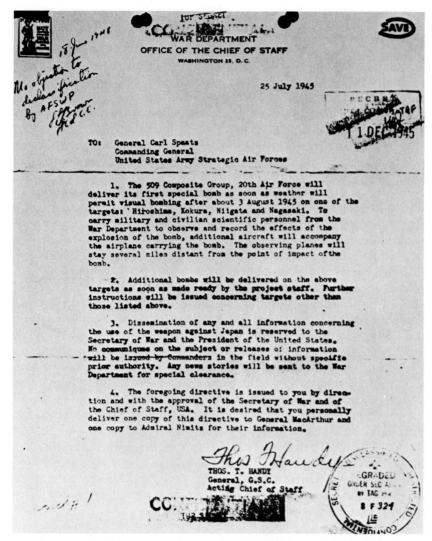

The letter outlining SOP *for dropping the bomb. It authorized the "509 Composite Group, 20th Air Force" to "deliver its first special bomb as soon as weather will permit visual bombing after about 3 August 1945 on one of the targets: Hiroshima, Kokura, Niigata and Nagasaki." In a reflection of protocol, as well as a hint of the rivalry between the Army and Navy, the letter instructs General Spaatz, in paragraph four, to inform General MacArthur and Admiral Nimitz of the decision personally.*

It remained, then, only to decide where specifically to drop the bombs and when to use them. Here, too, our models reveal both organizational processes and bureaucratic politics at work. To select the targets, Groves appointed a target committee composed of scientists and ordnance specialists. Their priorities reflected both the military's desire to end the war quickly and the scientists' hope to transmit a dramatic warning to the world. They sought cities that included military installations, but they also wanted a site with a large concentration of structures subject to the blast, in case the bomb missed its primary target. Kyoto, the ancient cultural and political center of Japan, topped their list.

Secretary of War Stimson vetoed that choice. As a former secretary of state and a person of broad cultural and political experience, he believed that the destruction of Kyoto would engender in the Japanese an undying bitterness toward the United States. Any hopes of integrating a revitalized and reformed Japan into a healthy postwar Asia might die with Kyoto. Stimson's position near the top of the organizational hierarchy gave him a different perspective from lower-level planners who weighed other issues. On the final target list Hiroshima ranked first, Nagasaki ranked fourth, and Kyoto not at all.

It was the weather and the routines of organization, not diplomatic or military strategy, that sealed Nagasaki's fate. After the bombing of Hiroshima and the Russian declaration of war, Japanese leaders decided to sue for peace. Advocates of surrender needed only enough time to work out acceptable terms and to reconcile military officers to the inevitable. As the Japanese discussed policy, the Americans followed standard military procedure. Control shifted from the commander in Washington, President Truman, to the commander of the bomber squadron on the island of Tinian in the Pacific. Plans called for Fat Man, a plutonium bomb, to be ready by August 11. Since work went faster than expected, the bomb crew advanced the date to the ninth. The forecast called for clear skies on the ninth, followed by five days of bad weather. Urged on by the squadron commander, the crew had Fat Man armed and loaded on the morning of the ninth. And again following military SOP, the pilot shifted his attack to Nagasaki when clouds obscured his primary target.

Had the original plan been followed, Japan might well have surrendered before the weather cleared. Nagasaki would have been spared. But the officer who ordered the attack had little appreciation of the larger military picture that made Nagasaki a target or that made the Soviet Union a diplomatic problem connected with the atom bomb. He weighed factors important to a bomb squadron commander, not to diplomats or political leaders. The bombing of Nagasaki slipped from the hands of policymakers not because of some rogue computer or any power-mad, maniacal general, but simply because of military SOPs.

And so two bombs were dropped and the world entered the atomic age.

If historians based their interpretations on a single model, they would never satisfy their desire to understand the sequence of events leading to Nagasaki. Each model provides its own particular perspective, both clarifying and at the

The reaction of scientists *watching the detonation of the first atomic bomb in New Mexico was recalled by Robert Oppenheimer: "A few people laughed, a few people cried, more people were silent. There floated through my mind a line from the* Bhagavad-Gita *in which Krishna is trying to persuade the Prince that he should do his duty: 'I am become death, the shatterer of worlds.' I think we all had this feeling, more or less." The photograph is of an atomic blast detonated at Bikini Island in July 1946.*

same time limiting. The use of several models allows the historian the same advantage enjoyed by writers of fiction who employ more than one narrator. Each narrator, like each model, affords the writer a new vantage point from which to tell the story. The facts may not change, but the reader sees them in another light. As organizations grow more complex, models afford historians multiple perspectives from which to interpret the same reality.

And yet, we must remind ourselves that models do not work miracles, for their potential to reveal new insights depends on the skills of the people who build and apply them. If poorly applied, their seeming precision, like reams of computer printout, conveys a false sense of empirical legitimacy. Data specialists have coined the acronym GIGO to suggest the limits of such mechanical devices—"garbage in, garbage out." In the end historians must remember that organizations are open systems existing within a broader historical and cultural context. Even when our models have accounted for goals, strategies, SOPs, and political influence, there remain those pieces of the picture which are still irreducible: from Robert Oppenheimer's uneasy, almost mystical vision out of the *Bhagavad-Gita* to the inanimate, complex meteorological forces that combined to dissipate the clouds over Nagasaki in August 1945.

Some elements of history will always remain stubbornly intractable, beyond the reach of the model builders. The mushroom clouds over Japan did not merely serve as a dramatic close to World War II. The afterglow of their blasts destroyed a sense of security that Americans had enjoyed for almost 150 years. After the war, the nuclear arms race turned the United States into an armed camp. Given the limits of human understanding, who in 1945 could have appreciated all the consequences that would result from the decision to drop the atom bomb?

ADDITIONAL READING

The recent easing of cold war tensions has only emphasized the terror much of the world has felt during the previous half century. That profound unease has informed the debate over the decision to drop the first atomic bombs on Japan. Indeed, the creation and uses of nuclear energy must rank with slavery, democratic reform, civil liberties, and economic justice as issues critical to the study of the American past, a point made in Jack Holl and Sheila Convis, eds., "Teaching Nuclear History," available from the Department of Energy (Washington, D.C., 1990). Holl and Convis provide comprehensive bibliographies from courses taught on the scientific, military, diplomatic, and political aspects of nuclear energy and weapons.

Many who first lived with the bomb, however, did not initially see it as quite so threatening, as Paul Boyer reveals in *By the Bombs Early Light: American Thought and Culture at the Dawn of the Atomic Age* (New York, 1985). The same point is made with wry irreverence in the film documentary, *The Atomic Cafe* (1982). During the early cold war, most Americans willingly accepted the rationale for dropping the bombs offered in official accounts such as Harry S Truman, *Memoirs, 1945: Year of Decisions* (New York, 1955), Henry Stimson (with McGeorge Bundy), *On Active Service in Peace and War* (New York, 1947), Leslie Groves, *Now It Can Be Told* (New York, 1962), and Richard Hewlett and Oscar Anderson, *The New World: 1939-1946: Volume I of a History of the United States Atomic Energy Commission* (University Park, Pa., 1962).

Then in 1965 came Gar Alperovitz's bombshell, *Atomic Diplomacy* (New York, 1965, rev. ed., 1985). Suddenly the rationale for building and using the bomb seemed much less obvious. Alperovitz raised difficult questions about the decision to drop the bomb at a time when the Vietnam War led many Americans to doubt the explanations of their government. Herbert Feis defended the official view in *The Atomic Bomb and the End of World War II* (Princeton, N.J., 1966). The debate has continued with critical studies by Martin Sherwin, *A World Destroyed* (New York, rev. ed., 1985), and Barton Bernstein, "Roosevelt, Truman, and the Atomic Bomb: A Reinterpretation," *Political Science Quarterly*, 90 (Spring, 1975), 23-69. McGeorge Bundy reviews the moral and political debates about the bomb in *Danger and Survival* (New York, 1988). George Kennan, the father of the cold war policy of containment, became more cautionary of nuclear diplomacy in later years, as reflected in *The Nuclear Delusion* (New York, 1982).

The military context of the bomb's development is important for understanding the implications of atomic weaponry. The evolution of military weapons and strategy is traced broadly in William H. McNeill, *The Pursuit of Power* (Chicago, Ill., 1982) and Robert O'Connell, *Of Arms and Men: A History of War, Weapons, and Aggression* (New York, 1989). Russell Weigley discusses *American Way of War* (Bloomington, Ind., 1977), while Ronald Spector, in *The Eagle inst the Sun* (New York, 1985), examines the Pacific campaigns of World War II. Some critics have suggested that racism made it easier for American leaders to use the bomb against Japan than against Germany. John Dower, *War without Mercy: Race and Power in the Pacific War* (New York, 1986), demonstrates that both Japan and the United States allowed racist misperceptions to inform key decisions. The bombing of Hiroshima and Nagasaki was an outgrowth of the rise of air power and doctrines of strategic bombing, discussed in Michael Sherry, *The Rise of American Air Power* (New Haven, Conn., 1987), and Ronald Schaffer, *Wings of Judgment: American Bombing in World War II* (New York, 1985). The impact of the bombing on the Japanese is movingly explored in John Hersey, *Hiroshima* (1946), and the French film *Hiroshima Mon Amour* (1960).

Issues of nuclear policy have attracted a rich variety of films, videos, and documentaries. The most comprehensive, taking the Soviet as well as the American side, is *War and Peace in the Nuclear Age* (PBS, 1988). *The Day After Trinity* (1980) focuses on Robert Oppenheimer, the Manhattan Project, and the scientists' views on the bomb. Four documentaries that look at the bombing of Hiroshima and Nagasaki are *Decision to Drop the Bomb* (NBC, 1965); *Hiroshima* (Thames TV, 1975), from The World at War series; *Ten Seconds that Shook the World* (Wolper, 1963); and *Hiroshima and Nagasaki: The Harvest of Nuclear War* (1975). The growing disenchantment with nuclear weapons during the 1960s is reflected in Stanley Kubrick's masterpiece, *Dr. Strangelove, or How I Learned to Stop Worrying and Love the Bomb* (1964).

An excellent collection of primary documents on the bomb's development can be found in Michael Stoff, Jonathan Fanton, and R. Hal Williams, eds., *The Manhattan Project: A Documentary Introduction to the Atomic Age* (New York, 1990). Many of the diaries, letters, and top-secret memoranda are reproduced in facsimile form. A brief history of the bomb project is offered by the Department of Energy, F. G. Gosling, *The Manhattan Project: Science in the Second World War* (Washington, D.C., 1990). The decision-making models we discuss are more fully developed in another context in Graham Allison, *The Essence of Decision: Explaining the Cuban Missile Crisis* (Boston, Mass., 1971). Richard Rhodes, *The Making of the Atomic Bomb* (New York, 1986), has written the most comprehensive and readable account of the bomb project. Daniel Kevles, *The Physicists* (New York, 1977), and Nuel Pharr Davis, *Lawrence and Oppenheimer* (New York, 1986 reprint), provide background on members of the science community who helped create the bomb. Many went on to raise profound questions about what they had done and how their work was put to use.

CHAPTER THIRTEEN

From Rosie to Lucy

It was 1957. Betty Friedan was not just complaining; she was angry—for herself and uncounted other women like her. For some time, she had sensed she was not alone. Now she was certain, as she read the results of a questionnaire she and about 200 graduates of Smith College had completed. The alumni office, no doubt, had been seeking responses designed to show how well a college education fitted Smith students for their roles in later life. But many of the women who answered, it seemed, were frustrated with their lives. They resented the wide disparity between the idealized image society held of them as housewives and mothers and the realities of their daily routines.

True, most were materially well off. The majority had families, a house in the suburbs, and the amenities of an affluent society. But amid that good fortune they felt fragmented, almost as if they had no identity of their own. And it was not only college graduates. "I've tried everything women are supposed to do," one woman confessed to Friedan; "hobbies, gardening, pickling, canning, being very social with my neighbors, joining committees, running PTA teas. I can do it all, and I like it, but it doesn't leave you anything to think about—any feeling of who you are. . . . I love the kids and Bob and my home. There's no problem you can even put a name to. But I'm desperate. I begin to feel I have no personality. I'm a server of food and putter-on of pants and a bedmaker, somebody who can be called on when you want something. But who am I?" A similar sense of incompleteness haunted Friedan. "I, like other women, thought there was something wrong with me because I didn't have an orgasm waxing the kitchen floor," she recalled with some bitterness.

A growing sense of doubt led to a period of questioning. Why, she wondered, had she chosen fifteen years earlier to give up a promising career in psychology for marriage and motherhood? What was it that kept women from using the rights and prerogatives that were theirs? What made them feel guilty for anything they did in their own right rather than as their husbands' wives or children's mothers? Women in the 1950s, it seemed to Friedan, were not behaving quite the way they had a decade earlier. During World War II the popular press extolled the virtues of women like "Rosie the Riveter"—those who left homes and families to join the work force. Now, Rosie was no longer a heroine. The media lavished their praise on women who devoted themselves to family and home. In the closing scene of one 1957 *Redbook* story, the heroine, "Junior" (a "little freckle-faced brunette" who had decided to give up her job), nurses her baby at two in the morning sighing, "I'm glad, glad, glad I'm just a housewife." What had happened? "When did women decide to give up the world and go back home?" Friedan asked herself.

That question might engage a historian in the 1990s, but it was not one housewives of the 1950s were encouraged to ask. For a red-blooded American to doubt something as sacred as the role of housewives and mothers was to show symptoms of mental distress rather than a skeptical or inquiring mind. Whatever the label attached to such feelings—neurosis, anxiety, or depression—most people assumed that women like Friedan needed an analyst, not a historian, to explain their discontent. The malaise was a problem with individuals, not with society. To cure themselves, they needed only to become better adjusted to who and what they were.

Friedan, however, was no ordinary housewife. Before starting her family, she had worked as a newspaper reporter; even after her children came, she wrote regularly for the major women's magazines. By 1957 she was fed up with the endless stories about breast-feeding, the preparation of gourmet snails, and similar domestic fare that was the staple of *Redbook, McCall's,* and *Ladies' Home Journal.* She had noticed, too, that many women like herself who worked outside the home, even part time, felt guilty because their jobs threatened their husbands' roles as providers or took time away from their children. Thus Friedan began to wonder not only about herself as a woman, a wife, and a mother but also about the role society had shaped women to play.

Having seen the results of the Smith questionnaire, Friedan's reportorial instincts took over. She sensed she was onto a story bigger than anything she had written. But when she circulated an article describing the plight so many women were experiencing, the male editors at the women's magazines turned it down flat. It couldn't be true, they insisted; women could not possibly feel as guilty or discontented as Friedan claimed. The problem must be hers. "Betty has gone off her rocker," an editor at *Redbook* told her agent. "She has always done a good job for us, but this time only the most neurotic housewife could identify."

Friedan was not deterred. If the magazines would not print her story, she would do it as a book. For five years, she researched and wrote, describing the "feminine mystique" that she saw American culture promoting.

> The new mystique makes the housewife-mother, who never had a chance to be anything else, the model for all women . . . it simply makes certain concrete, finite, domestic aspects of feminine existence—as it was lived by women whose lives were confined by necessity to cooking, cleaning, washing, bearing children—into a religion, a pattern by which all women must now live or deny their femininity.

By the time Friedan was finished, the book had become a crusade. "I have never experienced anything as powerful, truly mystical, as the forces that seemed to

A happy housewife with a week's work. *By 1947 many women laborers were back in the home full-time and the baby boom was under way.* Life *magazine celebrated the labors of a typical housewife by laying out a week's worth of bedmaking, ironing, washing, grocery shopping, and dishwashing for a family of four. An incomplete tally shows over 250 plates being washed and thirty-five quarts of milk consumed a week. Did the wife drink the majority of the six cups of coffee which seem to have been consumed per day? (Nina Leen,* Life Magazine, © *Time Warner Inc.)*

overtake me as I wrote *The Feminine Mystique*," she later admitted. Published in 1963, the book soon joined the ranks of truly consequential books in American history. What Harriet Beecher Stowe did for slaves in *Uncle Tom's Cabin*, Jacob Riis for the urban poor in *How the Other Half Lives*, Upton Sinclair for public health in *The Jungle*, or Rachel Carson for the environment in *Silent Spring*, Friedan did for women. No longer would they bear their dissatisfaction in silence as they confronted the gap between their personal aspirations and the limited avenues society had left open to them. Friedan helped inspire a generation of middle-class women to demand the equal rights and opportunities men routinely claimed. Together with other activists, she founded the National Organization for Women (NOW) in 1965 to press for reforms on an institutional level, donating royalties from her book to support it.

Retreat from Revolution: A Demographic Profile

The feminist movement that blossomed from the actions of NOW and other women's groups had a profound impact on the study of history as well. After all, many of the questions Friedan raised were the sort that historians are trained to explore. Why hadn't women followed up on the gains in employment they experienced during World War II? What caused society in postwar America to place so much emphasis on home and family? What was the image of women that the mass media, scholars, and other opinion makers presented? In seeking answers, Friedan adopted many methods common to both history and the social sciences. She canvassed articles in popular women's magazines, studied the recent scholarship, and talked to psychologists, sociologists, and marriage counselors who regularly treated women. She conducted in-depth interviews with women of varying ages, backgrounds, and social classes.

It was not so much her methods that affected the study of history, however, as the subjects she chose to probe. Prior to the 1970s, history as a discipline gave slight attention to the experience of women, even though they constituted over half the world's population. The vast majority of studies (most of which were written by men anyway) concentrated on topics in the public arena. Politics, business, intellectual life, diplomacy, war—all were areas in which males defined the terms of action. The few women who did enter the history books were there most often because, like Eleanor Roosevelt, they had lived a public life; like Jane Addams, they initiated political reform; like Margaret Mead, they contributed in major ways to the social sciences; or like Willa Cather, they stood among the nation's leading writers and artists. Those were exceptional women, and it was the exceptional, not the commonplace, that historians generally preferred to study.

Still, history has by no means been confined to the rich, powerful, and famous—as we have seen in earlier chapters. And particularly for the twentieth century, there are documentary materials that make it possible to study ordinary people, either on a small scale, focusing on the personalities and motivations of individuals, or in a macrocosmic sense, looking at the actions of millions of people in the aggregate. The latter approach in particular is possible because of today's modern bureaucracies. Whether they are governmental, private, or academic, all are designed to collect data and store it in systematic ways. The New Deal, which expanded the role of government in so many areas, provided a prime impetus for the collection of statistics. Accustomed as we are to periodic reports on the gross national product, employment, and trade deficits, it is easy to forget that when the Great Depression struck in 1929, the Hoover administration had no way of knowing how many Americans had been put out of work by the crash. No department was charged with collecting such statistics, and one way the government made unemployment estimates was to fan out in several cities, count the number of people waiting in breadlines, and multiply by 10. With the New Deal, government agencies proliferated—and so did their statisticians.

➤The 1930s was also the decade when George Gallup began developing sophisticated polling operations to determine mass opinions on a multitude of issues. Polling had been done before Gallup began his work, but he and his rivals undertook it much more systematically, devising better ways of recording opinions, more sophisticated techniques for minimizing margins of error, and more scientific means of asking questions. In the academic world, the expansion of social science theory enlarged the kinds of information people thought worth having as well as the means for collecting such data. And as we have seen in the previous chapter, the scientific bureaucracy grew rapidly during this era. Thus when historians began investigating women's status in the mid-twentieth century, they could draw upon a good deal of statistical information. The data they found in some ways challenged Friedan's picture of women being pushed out of the work force, but in other ways her view was strikingly confirmed.

Census data and other governmental records indeed show that many women entered higher-paying and more skilled jobs as early as World War I. But those gains were short-lived. With the return of peace, women faced layoffs, renewed wage discrimination, and segregation into female-only jobs, such as secretarial and clerical work. They made little headway over the next decade, despite the hoopla about the emancipated "new woman" of the twenties. Behind the stereotype of the smart-talking flapper with her cigarette, bobbed hair, and boyish clothes, traditional ideas about women and their proper roles prevailed in the labor marketplace. In 1920, 23 percent of women worked; by 1930, the figure was only 24 percent. Access to the professions, while increased, remained heavily restricted. For example, women earned over 30 percent of all graduate degrees but accounted for only 4 percent of full professors on college faculties. Most women workers toiled at unskilled jobs; most were young, single, and without children. Between 1920 and 1930, the percentage of women in manufacturing fell from 22.6 (the same as 1910) to 17.5, while percentages of women in both domestic service and clerical work—the lowest-paying jobs—rose.

Real gains for women came during World War II. A rapidly expanding war economy absorbed most of the reserve labor force of under- or unemployed male workers. The military alone siphoned off some 15 million men and women. That left married women as the single largest untapped labor reserve. Suddenly, the propaganda machinery that had once discouraged women from competing with men for jobs urged them to enlist in the work force. The patriotic appeal had the desired effect. What faithful wife could sit at home when the media warned that her husband in the service might die from the lack of ammunition? "Commando Mary" and "Rosie the Riveter" became symbols of women who heeded their country's call.

Patriotism by itself did not explain the willingness of married women to take jobs. Many found higher war wages an attractive inducement. Indeed, with so

Women of the Saturday Evening Post, Part One. *In the midst of the war, the* Post's *"cover girl" was this nonchalant and confident Rosie, patriotic buttons across her chest, goggles over her eyes, macho watchband around the wrist, and biceps calculated to make Charles Atlas envious. As one real-life Rosie commented about welding, "We were happy to be doing it. We felt terrific. Lunch hour would find us spread out on the sidewalk. Women welders with our outfits on, and usually a quart of milk in one hand and a salami sandwich in another. It was an experience that none of us had ever had before." (Printed by permission of the Norman Rockwell Family Trust. Copyright © 1943 the Norman Rockwell Family Trust.)*

many husbands earning low military pay, families needed additional income to survive. Absent husbands also meant a lower birthrate and fewer demands for household services. That left women more time and opportunity for work outside the home. And wartime restrictions on leisure activities made jobs a more attractive outlet for women's energies. Whether stated as raw numbers or percentages, the statistical gains for women were impressive. From 1940 to 1945, some 6.5 million women entered the work force, over half of them for the first time. Women accounted for just 25 percent of workers in 1940 but 36 percent in 1945.

Perhaps more significant were the kinds of women who now found employment outside the home. Young, single women no longer dominated. By 1950 married women were a majority of the female work force, compared with only a third in 1940. Similarly, older women between ages fifty-five and sixty-four became a major group, rising from 17 percent in 1940 to 35 percent by 1960. It was not only the numbers of working women that soared but also the quality of their jobs. Women had an opportunity to work in skilled areas of manufacturing and to earn much higher wages. Black women in particular, who had been concentrated in low-paying farm and domestic jobs, rushed to the factories that offered higher pay and better hours. Women on the assembly lines—shaping sheet metal, building airplanes, and performing a host of skilled tasks—shattered many stereotypes about traditional male and female roles.

Yet for all these undeniable gains, the situation brought about by a world at war was a special case, and most Americans perceived it that way. The men returning home intended to pick up their jobs, while most assumed that women would return to their traditional household duties. As a result, the war led to few structural changes affecting women's economic roles. For example, working mothers needed some form of day care for their young children. The government was slow to provide it and, even where it existed, many mothers were reluctant to use it. They or other family members continued to have primary responsibility for children. One result was a much higher absentee rate for working mothers. In addition, those mothers worked shorter hours. For them, the responsibilities of the job were secondary to those of the home.

Most professions continued to maintain barriers against women. Although female workers flooded government bureaucracies and factories, few received managerial status. And many employers found ways to avoid government regulations requiring equal pay for men and women. General Motors, for example, simply changed its job classifications from overtly segregated male-female categories to "heavy-light," thus leaving women in the "light," lower-paying categories. Fearful that rapidly rising wages would spur inflation, the government was slow to enforce its own rules protecting women from discrimination.

Certain social trends seemed to underscore the traditional resistance to working mothers. Statistics indicated that wartime stresses threatened to undermine the family. Alcohol abuse, divorce, and juvenile delinquency all increased, and some observers blamed those problems on working mothers. In fact, there was no clear evidence that the families of those women had any disadvantage over those whose mothers stayed home. Extraordinary wartime mobility, not the fact that the mothers worked, seems to have accounted for many of those problems. The sudden rush of workers, both male and female, to industrial centers overtaxed all manner of public services, including housing and schools, which were of particular importance to families with young children. The war disrupted families whether mothers worked or not.

What is striking is that by 1945, despite all the gains women had made, most attitudes about women and work had not changed substantially. Surveys showed that Americans, whether male or female, continued to believe that child rearing was a woman's primary job. Thus the marked demographic shift of women into the work force was revolutionary in import, but it brought no revolution in cultural attitudes toward sex roles. As historian William Chafe commented, "The events of the war years suggested that most Americans would accept a significant shift in women's economic activities as long as the shift was viewed as 'temporary' and did not entail a conscious commitment to approve the goals of a sexual revolution."

Despite the general expectation that women would return to the home after the war, female laborers did not simply drop their wrenches and pick up frying pans. Many continued to work outside the home, although mostly to support their families, not to find career alternatives. As peace came in 1945, polls indicated that over 75 percent of all working women wanted to continue at their jobs. About 88 percent of high school girls surveyed said they hoped for a career as well as the role of homemaker. Though employment for women did shrink slightly, a significantly higher percentage of women were working in 1950 than in 1940 (28 percent versus 24). Even more striking, that figure continued to rise, reaching 36 percent by 1960. Those numbers included older women, married women with children, and women of all social classes.

Such statistics would seem at first to undercut Friedan's notion that the vast majority of American women accepted the idea of total fulfillment through housework and child rearing. Some 2.25 million women did voluntarily return home after the war and another million were laid off by 1946. At the same time, 2.75 million women entered the job market by 1947, leaving a net loss of only half a million.

But if Friedan was mistaken in seeing a mass female exodus from the work force, a significant shift did take place in the types of work performed. When women who had been laid off managed to return to work, they often lost their seniority and had to accept reduced pay in lower job categories. Employment in almost all the professions had decreased by 1960. Despite gains in some areas, women were concentrated in jobs that were primarily extensions of their traditional responsibility for managing the family's physical and emotional well-being: they were nurses, not doctors; teachers, not principals; tellers, not bankers. Far more worked in service jobs (as maids or waitresses, for example) than in manufacturing. Overwhelmingly, job opportunities were segregated by gender. About 75 percent of all women workers held female-only jobs. In fact, gender segregation in the workplace was worse in 1960 than in 1900—and even worse than segregation by race. Thus, even though women's participation in the work force remained comparatively high, it did not inspire a corresponding revolution in attitudes about women's roles in society.

Retreat from Revolution: The Role of Mass Media

Attitudes, of course, were at the center of Friedan's concerns in *The Feminine Mystique*; and the demographic profile we have sketched underlines the reason for her focus. If the percentage of women holding jobs continued to increase during the 1950s and young women, when polled, said they hoped to combine work in some way with motherhood, how did the cult of the "feminine mystique" become so firmly enshrined? If wartime laboring conditions produced a kind of revolution in fact but not in spirit, what elements of American culture reined in that revolution and kept it from running its course?

As Friedan was well aware, economic and demographic factors played a crucial role in renewing the concern with home and family living. During the war, millions of American men fought overseas, which meant that, correspondingly, millions of wives at home could not have children. Even before the war, the hard times of the Depression had discouraged couples from starting large families. But in 1945, when the home front saw the return of peace and prosperity and GIs were eager to do more than kiss their wives hello, the well-nigh inevitable pressures set off a postwar baby boom. For the next fifteen years the United States had one of the highest birthrates in the world, rising from an average of 1.9 to 2.3 children for each woman of childbearing age. Large families became the norm. The number of parents with three children tripled, while those with four quadrupled. Women also married younger. The average age of marriage dropped from 22 in 1900 to 20.3 in 1962. With the highest rate of marriage of any nation in the world, American men and women clearly chose to organize their lives around family.[1]

Clearly, material conditions not only pushed women out of the workplace as GIs rejoined the peacetime economy but also pulled women back into the home as the birthrate rose. Friedan acknowledged these changes but noted that the birthrates of other economically developed nations—such as France, Norway, and Sweden—had begun to decline by 1955. Even more striking, the sharpest rise in the United States came among women aged fifteen to nineteen. In Great Britain, Canada, and Germany, on the other hand, the rise was more equally distributed among age groups. What was it that made so many American "teen brides" give up the chance of college and a career for early marriage and homemaking?

Friedan's answer was to look more closely at the mass media. Magazines, radio, movies, television—all these had come to play a predominant role in modern culture. They exposed Americans by the millions to powerfully presented messages conveying the standards and ideals of the culture. The media, observed sociologist Harold Lasswell in 1948, had come to perform many of the tasks that, in medieval Europe, were assumed by the Catholic church. Like the church, the media possessed the capacity to send the same message to all classes at the same time, with confidence in their authority to speak and to be heard universally. Friedan, for her part, found it significant that in the postwar era the media's message about women—what they could dream of, set their sights on, and accomplish—underwent a marked shift. The purveyors of popular culture suddenly seemed determined to persuade women that they should not just

---

[1] At the same time, the United States had the world's highest divorce rate. Enthusiasm for marriage was apparently no guarantee of success.

accept but actually embrace the idealized image of women as wives and mothers.

Having written for the mass-circulation women's magazines, Friedan already knew the part they played in promoting the feminine mystique. What surprised her was how much the image of women had changed. In the 1930s, the woman most likely to appear in a magazine story had a career and was as much concerned with a goal of her own as with getting her man. The heroine of a typical *Ladies' Home Journal* story in 1939 is a nurse who has "strength in her hands, pride in her carriage and nobility in the lift of her chin. . . . She had been on her own ever since she left training, nine years ago. She had earned her way, she need consider nothing but her heart." And unlike the heroines of the 1950s, these women did not have to choose invariably between marriage and career. If they held strongly to their dreams, they could have both. Beginning in the 1950s, however, new heroines appeared. These, Friedan noted, were most often "young and frivolous, almost childlike; fluffy and feminine; passive; gaily content in a world of bedroom and kitchen, sex, babies, and home." The new women did not work "except housework and work to keep their bodies beautiful and to get and keep a man." "Where," Friedan asked rhetorically, "is the world of thought and ideas, the life of the mind and the spirit?"

Talking with some of the few remaining editors from the 1930s, Friedan discovered one reason for the change. "Most of the material used to come from women writers," one explained. "As the young men returned from the war, a great many women writers stopped writing. The new writers were all men, back from the war, who had been dreaming about home, and a cozy domestic life." Male editors, when queried, defended themselves by contending that their readers no longer identified with career women, no longer read serious fiction, and had lost almost all interest in public issues except perhaps those that affected the price of groceries. "You just can't write about ideas or broad issues of the day for women," one remarked.

Just as the image of women changed in mass magazines, so too did women's fashions follow Rosie the Riveter out of the factory. As historian Lois Banner has observed, in the 1930s only a movie star like Katherine Hepburn could get away with wearing slacks. During the 1940s, however, a boyish or mannish look for women became popular. Narrow skirts, padded shoulders, and suits all had a vogue. That ended in 1947, when Parisian designer Christian Dior introduced the "new look." Dior-inspired fashion emphasized femininity. Narrow waistlines drew attention to shapely hips and a fully defined bosom. Most women had to wear foundation garments to achieve the necessary look. The new styles reached their extreme in the "baby doll" fashions, with cinched-in waists that set off full bosoms and bouffant skirts held out by crinoline petticoats. Women's shoes ushered in a bonanza for podiatrists. Toes became pointier and heels rose even higher, until it became dangerous for women to walk. Banner concluded that "not since the Victorian era had women's fashions been so confining." That fashion was a male image of the ideal feminine look.

In the 1930s, magazines and movies had set the fashion. By the 1950s, both those media had begun to lose their audience to television. Women who had once gone to the matinee stayed home to watch the latest episode of *As the World Turns*. In 1951, cities with television networks reported a 20 to 40 percent decline in movie attendance. Almost overnight, television became the preeminent mass medium, carrying images—feminine or otherwise—of American culture into the home. By 1949 there were about a million sets and 108 licensed stations, most in large urban markets. By 1952, 15 million Americans had bought sets; by 1955, the figure had jumped to 30 million; by 1960, television had entered 46 million homes. In fact, more American homes had television sets than had bathrooms! Obviously, if we are to understand how the mass media of the 1950s shaped the image of women, television must be at the center of our focus.[2]

And indeed, television portrayed women of the fifties in predictable ways. Most often they were seen in domestic dramas or comedies, in which Mom and Dad were found living happily with their two or three cute children and possibly a live-in maid or relative to provide additional comic situations. The homes in which they lived, even that of blue-collar airplane riverter Chester Riley (*The Life of Riley*, 1949-50, 1953-58), were cheerfully middle class, with the antiseptic look of a furniture showroom. As for Mom herself, she never worked outside the home and seldom seemed to do much more than wave a dust cloth or whip up a three-course meal at a moment's notice. Sometimes, as in *The Adventures of Ozzie and Harriet* (1955-66), she is competent, cool, and collected. Ozzie, in fact, often seems rather a lost soul when he is turned loose in his own castle, having to be guided gently through the current week's predicament by Harriet. In other series, such as *The Burns and Allen Show* (1950-58), women like Gracie Allen and her friend Blanche played more the role of "dizzy dames," unable to balance checkbooks and sublimely oblivious to the realities of the business world. When Harry Morton announces to his wife Blanche, "I've got great news for you!" (he's been offered a new job), Blanche replies, "When can I wear it?"

Perhaps the domestic comedy that best portrayed the archetypical family woman was *Father Knows Best* (1954-62). The title says it all: Robert Young, playing Jim Anderson, never lacks a sane head, while his wife Margaret is devoted, though something of a cipher. She lacks Gracie Allen's originality yet still can be counted on as a source of genial humor as she tries vainly, for instance, to learn to drive the family car. Warmhearted, attractive, submissive, competent only within the sphere of her limited domain, she is the fifties housewife personified.

In one sense, then, Friedan does have a case. The mass media of the 1950s, television prime among them, saturated the American public with the image of the new feminine mystique. But to establish that merely raises a much thornier issue: What sort of relationship is there between the media and reality? Friedan

---

[2] The technology of broadcasting had been available in the 1920s, but only after World War II did commercial application begin in earnest. As secretary of commerce, Herbert Hoover had his image transmitted in 1927, making him the first president to have appeared on television, although this occurred before his election in 1928. "Trivial Pursuit" buffs will recall that Franklin Roosevelt was, in 1939, the first president in office to appear on television.

***Women of the* Saturday Evening Post, *Part Two.** Biceps and riveting guns had deserted* Post *covers by 1956. Instead, these two women—like Margaret in* Father Knows Best—*can barely get their cars out the driveway, let alone down the street. No doubt, however, they could stir up a mean Jell-O salad. (© The Curtis Publishing Company.)*

is arguing not merely that the institutions of mass communication promoted the feminine mystique. She is suggesting that, through their influence and pervasiveness, the media were actually able to stifle women's aspirations and shape their attitudes. In that case, it becomes much more understandable why women's gains during the war were not translated into a revolution of the spirit.

Reflection versus Manipulation

What effect do the mass media have on real life? Obviously, that is a complex question. But in sorting out the possible answers, we can see that there are two sharply contrasting ways of responding. On the one hand, it is possible to argue that, in fact, the media have very little effect on the real world, since they merely reflect tastes and opinions that mass audiences already hold. Confronted with a need to attract the largest number of consumers, media executives select programs that have the broadest appeal. Advertisers seek less to alter values than to channel existing ones toward a specific choice. Americans already value romantic love; once Lever Brothers has its way, they brush with "Close-Up" to achieve it. In the most extreme form, this "reflection hypothesis" would see the media as essentially passive—a simple mirror to society. And in that case, a good deal of Friedan's examination of female imagery might be instructive but beside the point. Women of the fifties were portrayed the way they were because, for whatever reasons, they had been transformed by the conditions of postwar culture.

But that extreme form of the reflection hypothesis breaks down for several reasons. First, if we argue that the mass media are merely reflections, then what are they reflecting? Surely not "real life" pure and simple. Only in commercials do the people who brush with Close-Up make their mates swoon. The parents on *Father Knows Best* are happily married, with two children, hardly the statistical norm in America even then. Divorced, single-parent mothers were unknown in sitcom land. Black families were virtually nonexistent. Obviously, while the media reflect certain aspects of real life, the reflection hypothesis must be modified to admit that a good deal of what is reflected comprises idealized values—what people would like to be rather than what they really are.

But if mass communications reflect ideals as much as reality, whose ideals are these? As Friedan pointed out, most of the editors, producers, directors, and writers of the 1950s were men. If male rather than female ideals and aspirations were being communicated (or, for that matter, white rather than black, middle-class rather than lower-class, or the ideals of any limited group), then it again becomes legitimate to ask how much the ideals of one segment of America are shaping those of a far wider audience.

Of course, many of the people involved in producing mass culture would argue that in the matter of dreams and ideals, they are not selling their own— merely giving the audience what it wants. But do audiences know what they really want? Surely they do sometimes. But they may also be influenced, cajoled, and swayed. Persuasion, after all, is at the heart of modern advertising. A fifties marketing executive made the point quite freely, noting that

> In a free enterprise economy, we have to develop the need for new products. And to do that we have to liberate women to desire these new products. We help them rediscover that homemaking is more creative than to compete with men. This can be manipulated. We sell them what they ought to want, speed up the unconscious, move it along.

Perhaps the most obvious case of an audience susceptible to persuasion is that made up of children. Psychological research has indicated that among children, a process called "modeling" occurs,

> simply by watching others, without any direct reinforcement for learning and without any overt practice. The child imitates the model without being induced or compelled to do so. That learning can occur in the absence of direct reinforcement is a radical departure from earlier theories that regarded reward or punishment as

indispensable to learning. There is now considerable evidence that children do learn by watching and listening to others even in the absence of reinforcement and overt practice.

Obviously, if young girls learn week in and week out that father does indeed know best and that a woman's place *is* in the home, the potential for manipulation is strong.

The hypothesis that the media may be manipulative contrasts sharply with the theory that they are only reflective. More realistically, though, the two alternatives are best seen as the poles of a continuum. In its extreme form, the reflection hypothesis sees the media as entirely passive, with no influence whatever. In its extreme form, the manipulative hypothesis sees the media as highly controlling, "brainwashing" viewers (to use a term popular in the anticommunist fifties) into believing and acting in ways they never would have on their own. But a young girl, no matter how long she watches television, is also shaped by what she learns from her parents, schoolteachers, religious instructors, and a host of other influences. Given those contending factors, how decisive a role can the media play?

Ironically, the more extreme forms of the manipulative hypothesis have been supported by both the left and right of the political spectrum. During the 1950s, for example, with worries of foreign subversion running high, conservative ideologues warned that communists had come to rely "more on radio and TV than on the press and motion pictures as 'belts' to transmit pro-Sovietism to the American public." On the other hand, liberal intellectuals charged that mass culture, at its worst, threatened "not merely to cretinize our taste, but to brutalize our senses by paving the way to totalitarianism."

Historians have stepped only gingerly into the debate over media influence. In part this may be because, like most scholars, they tend not to be heavy consumers of mass culture themselves. Preferring a symphony by Strauss to MTV or Madonna, Federico Fellini's *8 1/2* to Burt Reynolds's *Smokey and the Bandit, Part 6*, or *Masterpiece Theater* to *The Simpsons*, their instinctive reaction is to deem popular fare "worthy of attention only if it is created by unpaid folk and 'serious' artists who do not appear to think about making a living," as sociologist Herbert Gans has tartly remarked.

By temperament and training, most historians are also more comfortable with the traditional print media. When they seek to explicate a document, book, or diary, they can readily find the text and use common critical strategies to identify major thematic, symbolic, or cultural content. Insofar as the "author" of the document is sensitive to issues that concern some significant sector of society, the text can be said to reflect on social reality.

But what if the "text" is a series of commercials plugging the virtues of a toothpaste or a year's worth of *Guiding Light* soap operas? In that case, historians confront two difficulties. A vast amount of broadcast material is ephemeral—not permanently recorded at the time it was broadcast and recoverable now only in the vast reaches of outer space, where the signals are still radiating, ready either to bore or boggle the minds of another galaxy. The actual content of many broadcasts can be reconstructed only from file scripts or memories of viewers or participants, if at all. Even where television material has been saved and can be analyzed for its cultural content, a knowledge of how the audience received a program or commercial is crucial. As Herbert Gans has insisted, "cultural values cannot be determined from cultural content, until we know why people chose it." Do they watch a program intensely, or do they turn it on only because it's the best of a bad lot? Historians seldom have the means to answer those questions satisfactorily.

→ Sociologists are the allies most likely to help historians determine the effects of the media—particularly television—in modern life. But while sociologists have run a number of interesting studies involving the effect of television violence and racial stereotypes on viewers, much less systematic evidence has been gathered on television's effect on women. The most promising work has centered on what is known in the trade as content analysis. A content-analysis researcher examines a body of evidence, scanning it systematically in order to answer a few objective questions. How often are sex and violence linked in network crime shows? The researcher picks a sample group of shows, views them on a regular basis, and counts the number of incidents that include sex and violence. The results, of course, are descriptive within fairly limited bounds. They can tell us, for example, how often women appear in certain roles, but not how the audience perceives or values those roles. Nor can we know, except indirectly, what the shows' producers actually intended. If women are always portrayed in inferior positions, we can infer that the producers saw women as inferior; but the inference remains unproved.

Content analysis of early television programming has led sociologist Gaye Tuchman to conclude that television practiced the "symbolic annihilation of women." By that she meant that women were "demeaned, trivialized, or simply ignored." Surveys of television programs revealed that women, who were over half the population, accounted for just 32 percent of the characters in prime-time dramas. Most of the women who did appear were concentrated in comedy series. Children's cartoons had even fewer female characters. Even where women appeared most often—daytime soap operas—they still held inferior positions. A 1963 survey showed, in fact, that men held 80 percent of all jobs in prime-time shows.

Women were demeaned in other ways. They were most often the victims of violence, not the perpetrators. Single women were attacked more frequently than married women. The most favorably portrayed women were either courting or in a family role. In the 1950s, two-thirds of all the women characters on television shows were married, had been married, or were engaged. Even in soap operas, usually set in homes where women might presumably be allowed to act as leaders, women's roles were trivialized, for it was usually men who found the solutions to emotional problems.

Much early content-analysis research was not designed to focus specifically on women. But studies analyzing the settings of shows and the psychological characteristics of heroes, villains, and supporting characters indirectly support Tuchman's conclusion, since they show that the world of television drama was overwhelmingly white, middle-class, suburban, family-centered, and male-dominated. In eighty-six prime-time dramas aired during 1953, men outnumbered women 2 to 1. The very young (under twenty) and the old (over sixty) were underrepresented. The characters were largely of courting or childbearing age and employed or employable. High white-collar or professional positions were overrepresented at the expense of routine white- or blue-collar jobs. Most characters were sane, law-abiding, healthy, and white (over 80 percent). Blacks, who accounted for 12 percent of the population, appeared in only 2 percent of the roles. Heroes outnumbered heroines 2 to 1; and since heroic foreigners were more likely to be women, that left three American heroes for each American heroine.

In these same eighty-six shows, male villains outnumbered female villains. On the one hand, feminists might take heart at this more positive presentation of women. On the other, villains had many traits that Americans admired. While more unattractive, dishonest, disloyal, dirty, stingy, and unkind, they were also braver, stronger, sharper, or harder than most heroes, and had inner strength. Thus they were effective even if undesirable. By minimizing women as villains, television denied them yet another effective role. Similarly, television dramas presented the most favorable stereotypes of professions in which men dominated. Journalists, doctors, and entertainers all had positive images, while teachers—a large majority of whom were women—were treated as the slowest, weakest, and softest professionals (though clean and fair).

So far as content analysis is able to go, then, it confirms that television did systematically reinforce the feminine mystique Betty Friedan found so prevalent elsewhere. But along with the advantages of content analysis come limits. To be rigorous, the method of measuring must be standardized and the questions asked must be fairly limited and objective. For example, one content analyst described her approach in this way:

> Between March 18 and March 31, 1975, I watched and coded the shows, according to pretested categories. Using a specially prepared timer, I examined the first verbal or nonverbal interaction clearly between two people in thirty seconds of one-minute segments of the programs. I recorded who was dominant, dominated, or equal in each interaction and noted the relevant occupation status, sex, race, and family role of each participant.

This is admirably systematic, but it leaves little room for more qualitative judgments—for evaluating the nuances of an image as well as its overt content. Sociologists, of course, would say that such subjective analysis is precisely what they are trying to avoid, because any "nuances" are likely to incorporate the prejudices of the researcher. As we know by now, however, historians have traditionally felt that this was a risk worth taking in order to examine documents for what they hint at or even do *not* say as much as for what they do. Since we are not in a position to undertake field research on how audiences of the fifties were affected by programs involving women, let us instead resort to a subjective analysis of television's product itself and see what its leading characters and dramatic themes reveal.

Male Frames and Female Energies

The most promising programs for exploring gender issues are the situation comedies, or "sitcoms." As we have seen, other genres popular in the 1950s—crime shows, westerns, quiz programs, and network news—tended to ignore women or place them in secondary roles. A majority of the sitcoms, however, take place in a domestic or family setting in which women are central figures. The plots regularly turn on misunderstandings between men and women over their relationships or the proper definition of gender roles. As a consequence, of all television programs, sitcoms had the most formative influence on the image of women.

As a genre, sitcoms had their roots in radio shows like *Jack Benny, Burns and Allen,* and *Amos 'n' Andy*—an influence that helps explain why their comedy came to be more verbal than that of film, which blended physical and verbal humor.[3] Sitcoms derived most of their laughs from puns, repartee, or irony. What the camera added was the visual delivery of the comedians: a raised eyebrow, a curled lip, or a frown. Thus closeups and reaction shots were key to the humor, especially since the small television screen limited the detail that could be shown. "You know what your mother said the day we were married, Alice?" grumps the obese Ralph Kramden on *The Honeymooners.* [A close-up, here, for emphasis; the double-chin juts in disdain.] "You know what she said? I'm not losing a daughter; I'm gaining a ton." Or another time, when Ralph's vanity gets the better of him, he brags, "Alice, when I was younger, the girls crowded around me at the beach." "Of course, Ralph," replies Alice, "that's because they wanted to sit in the shade." [Cut to Ralph's bulging eyes.]

From the historian's point of view, the more intriguing sitcoms are not the predictable ones like *The Adventures of Ozzie and Harriet* or *Father Knows Best* but those that do not seem to fit the standard mold. It is here—where the familiar conventions come closest to being broken—that the tensions and contradictions of the genre appear most clearly. In different ways, *Our Miss Brooks, I Love Lucy*, and *The Honeymooners* all feature unconventional characters and unusual plot situations. *Our Miss Brooks* stars Eve Arden as an aging, unmarried schoolteacher whose biting humor makes her a threat to the bumbling men around her. *I Love Lucy*, with Lucille Ball, follows the wacky attempts of Lucy Ricardo to break out of her narrow domesticity into the larger world of show business or into some moneymaking venture. Though the Ricardos had a child midway through the series, he was not often featured in the show. *The Honeymooners* was perhaps the most offbeat sitcom of the fifties. It featured the Kramdens, a childless couple, who lived in a dreary Brooklyn flat with their neighbors Ed and Trixie Norton, also childless. Ralph, a bus driver, and Ed, a sewer worker, seem unlikely subjects to reinforce the middle-class values of Friedan's feminine mystique.

---

[3]*Amos 'n' Andy*, a show about a taxicab company operated by blacks, presented a special crossover problem. The white radio actors who started in the show were hardly appropriate for a visual medium.

Despite their unusual formats, all three sitcoms were among the most popular shows of the fifties, and *Lucy* stayed at the top of the ratings for almost the entire decade. By looking at them, we can better understand on what basis a show could deviate from traditional forms and still remain successful.

As it happens, none of these shows is as exceptional as it might first seem. All incorporate elements of the traditional family show structure, with male authority remaining dominant, middle-class values applauded, and the proper order of society prevailing by the end of each episode. Still, there is more to them than the simple triumph of the feminine mystique. The three leading female characters—Connie Brooks, Lucy Ricardo, and Alice Kramden—reveal through the force of their comic personas certain tensions that slick production styles and pat plot resolutions cannot hide. We see glimpses of women's discontent as well as women's strength in coping with adversity.

The comic tensions in *Our Miss Brooks* arise from two primary sources: Connie constantly clashes with her authoritarian and pompous principal, Osgood Conklin, and—at the same time—has her amorous eye on the biology teacher, Mr. Boynton. He seems oblivious to her sexual overtures yet is the best prospect to save her from spinsterhood. In one show she walks in with her arms full of packages. "Can I hold something?" he asks. "Sure, as soon as I put these packages down," she cracks. He overlooks the sexual innuendo that she is forced to use in her constant attempts to stir his interest.

Miss Brooks is oppressed on several levels. She recognizes that society places little value on her role as a teacher. There is no future in her job, where she is bullied, exploited, and underpaid. Marriage offers the only way out, but since she is superior in intellect and personality to the men and no longer young and fresh, her prospects are dim. Thus she faces a future in which she cannot fulfill the feminine mystique. Her only hope is to use her wiles to trick Mr. Boynton into marriage. She must be passive-aggressive, because convention prevents her from taking the initiative. At the same time, she must accept an economic role that is far beneath her talents. Rather than challenge the system that demeans her, she survives by treating it as comical and transcending it through the force of her superior character.

The first episode of the series establishes many of those themes as well as a somewhat irreverent style. Connie gets an idea that she can arouse Mr. Boynton's interest by starting a fight. That leads to a number of laughs as Boynton ducks each of her attempts at provocation. Before she makes headway, she is called on the carpet by Mr. Conklin, the principal. In his office, he radiates authority, glowering from behind his desk and treating her with disdain. But Miss Brooks hardly folds before the onslaught. She tricks him into reminiscing about his youth and, as he becomes more mellow (and human), she assumes greater familiarity, until she is sitting casually on the corner of his desk. By the end of the meeting, Connie has sent Mr. Conklin on a wild-goose chase that leads to his arrest by the police. In his absence, she becomes acting principal and clearly relishes the sense of authority she gains sitting in the seat of power. The duly constituted hierarchy has been bearded and stood on its head. Of course, all is set right in the end, but before order returns, we have had a glimpse of a world where women have power.

The liberties taken in the show, however, amount to scarcely more than shore leave. Even if Miss Brooks is unmarried, the show does have a kind of surrogate family structure. Despite her relatively advanced age, Connie's real role is more that of an impish teen daughter. She lives in an apartment with a remarkably maternal housekeeper. One of the students at school, Walter (who these days would be classified as an eminent nerd), serves as a surrogate son, while Mr. Conklin, of course, is the father figure. That leaves Mr. Boynton to be paired off as Miss Brooks's reticent steady. As for Connie's challenges to Mr. Conklin's male authority, they are allowed only because the principal is pompous, arbitrary, or abusive of his position. And Mr. Boynton turns out not to be as dumb as he acts; indeed, at the end of the first episode, as Miss Brooks waits eagerly for a kiss that will demonstrate his interest, he holds back, his wink to the audience indicating that he can dish it out too. With Mr. Conklin back in charge and Mr. Boynton clearly in control, the male frame is reestablished, Connie has been chastened for her presumption, and the normal order of things has been restored.

Lucy (Lucille Ball), Ethel Mertz (Vivian Vance), and Ricky Ricardo (Desi Arnaz) *look on anxiously as French film star Charles Boyer straightens his pocket handkerchief in an episode of* I Love Lucy. *Lucy, who could not confront a celebrity without causing trouble, had torn Boyer's raincoat and crushed his hat. For all her zaniness Lucy generally appeared dressed in the latest fashions and her apartment reflected tasteful middle-class decor. (Courtesy of CBS, Inc.)*

Similar tensions operate in the *I Love Lucy* show. Lucy's efforts to escape the confines of domesticity threaten her husband Ricky and the well-being of the family. The plot generally thickens as Lucy cons her neighbor Ethel Mertz into joining her escapades. Ethel and Lucy then become rivals of their husbands. In an episode that could have generated biting commentary, Lucy and Ethel challenge Fred Mertz and Ricky to exchange roles. The women will be the breadwinners, the men the housekeepers. Both, of course, prove equally inept in the others' domain. Ethel and Lucy discover they have no significant job skills. After much frustration, they end up working in a chocolate factory under a woman who is far more domineering and arbitrary than Mr. Conklin ever was. In a parody of Charlie Chaplin's *Modern Times*, they fall hopelessly behind as they pack candies off a relentless conveyor belt. By the end of the day they are emotionally drained, humbled, and thwarted.

In the meantime, Ricky and Fred have virtually destroyed the apartment. How much rice do they need for dinner? They decide on several pounds, so that the kitchen is soon awash. Just as Ethel and Lucy are relieved to return home, Fred and Ricky are overjoyed to escape the toils of domestic life. Each side learns a new regard for the difficulties faced by the other.

Despite the schmaltzy ending, there is a real tension in the structure of this episode and the series as a whole. Within the orthodox framework (Lucy and Ricky are firmly middle class, worrying about money, friends, schools, and a house in the suburbs), the energy and spark of the show comes precisely because Lucy, like Miss Brooks, consistently refuses to recognize the male limits prescribed for her. Although Ricky manages to rein her in by the end of each episode, the audience realizes full well that she is too restless, too much restricted by four walls and a broom, and far too vivacious to accept the cult of domesticity. She will be off and running again the following week in another attempt to break loose.[4]

More than any sitcom of the 1950s, *The Honeymooners* seems to deviate from middle-American stereotypes. As lower-class, childless couples living in stark apartments, the Nortons and Kramdens would scarcely seem ideal reflections of an affluent, family-centered society. Ralph and Alice struggle to get by on his $67.50 a week salary as a bus driver. Sewer worker Ed Norton and his wife Trixie live off credit. Whenever their appliances or furniture are repossessed, Ed starts over at another store. The Kramdens have no television set, telephone, vacuum cleaner, or other modern appliance. Their living room/kitchen, the

---

[4] The show's most successful moment might also serve as a model of 1950s family life. In its early years, television honored all the middle-class sexual mores. Even married couples slept in separate beds and the word "pregnant" was taboo (since it implied that a couple had been sexually active—at least once). The producers of *Lucy* thus faced a terrible dilemma when they learned that their star was indeed with child. What to do? They made the bold decision to incorporate Lucille Ball's pregnancy into the show. For months, television audiences watched Lucy become bigger and more uncomfortable. On January 19, 1953, the big day arrived. The episode "Lucy Has Her Baby" (filmed earlier in anticipation of the blessed event) scored the highest rating (68.8 percent) of any show of the decade. News of the birth of Desi Arnaz, Jr., rivaled the headlines for the inauguration of Dwight D. Eisenhower, which occurred the following morning.

main set for the show, had only a bureau, a table and chairs, a sink, an icebox (literally), and a stove. It had the look of the Depression era, not the 1950s.

The show turns on Ralph's obsession with money and status. He is forever trying to get rich quick, earn respect, and move up in the world. All that saves him from himself and disaster is Alice's stoic forbearance. She has had to live through all his efforts to assert his authority—"I'm the boss, Alice and don't you ever forget it!"—and to resist his hare-brained schemes (diet pizza parlors, wallpaper that glows in the dark to save electricity). And it is Alice who cushions his fall when each new dream turns to ashes. Like most middle-class American couples, Ralph and Alice bicker over money. Ralph is a cheapskate, not by nature but to mask his failure as a breadwinner. Alice must use her feminine wiles to persuade him to buy anything, even a TV or a telephone. To protect his pride, Ralph accuses her of being a spendthrift. Their battles have far more bite than those seen in any other sitcom of that era. In no other show do the characters so regularly lay marriage, ego, or livelihood on the line.

In a typical scene *from* The Honeymooners, *Ralph Kramden (Jackie Gleason) adopts a pompous pose before his skeptical wife Alice (Audrey Meadows) and her anxious friend Trixie Norton (Joyce Randolph), while his friend Ed Norton (Art Carney) looks on with bug-eyed disbelief. Inevitably Ralph's confidence shattered in the face of his bungling attempts to get rich quick, leaving Alice to pick up the pieces and put him back together again. (Courtesy of CBS, Inc.)*

Why, then, did the audience like this show? For one thing, it is very funny. Ed Norton's irrepressible deadpan is a perfect foil to Ralph's manic intensity. It is a delight to watch Norton take forever to shuffle the cards while Ralph does a slow burn. And Alice's alternately tolerant and spirited rejoinders complete the chemistry. In addition, there is a quality to the Kramdens' apartment that separates it in time and space from the world in which middle-class viewers live. The mass audience is more willing to confront serious questions if such issues are raised in distant times or places. Death on *Gunsmoke* does not have the same implications as a death on *Lassie*. Divorce for Henry VIII is one thing; even a hint of it for Ozzie and Harriet would be something quite different. Thus the Depression look of the Kramdens' apartment gives the audience the spatial and temporal distance it needs to separate itself from the sources of conflict between Ralph and Alice. The audience can look on with a sense of its material and social superiority as Alice and Ralph go at it:

RALPH: You want this place to be Disneyland.

ALICE: This place is a regular Disneyland. You see out there, Ralph? The back of the Chinese restaurant, old man Grogan's long underwear on the line, the alley? That's my Fantasyland. You see that sink over there? That's my Adventureland. The stove and the icebox, Ralph, that's Frontierland. The only thing that's missing is the World of Tomorrow.

RALPH: (doing his slow burn): You want Tomorrowland, Alice? You want Tomorrowland? Well, pack your bags, because you're going to the *moon*! [Menaces her with his raised fist.][5]

Underneath it all, however, *The Honeymooners* is still a middle-class family sitcom. Alice and Trixie don't have children; they have Ralph and Ed. In one episode Trixie says to Alice, "You know those men we're married to? You have to treat them like children." A trick of social class makes this arrangement work without threatening the ideal of male authority. Since the middle classes have always equated the behavior of the poor with that of children—and Ralph and Ed are poor—no one is surprised by their childish antics. Trixie and Alice, both having married beneath them, maintain middle-class standards. At the end of almost every episode, Alice brings Ralph back into the fold after one of his schemes fails. Surrounding her in an embrace, he rewards her with his puppydog devotion: "Baby, you're the greatest."

One episode in particular reveals the price Alice paid to keep her man-child, marriage, and selfhood intact. A telegraph arrives announcing, "I'm coming to visit. Love, Mom." Ralph explodes at the idea of sharing his apartment with his dreaded mother-in-law, for her disapproval and insults wound his brittle pride whenever she visits. There are numerous jokes at Ralph's expense as well as some cutting commentary on mothers-in-law, after which Ralph moves in with the Nortons upstairs, where he sparks a similar fight between them. Finally, marriage and family prevail over wounded pride. An unrepentant Ralph returns

---

[5] Similarly a show like *M*A*S*H* could more easily explore topical issues like racism because it was set in Korea, not the United States, and in the 1950s, not the 1970s during which it was broadcast, even though the issues were contemporary.

home, only to find out that "mother" is Mother Kramden, whom Alice, of course, is treating with the very warmth Ralph denies *her* mother. He is once again reduced to a shamefaced puppy.

Alice's victory is so complete that it threatens to destroy her relationship with Ralph. As if to soften the blow, she sits down to deliver her victory speech. She lowers her eyes, drops her shoulders, and speaks in tones of resignation rather than triumph, finally reading to Ralph a letter in praise of mothers-in-law, who have the "hardest job in the world." It turns out to be a letter Ralph wrote fifteen years earlier to Alice's mother. The sentiments are so sappy that they virtually destroy the comedy. Like Ralph, the producers must have thought it better to eat crow than leave a residue of bitterness or social criticism. They must have recognized that their material had been too extreme, the humor too sharp, and the mother-in-law jokes too cruel for middle-American tastes.

Even after its apology, the show ends with what appears to be an unintentional image of Alice in a domestic prison. Mother Kramden has gone off to "freshen up." A penitent Ralph admits his defeat, then announces he is going out for some air—in essence to pull himself back together. But what of Alice? She is left holding nothing more than she had before—dominion over her dreary kitchen. Her responsibility to Ralph's mother prevents her from escaping also, and she is no better off than before the battle began. Her slumped posture suggests that she understands all too well the hollowness of her triumph. We must believe that many women in videoland identified with Alice.

The Honeymooners, I Love Lucy, and *Our Miss Brooks* all suggest that, while the male characters in the series maintain their ultimate authority, the "symbolic annihilation" of women that Gaye Tuchman spoke of is, in these comedies at least, not total. A battle between the sexes would not be funny unless the two sides were evenly matched; and setting sitcoms in the home placed women in a better position to spar. Further, where men's roles gave them the advantage in terms of social position, rank, and authority, women like Connie, Lucy, and Alice vied equally through the sheer strength of their comedic personalities. The producers, of course, were not closet feminists in permitting this to occur; the circumstances simply made for popular shows. And their ratings were high, we would argue, partly because they hinted at the discontent felt by many women, whether its strength was recognized or not.

If that conclusion is correct, it suggests a common weakness in the ways both the reflective and manipulative hypotheses treat the mass media. At bottom, the extreme forms of each explanation slight one of the constants in historical explanation: change over time. If the mass communications industries simply reflected public taste and never influenced it, they would become nonentities— multimillion-dollar ciphers in any explanation that seeks to account for change. On the other hand, if we assign too manipulative a role to the media, it becomes difficult to explain any change at all. How was it that hundreds of thousands of girls who watched themselves being symbolically annihilated during the 1950s supplied so many converts to the women's movement of the sixties?

In sum, while the mass media are influential forces in modern society, they are perhaps not as monolithic in outlook as they sometimes seem. The comparison to the medieval church is apt as long as we remember that the church, too, was hardly able to impose its will universally. Even where orthodoxy reigned, schismatic movements were always springing up. Today's heretics may be feminists rather than Anabaptists, but they are responding to pressures growing within society. From a feminist point of view, we may not have reached utopia merely because, by 1984, a female television producer could launch the series *Cagney and Lacey*, in which two female career police officers energetically catch murderers as well as live through the traumas of being diagnosed for breast cancer. All the same, there is change. Lucy is not Lacy, any more than Rosie was Gracie. And the same mass culture industry that threatened women with symbolic annihilation also published *The Feminine Mystique*.

ADDITIONAL READING

This chapter draws on material from three different fields—women's history, social history and popular culture, and the history of television. Among broad surveys of the 1950s we suggest John Patrick Diggins, *The Proud Decades* (New York, 1988); Ronald Oakley, *God's Country: America in the 1950s* (New York, 1986); and William O'Neill, *American High* (New York, 1986). James Gilbert, *A Cycle of Outrage* (New York, 1986), has provided a look at juvenile delinquency that also offers insights into family life and popular culture.

For overviews of the image of women in our culture, see Lois Banner, *American Beauty* (New York, 1983); Ann Douglas, *The Feminization of American Culture* (New York, 1977); and Molly Haskell, *From Reverence to Rape* (New York, 1974). Haskell's study of the image of women in movies confirms what we learn from examining other areas of popular culture. A most intriguing strategy for decoding gender signs in the mass media is Erving Goffman, *Gender Advertisements* (New York, 1976).

For readers more concerned with the feminist movement and women's history, Betty Friedan, *The Feminine Mystique* (New York, 1963), is one place to start. Her book retains the vitality that spurred its wide popularity and remains an interesting social history of the 1950s. Kate Millett's *Sexual Politics* (New York, 1970) is another important feminist essay. For an overview of women in twentieth-century America, see Lois Banner, *Women in Modern America* (New York, 1974). In this brief history, Banner resists the argument of two leading male historians writing on women—Carl Degler, *At Odds* (New York, 1980), and William Chafe, *The American Woman* (New York, 1972)—who both stress demographic and economic patterns to explain changing roles for women. Banner gives more credit to the political efforts women have exerted.

The explosion of thinking and writing in women's history makes it impossible to mention more than a few valuable studies. Carroll Smith-Rosenberg has been a leader among women historians; her article "The New Woman and the New History," *Feminist Studies*, 3 (1975-76), 185-98, offers useful perspectives. Similarly, Rosalind Rosenberg, *Beyond Separate Spheres: The Roots of Modern Feminism* (New Haven, Conn., 1982), is worthwhile. In addition to Chafe and Degler on women, work, and politics, we found useful Ruth Schwartz Cowan, *More Work for Mother: The Ironies of Household Technologies from Open Hearth to Microwave* (New York, 1983); Eleanor Flexner, *A Century of Struggle*, rev. ed. (Cambridge, Mass., 1975); Susan Estabrook Kennedy, *If All We Did Was to Weep at Home: A History of White Working-Class Women in America* (Bloomington, Ind., 1981); and Barbara M. Wertheimer, *We Were There: The Story of Working Women in America* (New York, 1977). Carol Warren, *Madwives: Schizophrenic Women in the 1950s* (New York, 1987), treats a dark chapter in women's experience. For anyone curious about the European scene, we recommend John C. Fout, ed., *German Women in the Nineteenth Century* (New York, 1984), because it reveals a variety of methodologies and includes a comprehensive bibliography of women's history.

As we mentioned, historians have not written extensively about television. Clearly, the best place to begin is Eric Barnouw, *Tube of Plenty* (New York, 1975), which is a condensed version of his three-volume history of television and broadcasting. His study *The Sponsor* (New York, 1978) takes a highly critical look at TV advertising. Several collections of essays are quite interesting: John O'Connor, ed., *American History/American Television* (New York, 1983); Horace Newcomb, ed., *Television: The Critical View* (New York, 1976); E. Ann Kaplan, ed., *Regarding Television* (Los Angeles, Calif., 1983); and Alan Wells, ed., *Mass Media and Society* (Palo Alto, Calif., 1972) all contain useful historical and critical materials. Raymond Williams, *Television: Technology and Cultural Form* (New York, 1975), has some of the most interesting insights into the evolution of television and its impact on society. David Marc, *Demographic Vistas: Television in American Culture* (Philadelphia, Pa., 1984) and Robert Sklar, *Prime Time America* (New York, 1980), are two critical essays on television.

When we turned to sociology and the fields of popular culture, we found a rich though uneven literature. Gaye Tuchman, Arlene Kaplan Daniels, and James Benet, eds., *Hearth and Home: Images of Women in the Mass Media* (New York, 1978), is an invaluable source of statistics and ideas. The often sharp debate over popular culture in the 1950s still makes lively reading in the essay collection edited by Bernard Rosenberg and David White, *Mass Culture* (New York, 1957). Herbert Gans, *High Culture and Popular Culture* (New York, 1974), may have gotten in the final and most persuasive word for the functional school of sociological thought. Charles Wright, *Mass Communications* (New York, 1959), provides a sociological approach to the mass media in the 1950s, while Klaus Krippendorff, *Content Analysis* (London, 1980), covers the topic named.

In the second edition of this book, we invited readers to do their own sleuthing into 1950s television programs, using the collections of the Museum of Broadcasting in New York City. Karen McHale, a student from Michigan, did not visit the museum but did write to inform us that the figure at far left in the photograph, page 321, was not Fred Mertz of *I Love Lucy*, as we had claimed, but Charles Boyer. We were skeptical: after all, we knew what Mertz looked like, even if the hat in the photo blocked some of his face. And both CBS and a photo-supply house had identified the man as Frawley. When we wrote McHale, sticking to our guns, she did us one better: she wrote Lucy. Lucille Ball was kind enough to set us straight—it *was* Boyer. As we sheepishly wrote to McHale, some of the fun of doing history is catching the "experts" in errors.

CHAPTER FOURTEEN

Instant Watergate

At 2:30 in the morning on Saturday, June 17, 1972, police arrested five men who had broken into Washington headquarters of the Democratic National Committee, located in the plush Watergate apartment complex. The men were a rather strange set of burglars. They wore business suits and rubber surgical gloves, and carried with them a walkie-talkie, forty rolls of unexposed film, two cameras, lock picks, two pen-size tear gas guns, and several bugging devices. Far from stealing into the complex in the dead of night, the burglars had dined earlier on lobster in a Watergate restaurant. Police discovered that among them, the five men carried $2,300, mostly in the form of hundred-dollar bills with sequential serial numbers.

When Bob Woodward of the *Washington Post* received a phone call from the paper requesting him to cover the story that Saturday morning, he had no knowledge of the case's puzzling aspects. To him, it seemed just another burglary assignment handed a cub reporter. He had joined the staff of the *Washington Post* only nine months earlier. That the editors rated the story as minor was confirmed when they allowed Carl Bernstein onto the case. Bernstein, another young reporter, covered the local ups and downs of Virginia politics.

But as the day wore on, the appearance of the burglary grew curiouser and curiouser. At the preliminary hearing for the five burglars, their spokesman, one James McCord, was asked his occupation. "Security consultant," he answered quietly. Woodward, covering the hearing, moved to the front row to hear better. McCord was saying that he had recently left a job with the government. Where in government, asked the judge. "CIA," whispered McCord.

Sunday night another *Post* reporter relayed Woodward the information that the police had found two address books on one of the suspects. Each listed the name Howard Hunt, with a telephone number listed as "W. H." in one book and "W. House" in the other. The next day Woodward called the White House and discovered that indeed, a man named E. Howard Hunt was a White House consultant. Woodward finally reached Hunt and asked him what his name was doing in the address book of two Watergate burglars. "Good God!" responded Hunt. He issued a quick no-comment and hung up. Official White House response was equally swift. Presidential Press Secretary Ronald Ziegler called the break-in "a third-rate burglary attempt" and warned, "certain elements may try to stretch this beyond what it is."

In the months that followed, Woodward and Bernstein began digging for more information. Both reporters assembled their own master lists of key telephone numbers: several hundred contacts who were each called at least twice a week. All notes, records of phone conversations, and first drafts of articles went into a filing system that soon filled four cabinets.

Increasingly, the information they pieced together linked the Watergate burglary with officials in the Nixon-reelection campaign, known as the Commit-

E. Howard Hunt, one of the convicted Watergate burglars, testifying at the Senate Watergate hearings. Hunt, a former CIA agent, possessed a flair for the dramatic. He had published a series of James Bond-style spy novels, and apparently attempted to live a similar life in his own career. On one secret mission for the White House, he flew to Denver, disguising himself with what one Justice Department official later described as "a cheap, dime-store, reddish colored wig." A similar wig was found in the Watergate hotel the day after the arrest of the burglars. (Wide World Photos.)

tee to Re-elect the President, or more popularly, CREEP. One of the burglars, it turned out, had opened a checking account containing $89,000. The money had come from checks which were traced back to fund-raising efforts by the reelection committee. Apparently CREEP Finance Chairman Maurice Stans had gone on a money-raising tour in the spring of 1972. To preserve contributors' anonymity, he "laundered" the funds through a Mexican bank. Somehow, some of the donations had turned up in the burglar's bank account.

Further investigation indicated that in addition to money spent for legitimate purposes, CREEP had a secret "slush fund" of over $350,000 that could be used for clandestine projects. Even more serious, use of the funds had been cleared by high-level White House officials, including Maurice Stans, the former secretary of the treasury; John Mitchell, former attorney general; and H. R. Haldeman, White House chief of staff. The two reporters also uncovered information indicating that the Watergate burglary was only one incident in a larger undercover effort to discredit the campaigns of various Democratic presidential candidates. That effort was coordinated by Donald Segretti; *Post* articles noted that Segretti's minions had been

> following members of Democratic candidates' families; assembling dossiers of their personal lives; forging letters and distributing them under the candidates' letterheads; leaking false and manufactured items to the press; throwing campaign schedules into disarray; seizing confidential campaign files and investigating the lives of dozens of Democratic campaign workers.

Although Segretti himself behaved much like a college prankster out on a romp, he had been hired directly by Dwight Chapin, President Nixon's personal appointments secretary.

Despite Woodward and Bernstein's exposés, the Watergate scandal had little effect on the Nixon reelection campaign. The president himself announced in August that White House counsel John Dean had conducted an investigation into the burglary and that "no one on the White House staff . . . was involved in this very bizarre situation. What really hurts in matters of this sort is not the fact that they occur," the president continued, "What really hurts is if you try to cover it up." In the closing days of the campaign, White House officials accused the *Post* of being little more than an appendage of the McGovern organization. "This is a political effort by the *Washington Post*," complained Ziegler, "well conceived and coordinated, to discredit this administration and individuals in it."

On election day Richard Nixon received nearly 61 percent of the popular vote, one of the largest majorities in American presidential elections. At the same time Woodward and Bernstein were finding it increasingly difficult to come up with new leads in their investigation. Ben Bradlee, the *Post*'s flamboyant editor, recalled in frustration that he had been "ready to hold both Woodward's and Bernstein's heads in a pail of water until they came up with another story."

The decisive break in the case came not from any investigative reporting, but from pressures arising out of the burglars' trial held in January 1973. Despite an extensive investigation, officials chose to prosecute only the five burglars, plus Howard Hunt and G. Gordon Liddy, a former FBI agent and finance counsel for CREEP, who had helped Hunt. The trial was concluded within a month, and the jury took less than an hour and a half to find all seven defendants guilty.

But the presiding judge, John Sirica, remained unsatisfied. None of the seven men had explained adequately why they had acted as they did and where they got their money. "These hundred dollar bills," Sirica complained of the bank account funds, "were floating around like coupons." He criticized the prosecution's handling of the case and concluded, "I have not been satisfied, and I am still not satisfied that all the pertinent facts that might be available—I say *might* be available—have been produced before an American jury." He set bond for McCord and Liddy at $100,000 each and threatened to impose particularly stiff sentences on them.

In March, McCord apparently decided not to chance the harsh sentence. He wrote Judge Sirica a letter maintaining that the burglars had been under political pressure to plead guilty, and so avoid any protracted questioning during the trial. Some witnesses had perjured themselves, he claimed; the names of others involved in the conspiracy had been kept out of the trial.

During March and April the prosecutors investigated McCord's claims. As the threat of exposure increased, some campaign officials scrambled for lawyers; others approached the prosecutors with their own revised stories. By April new disclosures had forced President Nixon to accept reluctantly the resignations of his two closest aides, H. R. Haldeman and John Ehrlichman, as well as Richard Kleindienst, the attorney general. The president also fired his White House counsel, John Dean, who had agreed to cooperate fully with the prosecutors.

Watergate stories were breaking daily throughout the spring of 1973; as spring turned to summer Americans got a firsthand look at the controversy when a special Senate committee, chaired by Senator Sam Ervin of North Carolina, convened to hear testimony about Watergate. During televised hearings, viewers saw a parade of witnesses testify that Attorney General John Mitchell, the highest law enforcement officer in the land, had been present at meetings where Gordon Liddy outlined his proposals for the Watergate burglary and other espionage attempts. Others testified that McCord, Liddy, and their associates had worked directly for John Ehrlichman as part of a security group called "the Plumbers," which investigated leaks to the press. The Plumbers, it was revealed, had burglarized the office of a psychiatrist to obtain damaging information about Daniel Ellsberg, a former government official being prosecuted for leaking a secret Pentagon study about the conduct of the Vietnam War.

The most astonishing witness to appear before the Ervin committee was John Dean. In a quiet, monotonous voice Dean testified that the president himself had maintained the cover-up as recently as April 1973. When McCord had threatened to tell prosecutors what he knew, Dean met with the president and his aides on March 21 and approved "hush money" of up to a million dollars to buy the Watergate burglars' silence. Of all the witnesses, only Dean claimed that Richard Nixon had participated in the cover-up. It was his word against the president's. Then came the most stunning revelation of all. Alexander Butterfield, an aide to H. R. Haldeman, informed committee members that for years a secret White House taping system had routinely recorded all presidential conversations. If the committee could listen to those tapes, it would no longer have to weigh one witness's word against another's. The tapes could tell all.

But obtaining that evidence did not prove easy. Archibald Cox, who in May had been appointed as special prosecutor to investigate the new Watergate disclosures, subpoenaed relevant tapes. When the courts backed Cox in his request, the president fired him on Saturday, October 20. Reaction was swift and vehement. Attorney General Elliot Richardson and his immediate subordinate resigned in protest. Reporters dubbed the firing and resignations the "Saturday Night Massacre." In Congress, twenty-two separate bills were introduced calling for possible impeachment of the president, and Representative Peter Rodino, chairman of the House Judiciary Committee, began deliberations on the matter.

Under immense pressure, President Nixon named a new special prosecutor, Leon Jaworski of Texas, and released the subpoenaed tapes to Judge Sirica. Then came yet another jolt. White House counsel J. Fred Buzhardt told the court that some sections of the requested tapes were missing. One tape contained a crucial eighteen-and-a-half-minute "gap." Experts testified that the missing materials had been deliberately erased. Alexander Haig, the president's new chief of staff, could only suggest lamely to Sirica that "some sinister force" was at work. By

Former White House counsel John Dean *consults a portion of his testimony, as Senator Sam Ervin (left) speaks with Dean's lawyers. Dean's low-key manner, meticulous testimony, and remarkable memory impressed many listeners, but until the existence of the tapes became known, it was Dean's word against the president's. (Wide World Photos.)*

April 1974, Special Prosecutor Jaworski and the House Judiciary Committee had requested additional tapes. At first the president refused; then he grudgingly agreed to supply edited transcripts. White House secretaries typed up over 1,200 pages, which the president with a show of virtue made public.

The transcripts were damaging. They revealed a president who was often vindictive, vulgar, and small-minded. The pivotal meeting with John Dean, on March 21, 1973, showed him discussing in detail how his aides might, as he put it, "take care of the jackasses who are in jail." "How much money do you need?" Nixon asked Dean. "I would say these people are going to cost a million dollars," Dean estimated. "We could get that," replied the president. " . . . You could get a million dollars. And you could get it in cash. I know where it could be gotten. I mean it's not easy, but it could be done."

In the following months events moved swiftly. Neither the Judiciary Committee nor Jaworski was satisfied with edited transcripts, and Jaworski appealed directly to the Supreme Court. In July, the court voted unanimously to order the president to produce the tapes. The same month, the Judiciary Committee passed three articles of impeachment, accusing the president of obstructing justice, misusing his presidential powers, and refusing to comply with the committee's requests for evidence. In August, the president's lawyers, J. Fred Buzhardt and James St. Clair, insisted that the president release transcripts of conversations recorded on June 23, 1972, only a few days after the Watergate burglary. The tapes demonstrated beyond all doubt that from the beginning the president had known of the burglars' connection to the White House and had acted to limit the FBI investigation. Even the president's staunchest supporters in Congress refused to defend him.

Bowing to the inevitable, Richard Nixon appeared on national television and announced his resignation, effective the following day at noon. On August 9 the new president, Gerald Ford, took the oath of office. "The Constitution works," he announced. "Our long national nightmare is over."

Two Journalists in Search of a History

At every turn in its two years of unwinding, the Watergate drama grew beyond the expectations of those who pursued its story. What had begun as a routine burglary assigned to a couple of young reporters had ended with the first resignation of a president of the United States. Woodward and Bernstein had fought to stay on top of events as they grew. When the *Post*'s national desk sought to take over the story, the two reporters successfully defended their claim to cover the case. For months it was their investigations and their byline that advanced public knowledge of the scandal. Yet even they were overtaken by the flood of events. In the months after McCord's letter to Sirica, when every day brought a new participant willing to tell his or her own version of events, Woodward and Bernstein's articles were joined by a host of others from major newspapers and newsweeklies.

Still, the two reporters recognized that from the beginning they had been as close as any reporters to the unfolding drama. Why not write a book about Watergate? Even in October 1972, before the election, Woodward and Bernstein pursued the idea with representatives of Simon and Schuster. The result of these conferences was *All the President's Men*, published in mid-1974 at the height of the Watergate crisis. It became an immediate bestseller.

All the President's Men was popular not merely because of its timing but also because it was an exciting, well-written detective story. The book's main characters were not really the president's men so much as the *Washington Post's*— Woodward and Bernstein themselves. The narrative outlined, day by day, the extensive, exhausting, and sometimes suspenseful maneuvers undertaken by the two reporters to get their story. It recounted late-night visits to CREEP accountants, clandestine attempts (of dubious legality) to obtain information from grand jurors hearing the Watergate case, and Woodward's periodic cloak-and-dagger visits to a source high in the Nixon administration, identified in the book only by the nickname "Deep Throat." On most occasions, Deep Throat agreed to meet only at two in the morning in a parking garage, and only after Woodward had taken two separate cabs in order to elude any possible tails. This emphasis on the reporters' own story made good sense. The detective work was worth describing, and in any case, Woodward and Bernstein remained very much outsiders: investigators trying to penetrate the secrets of the Palace Guard.

The two reporters probably recognized that this approach left the end of their book dangling. If the story was going to be about their detective work, then the unique part of the tale ended, for the most part, once the host of other journalists had joined them in the hue and cry. Thus 95 percent of *All the President's Men* describes events previous to April 1973; the book ends with the Watergate crisis itself unresolved. While it was only natural, then, that the two reporters would consider writing a second book, such a sequel would necessarily have to focus not on the reporters, but on the main participants in Watergate itself. It would be history, not autobiography.

Within a week of the Nixon resignation, Woodward and Bernstein began work on an account of the president's last days in office. Starting with their already impressive number of contacts, they interviewed anyone who had a part in the drama—from secretaries of state to secretaries of offices and presidential barbers. Within six months, they and two other research assistants had talked with 394 people. They collected unpublished notes, memos, diaries, transcripts, logs, and correspondence. In the spring of 1976 the fruits of this labor appeared in a voluminous account titled *The Final Days*.

Once again, the two reporters had a hit on their hands. Eager readers scrambled for the serialized excerpts in *Newsweek* magazine to discover the lurid, yet-untold highlights of the drama. And lurid highlights there were. The book's portrait of Richard Nixon revealed a leader obsessed with Watergate, largely incapable of concentrating on other matters, and at times driven to heavy drinking. At one point, the book told of the president's son-in-law, Edward Cox, sighting the president in the White House hallways late at night, talking to the pictures on the wall. The most dramatic moment of the book came when the president, having made his decision to resign, summoned Secretary of State Henry Kissinger to the Lincoln Room of the White House. As the two men talked, Nixon broke down and sobbed, "Henry, you are not a very orthodox Jew, and I am not an orthodox Quaker, but we need to pray." With both men on their knees, the president prayed for peace, rest, and love. And then, still sobbing, Nixon leaned over and struck his fist on the carpet, crying, "What have I done? What has happened?"

Given such riveting material, *The Final Days* sold well; yet praise from the press was much less overwhelming than it had been for *All the President's Men*. Most critics took exception to both the book's narrative style and its research techniques. In *All the President's Men*, where Woodward and Bernstein had written autobiographically, they dealt primarily with firsthand experiences. In crossing the line from autobiography to history, they had to reconstruct the activities of the president and his inner circle from a variety of documents and interviews. And this presented a problem. Most scholars undertaking such a project would have provided readers with footnotes, indicating which sources contributed to which sections of the narrative. But Woodward and Bernstein conducted all of their interviews "on background," with the understanding that the information would be used only if the source's identity remained confidential. Thus the book was written without footnotes.

"Hell, I trust Woodward and Bernstein," wrote Richard Reeves in his *New York Times* review (headlined "Lots of Footwork, No Footnotes"). "But how do you evaluate material this important without a guide to the sources?" Historian Max Lerner made the same point in an article entitled "Writing 'Hot History.'" "The self-interest of many of [the book's] sources—their public face, their desire to rid themselves of the Watergate taint and get a better role in the drama of history—seem to me an insurmountable obstacle, unless the reader knows who the sources are and can make his own assessment of them." In the *New Republic*, John Osborne angrily observed that Woodward and Bernstein "never once attribute a statement to the source or sources of the statement." Osborne called *The Final Days* "on the whole the worst job of nationally noted reporting that I've observed during 49 years in the business."[1]

---

[1] Osborne and Lerner were more adept at mustering righteous indignation than being consistent. Osborne admitted that his own writings were full of unattributed statements—"by preference" even—but weakly argued that Woodward and Bernstein's "piling statement upon unattributed statement for 450 pages" gave "a good method a bad name." The rest of the review was replete with rebuttals that began, "I was told recently on excellent authority. . . ." Lerner, for his part, attacked Woodward and Bernstein for claiming that Chief Justice Warren Burger's Supreme Court opinion on the Nixon tapes was so inadequate that Justice Potter Stewart undertook to co-author it. "As it happens," Lerner announced in his most authoritative deadpan, "I tried out this assertion on the Chief Justice, who was astounded by it. He told me that the process of shaping a unanimous opinion was a long one, but that he had been in charge all along and had no 'co-authors.'" Despite Lerner's own admonition that Watergate participants might distort their recollections in order to "get a better role in the drama of history," he apparently felt that if his friend the Chief Justice said it ain't so, that settled the case.

The widespread reaction of journalists against the missing footnotes may be partly explained by another feature of *The Final Days*; its "omniscient" narrative perspective. The book's characters are never made to say anything "according to reliable sources," or "based on a participant's notes made shortly after the meeting." Words are instead placed in their mouths as if the two inquiring reporters from the *Post* were invisibly present at all the crucial meetings. Such a style may pretend to omniscience, the critics argued, but Woodward, Bernstein, and Ben Bradlee were hardly Father, Son, and Holy Ghost.

At first glance, it would appear that professional historians might share the critics' disdain for *The Final Days*. As we have already seen, one of the prime requirements of historical research is the necessity of evaluating the perspectives of all primary sources. It is scant consolation to know that Woodward and Bernstein have pledged to deposit their notes and interviews in a library, to be made public at some distant future date. Their book is available to historians now; and the need to evaluate it exists now.

Yet historians are likely to judge the two reporters less severely than their colleagues in journalism, if only because historians are all too eager to obtain data from any quarter. Readers will recall that early on in our explorations we examined another piece of "hot history"—Captain John Smith's *Generall Historie of Virginia*. No doubt Smith's account would have been lambasted by today's reporters for the same reasons they chastised Woodward and Bernstein's. The captain includes no footnotes. He writes from an "omniscient" perspective, even referring to himself in the third person. Furthermore, he often blithely borrows passages from other published works, silently incorporating them in his own narrative as if he had written them himself. Smith gets terrible marks on all these counts, yet historians of early Virginia depend on his account continually.

And they do so without surrendering their ability to judge the material critically. Smith may not have left behind footnotes, but historians have their own ways of evaluating his prose. Henry Adams, we saw, questioned Smith's Pocohontas story by comparing the *Generall Historie* with earlier published versions of it. In our own investigation, we were able to judge Smith's stories of Indian life critically by making ourselves aware of the narrative's characteristic perspectives.

By the same token, historians reading *The Final Days* are not left quite as helpless by the lack of footnotes as journalists apparently believe. For the fact is, Woodward and Bernstein tell readers a good deal more about the identity of their sources than first appears. Their "omniscient" prose, like Smith's, is readily susceptible to analysis. It is worth examining how such an analysis might proceed.

Behind the Omniscient Narrative

Even the casual reader of *The Final Days* can guess the approximate source of information in many of the book's passages. When we read that Special Prosecutor Leon Jaworski considered compromising with the White House on access to the tapes, we cannot guarantee that Jaworski himself was the source, but the text says he "called a meeting of his most trusted assistants" to discuss the problem, and the book then goes on to recount the debate. Obviously, one or more of the assistants are prime candidates. All the major figures in the Watergate drama commanded their own entourage of aides, associates, and secretaries whom Woodward and Bernstein went to work on. It is the time-honored tactic, after all: start with the minnows and work slowly up to the big fish. Jaworski used it himself when he was investigating the cover-up.

But knowing the approximate source of information is not good enough. The more a story is passed ear to ear, the more likely it is distorted. Furthermore, different perspectives yield different accounts. James St. Clair is unlikely to narrate the challenges of his appearances before the House Judiciary Committee quite in the same manner as his disgruntled research assistant. So it is important to determine, wherever possible, which of the major characters are willing firsthand sources, and which appear only through the filtered accounts of either their subordinates or other major protagonists. The task is by no means easy.

But is the prose of *The Final Days* all that omniscient? Consider the realm of fiction. Novelists, who possess absolute control over their creations, have the license to be as omniscient as they please. Their writing does not require either the historian's footnote or the journalist's attributive clause. Yet they do not always exercise their prerogative. Charles Dickens, for instance, opens his novel, *Bleak House*, with a chapter that omnisciently enters the minds of all the

James St. Clair, *special counsel to the president for Watergate, surrounded by his entourage. Although there are smiles on all the faces, the narrative perspectives in* The Final Days *suggest that while St. Clair refused to talk with Woodward and Bernstein, several of his hardworked, disgruntled staff unburdened themselves to the two reporters.*

characters and explains their thoughts. But then in Chapter II Dickens decides to write with only partial omniscience. "We still use his eyes," E. M. Forster has noted, "but for some reason they begin to grow weak: he can explain Sir Leicester Dedlock to us, part of Lady Dedlock but not all, and nothing of Mr. Tulkinghorn. In Chapter III he is even more reprehensible: he goes straight across into the dramatic method and inhabits a young lady, Esther Summerson. . . . Logically, *Bleak House* is all to pieces, but Dickens bounces us, so that we do not mind the shiftings of the view-point."

Woodward and Bernstein are equally good bouncers, but for different reasons. Dickens keeps quiet about Lady Dedlock's inner thoughts because the plot demands it; Woodward and Bernstein keep quiet because they simply don't have certain information. But they are such good storytellers that, like Dickens, they keep us from noticing their elegant sleights of hand.

Take, for example, Edward Cox's well-publicized phone call to Senator Robert Griffin of Michigan, during which Cox anxiously reported that President Nixon had been walking the halls talking to pictures. Here is the way *The Final Days* introduces the episode:

> Griffin was worried. His call for resignation, a difficult thing for him to do, had fizzled. In his office that afternoon, he was notified that Ed Cox was on the phone. . . . He picked up the phone and found a very disturbed young man on the other end of the line.

It all seems perfectly omniscient. But the passage does take a point of view. Woodward and Bernstein might just as easily have written it this way:

> Ed Cox was worried. Later the previous evening while walking the corridors of the White House, he had witnessed something that disturbed him intensely. Now he picked up the phone and asked the operator to get him Senator Robert Griffin.

A novelist's option, certainly, and also the most direct approach. But it was not the phrasing Woodward and Bernstein chose, we may reasonably conclude, because their information came from either Griffin or an aide in his office. The reporters naturally retold the story from the same perspective that it came to them.

One example surely will not demonstrate that Cox refused to talk to Woodward and Bernstein. But when a similar pattern emerges (indeed, all of Cox's worries about the president's mental state are described from the far end of the telephone), then we begin to be on the lookout. We notice, for instance, that when relating Nixon family conversations, *The Final Days* appears much more omniscient about the thoughts of David Eisenhower than those of Ed Cox. We constantly learn what David felt directly (he *realized* he was doing a lot of repeating, he *sensed* the president was going to resign); whereas with Ed, we are often told only how an observer thought he felt: "Ed *appeared* irritated;" "He weighed both sides carefully, *as if* he were going to make a presentation." (Not, "*because he intended* to make a presentation. . . .") And the facade slips a little when the book refers to Ed Cox primarily as "Cox," but to David Eisenhower as "David."

It is often easier to discover who did not talk than it is to establish conclusively who did. Just because the text says, "David *thought*," it does not follow that Eisenhower was necessarily a firsthand source. "At no point in the book do we describe someone's thought processes," argued Bernstein in an interview. He cited Buzhardt as an example. "There's a sentence [in there] that says that Buzhardt thought that the President was the most transparent liar he had ever seen. That's not describing the thought process. That's not attributing thoughts to someone's head which were unexpressed. That's a statement Buzhardt said to a good number of people." In the case of David Eisenhower, *The Final Days* reports that he constantly confided in his close friend, Brooks Harrington. And of course Eisenhower also talked with other friends of the family like Pat Buchanan. So we must concede that the Eisenhower material may be second-hand, at least until we find other ways to pin down its origins.[2]

To identify sources more precisely, then, we must isolate material in the text that could have come from one person and one person only. Henry Kissinger's final meeting with the president in the Lincoln Room has attracted so much notice, in part, precisely because it fits this category. Nixon didn't talk, so Kissinger must have—to someone. Yet (as everyone has also pointed out) he *did* talk—to two of his aides, Brent Scowcroft and Lawrence Eagleburger, right after the meeting. The book comes right out and says so. And Scowcroft and Eagleburger would have to have possessed the resolution of saints to keep from retelling the story to a few trusted friends. With an event of such magnitude, it is only natural to expect word to spread.

So natural, in fact, that the curious footnote-hunters in the popular press ought to have kicked themselves for not making the final logical inference. If the big, dramatic stories are the ones passed from ear to ear, then the way to isolate the sources of *The Final Days* is to go back and look for the events so undramatic, so minuscule that *nobody* would bother to tell anyone else about them.

In a book jammed with dramatic events, the minuscule is hard to come by. But it is there, even as the curtain rings up on White House lawyers Fred Buzhardt and Leonard Garment winging their way south on Eastern Flight 177 to recommend that the president resign:

> For most of the travellers, the flight was an occasion for relaxation, the beginning of a vacation. But Buzhardt and Garment were grim and tense as they rehearsed their presentation. . . .
>
> Buzhardt nervously tapped his hand on the armrest. His West Point class ring struck the metal. The "1946" was nearly worn from the setting. A slightly hunched figure with thick glasses and a slow, deliberate manner, Buzhardt came out of the political stable of Senator Strom Thurmond. . . .

It is all done so well, so quickly, that we hardly stop to think that only two people saw that ring tapping the metal armrest. And chances are, even Buzhardt was

---

[2] Eisenhower has admitted that he contributed material, but we are concerned here not simply with who talked, but with the evidence that can be deduced from the text of *The Final Days* alone.

J. Fred Buzhardt, *special White House counsel for Watergate, wearing the tell-tale West Point class ring. Internal evidence indicates that Buzhardt was Woodward and Bernstein's most extensive source. (Wide World Photos.)*

unaware of his mannerism. But in either case, it is not the sort of fact that anyone would bother to pass along to an aide (or for that matter, the sort of fact aides would be likely to remember if they ever had been told). No, the tapping ring provides a good indication that either Buzhardt or Garment (and most probably Garment) spoke with Woodward and Bernstein.

Other such revealing details are sprinkled through the book. Attorney General Elliot Richardson might well confide to his aides that he had written a letter of resignation over the Archibald Cox affair, but would he mention that as he wrote, he could barely hear "the rush of the Potomac River" in the distance? Buzhardt would tell his friends that he guessed the president would resign by Friday, August 2, but would he bother to tell them that he also made that guess to his wife? And who but presidential speechwriter Pat Buchanan would know that Alexander Haig's office called just as Buchanan had "laced up his new blue-and-white track shoes"? Who would know that, as he went jogging that day, "he slowed down only at the guard post on West Executive Avenue between the White House and the EOB"? The probabilities are high that in each case, Richardson, Buzhardt, and Buchanan told those parts of the story directly to

Woodward and Bernstein; doubly high if other supporting evidence can be found.

➤ Critical readers might object that these conclusions depend too heavily on the assumption that Woodward and Bernstein are not indulging in what they might regard as innocent embellishment: making up details like the ring-tapping to dramatize the story. Certainly some reporters are not above fabrication. Journalist Richard Reeves admits to inventing secret sources to protect his information and regards it as so well-established a practice that he even doubts the existence of Deep Throat. But there are reporters and there are reporters; and each journalist deserves to be judged on his or her own merits. Maybe Woodward and Bernstein did take a little license with the ring-tapping or the jogging, but if so, why not embellish more consistently? Some narrative passages are so spare (as we shall shortly see) that they nearly beg for some imaginative, lively detail. That is simply not Woodward and Bernstein's style. When they lack information, they pass by in unnoticed silence. When they do have information, they print it—even when its actual value is marginal, as in a largely irrelevant presidential conversation with Milton Pitts, Nixon's barber.

In any case, the small telltale details are not so much proofs in themselves as indicators of larger confirming patterns embedded in the book's narrative perspectives.

Such patterns can be found, to take one example, in the syntax of the many conversations recorded in *The Final Days*. The human memory is both fallible and selective. It does not, like the tape recorder, indiscriminately record every syllable of a conversation. If Alexander Haig spends two hours alone with the president, and then comes out and gives a blow-by-blow account to his friend Buzhardt, Haig's account will be at best only a partial retelling. He may quote a few phrases verbatim, mention the president's more dramatic gestures, and paraphrase the remaining points. If Haig keeps a diary, he may be able to record the conversation with a fair amount of detail, but nothing approaching a verbatim report. Buzhardt too may keep a diary, but his record of Haig's meeting will suffer from the disadvantage of having to select highlights from highlights, rather than from the complete two-hour conversation. Thus Buzhardt's entry will be less detailed and much briefer.

Now, as can be seen, any presidential conversation may produce several types of records. And each type will tend to leave behind characteristic trademarks in Woodward and Bernstein's apparently omniscient prose.

If a tape transcript of the actual meeting is available, Woodward and Bernstein can quote extended passages of conversation. More important, they will quote it in the style of the mechanical recorder, which remembers each phrase exactly, complete with missteps, stutters, stops, and backtrackings. When we come to the conversation between Nixon and Ziegler on June 4, 1973, we hardly need a footnote to realize the account is based on a transcript:

> "That's the tragedy of the whole thing [says the President]. Mitchell would never step up to this. Well, I suppose, would you? No, no. Former Attorney General step up and say you bugged? Shit, I wouldn't. What I would step up and say—'Look, I haven't

approved a goddam thing and so forth, but I take responsibility for it—bah, bah, bah, bah, you know—and I'm going to take, uh, take, you know, a suspended sentence or misdemeanor slapped in the face or whatever the hell it's going to be.' But once denied—under oath—he was stuck. See? God damn."

This speech is set in the middle of a four-page, back-and-forth dialogue between Ziegler and Nixon—a dialogue no one could possibly remember in its entirety, not to mention all the *uhs, you knows,* and *bah, bah, bahs* of this particular passage.

Perhaps the most interesting example of "transcript syntax" occurs near the end of the drama, when Nixon is about to go before the cameras and announce his resignation. For two full pages, *The Final Days* presents a back-and-forth conversation between a nervous, distraught president and a nervous, uneasy television crew. All the little transcript stumbles are there, such as Nixon correcting himself when he mispronounces photographer Ollie Atkins's name. When the president laughs nervously or clears his throat, we are told; so also when his voice quavers. And when the lights shine in his eyes, we even learn he squinted. Yet the White House taping system was no longer in operation. What was the source of the transcript? The historian is inevitably led to conclude that the television crew was already videotaping as they tested lighting and microphone levels. Somehow the tape was never erased, and Woodward and Bernstein managed to view a copy of it.[3]

Transcripts are not often available, of course. Thus when Buzhardt first informs the president of his discovery of the famous eighteen-minute gap (Haig present also), the account is less detailed than a transcript but long enough to suggest that it is based on recollections and records of someone who was actually there. Questions and answers are related in a back-and-forth manner, but not, for the most part, enclosed in quotation marks.

> The President appeared concerned but calm as Buzhardt described the sounds of the two tones [during the gap].
> What did he think might have happened? the President asked.
> Buzhardt said he had no answers.
> What had been on the tape?
> Buzhardt didn't know that either.
> Nixon said he could not recall what had occurred in the conversation. He had tried, but. . . .

The construction of the account implies that one of the participants recorded its substance shortly after, but (naturally enough) did not include any verbatim statements. Sometimes *The Final Days* makes the presence of such notes even more explicit: "Buzhardt jotted furiously on his own legal pad as Nixon read from his notes" of the March 21st conversation. "Richardson gathered his

---

[3] Through an element of serendipity, we learned while writing this that such a videotape does indeed exist, although we have not viewed it.

assistants at the Justice Department" to try to resolve the conflict between Nixon and Archibald Cox: "An initial draft was made: 'A Proposal—ELR #1.'"

In contrast to the longer descriptions, notice this account of lawyer James St. Clair's meeting with the president, just after St. Clair appeared before the Justices of the Supreme Court:

> St. Clair had met with Nixon for forty minutes that afternoon. It had gone well, he told the President, very well. They had a good chance. He firmly believed it.

A forty-minute meeting, immediately after an appearance of momentous consequence for both Nixon and St. Clair, and the narrative lasts only four sentences. A log of some sort has likely indicated the duration of the meeting, but the only substance reported is the kind of cautious digest St. Clair might have given to another of the principals after the conference. If St. Clair spoke with Woodward and Bernstein, he surely refused them any information about this meeting.

Taken singly, none of these inferences conclusively indicates who contributed material to *The Final Days*. But when the entire context of the book is subjected to a similarly close contextual reading, patterns emerge that permit the historian to conjecture with fair probability the identities of *The Final Days'* principal sources. Since neither historian nor journalist has yet, to our knowledge, undertaken such an effort, it may be useful to present our major findings.

Henry Kissinger contributed virtually nothing. When *The Final Days* first appeared, the press devoted a great deal of attention to the Kissinger material, primarily because the book's revelations about him were almost as shocking as the revelations about Nixon. But the secretary plays a remarkably small role in the entire drama. He doesn't appear center stage until Chapters 14, 16, and 17, and then disappears again for all practical purposes until his final dramatic return. Furthermore, Chapters 14, 16, and 17 contain none of the extended conversations present in other parts of *The Final Days*; only a series of facts, opinions, and quotations that could easily have been strung together from immediate aides to Kissinger like Eagleburger and Scowcroft, and from minor assistants and secretaries.

For the fact of the matter is, the secretary of state left behind a wide trail of evidence generated by his system for monitoring and recording phone conversations. The system was elaborate enough to require a small army of transcribers to keep it going, and for sheer complexity, put to shame Richard Nixon's jerry-rigged Oval Office recorders. "On some calls," note Woodward and Bernstein, "the unsuspecting party might be talking simultaneously to Kissinger, Haig, a transcribing secretary, and the appointments secretary." And in Kissinger's basement office at the White House, eight other phones could monitor the direct line with Nixon. When the transcribing volume got too large for the regular secretaries, a night crew was put on the job. Thus, although Kissinger took great pains to conceal his true feelings from his commander-in-chief, there were plenty of secretaries and aides within transcribing distance, enough of them sufficiently disgruntled to remember and report any off-the-cuff retorts, as when the secretary reportedly referred to his superior as "our meatball President."

The video camera *(right) is the source of "transcript syntax" in the*
following excerpt from The Final Days, *which describes President Nixon*
before his resignation speech. Note the characteristic transcript patterns,
as well as the additional visual cues:

> *The President pointed to the backup camera. "That's an NBC*
> *camera, I presume?"*
> *"No, they're both CBS cameras."*
> *"Standard joke," the President said and laughed nervously. He*
> *cleared his throat loudly.*
> *"Let me see, did you get these lights properly?" They were shining*
> *in his eyes. He squinted. "My eyes always have . . . you'll find they get*
> *past sixty . . ." his voice trailed off.*

In addition, Kissinger seems to have enjoyed talking to his immediate
subordinates about the manipulation of power and about his own power politics
in particular. Much material in the Kissinger chapters is explicitly attributed to
assistants. The secretary could control Nixon on his Cambodia policy, he
"boasted to his aides." The president couldn't be pushed too far, he "warned his
associates." Deviousness was a part of the job, he "counseled his aides." Indeed,
when it comes right down to it, virtually all the material in these sections is
either explicitly or implicitly critical of Kissinger. No secretary of state with an
I.Q. above 75 would willingly volunteer any of it, especially while still in office.

David Eisenhower and Pat Buchanan are key sources for Nixon family material. Eisenhower admitted to having two interview sessions with Woodward and Bernstein. But even had he denied it, the book makes his contribution clear. His point of view dominates many of the family narratives, as we have seen. Some of his opinions and feelings could have been reported secondhand by Harrington and other friends (to his credit, Eisenhower appears to be one of the few family members at once loyal and yet willing to voice differing opinions). Still, many of the family conversations are detailed enough to suggest a firsthand source. On Friday, August 2, the president is seen with his feet up on an ottoman; David sits with his back to the fireplace and is thus able to see "the flames reflected in Nixon's glazed eyes."

Speechwriter Pat Buchanan, with his sharp journalist's eye, flavors his accounts with the small details that a firsthand source is privy to: the exact route he jogs, the sneakers he wears, his wife's white lie that he is already asleep when Julie Eisenhower tries to reach him. More to the point, the narrative often assumes the Buchanan point of view during family debates, especially the sequence on Saturday morning, August 3. We meet Buchanan, 9:30 at the office, and follow him along to the White House where we get a detailed reconstruction of the family meeting (aided also by Eisenhower's recollections). Buchanan's perspective is ever-present; "Buchanan sipped his coffee. . . . Buchanan understood. . . . Buchanan shifted uneasily. . . . Buchanan was swallowing hard. . . . Buchanan paused, searching for the right words."

When the discussion is over and Buchanan leaves, do we stay to hear the family's reaction? No, the narrator obediently trails Buchanan down the hall and observes a chat with Rosemary Woods. Then Rebozo comes along and he and Buchanan decide to see Haig. Haig is busy. They try the president. No response there, either, so Rebozo goes his own way. Do we go with Rebozo? No, back to the office with Buchanan, then come along to lunch in the senior staff mess. Finally, off to Buzhardt's office for a conference. Is it only coincidence that we shadow Buchanan from scene to scene the whole morning?

St. Clair kept his counsel. The extended conversations in which he participates either are a matter of public record (his Supreme Court and Judiciary Committee presentations) or are seen from an aide's point of view ("Presenting the transcript at this late date would be a public relations disaster, Speakes felt, but St. Clair was a $300,000-a-year lawyer and he must know what he was doing.") In the case of St. Clair's relations with the president, detailed conversations are reported only when Woodward and Bernstein sources are also present. Other times, as after the Supreme Court decision, we get either silence or a curt summary: "St. Clair met with Nixon and Haig for nearly two hours and spent the rest of the day preparing." St. Clair's silence may have been principled or it may have been pragmatic, but whichever, it surely resulted in his being on the receiving end of the book's biggest hatchet job.

Alexander Haig did not talk. This is perhaps the most surprising conclusion of them all; not because Haig would be expected to talk, but simply because he is the focus of so much of *The Final Days.* Even in *Newsweek,* where *The Final Days* first appeared, the book reviewer assumed that the general had contributed. Yet however much we see of Haig, we miss even more. If he talked, why is there silence at so many key points? During the Richardson negotiations over the fate of Archibald Cox, Haig goes to Nixon's office to persuade the president to keep Cox. We wait back with everyone else in Haig's office. He returns: the scene with Nixon has been "bloody, bloody," he says. But once again, we get no details. The same pattern appears throughout the book. (Page 62: "Haig said he would present the idea to the President. Within an hour he was back on the phone with good news for Richardson." Page 264: "The general had gone to the residence 45 minutes earlier to brief the President and had just come back, his mouth set in a tight line.")

Small wonder, then, that when the first excerpts appeared in *Newsweek*, Haig sent a telegram to Nixon denying any participation and noting that he was "genuinely shocked by the excerpts." In their quest for material, Woodward and Bernstein had pursued him all the way to the Netherlands, where he had been stationed, and still the loyal general remained silent. Suddenly he was confronted with an account so detailed, it approached a minute-by-minute narrative of his actions—indeed, sometimes even presented his thoughts in the same omniscient way it did David Eisenhower's. Haig may be forgiven for wondering ruefully whether the *Post* reporters had somehow stumbled onto his obliging double.

In fact, they had stumbled onto his double, or the nearest thing to it. The man who very likely contributed more to *The Final Days* than any other major participant was the man also closest to Alexander Haig: White House lawyer Fred Buzhardt.

The loquacious J. Fred Buzhardt was a key source. Buzhardt admitted that he talked to Woodward and Bernstein but did not let on just how much. Internal evidence indicates that he was a key contributor. The small, personal details are there, the extended paraphrases of presidential conversations, the blow-by-blow accounts of Buzhardt's first hearing of the tapes.

And the larger narrative pattern is equally revealing. The detailed accounts of White House strategy sessions among Nixon, Haig, and White House lawyers decrease significantly after Buzhardt suffers a heart attack in mid-June 1974. They do not resume until he is back on the job later in the summer. Where in earlier sections, much light is shed on the president's wavering resolution to surrender the tapes, we hear little about the July decision to provide the Judiciary Committee with an additional snippet of exonerating evidence. Did the president object to release as much as he did with the earlier transcripts? Who discovered the exonerating evidence? How much did Nixon want to edit the transcript? These kinds of questions, which the book readily answers when Buzhardt is on the scene, are now silently passed over. The absence goes unnoticed because the Kissinger chapters are conveniently introduced at the point of Buzhardt's illness, and personal glimpses of the president are inserted based on the Eisenhower-Harrington material.

Because Buzhardt is such a helpful source, Woodward and Bernstein can fill in many details about Haig's attitudes, even though Haig himself remained silent. Both aides were West Point graduates. Both decided early on that they were treading on slippery ground and thus "sought each other's counsel." "They could protect themselves," Haig is said to suggest, "if they trusted each other totally. But no one else." So the two men "began meeting regularly in the general's office to debate the ethics of the situation and calculate their next moves." This close relationship enables Woodward and Bernstein on several occasions to re-create private conversations between the president and Haig, since Buzhardt got a replay of the action immediately afterward. (E.g., Thursday, August 1: "When Haig got back to his office, Buzhardt was there waiting for him.")

Fred Buzhardt's vantage point, in other words, functions as one of the major narrative perspectives within *The Final Days*—perhaps the most prominent perspective of all, at least for the political and legal portions of the book. Woodward and Bernstein indicate that while "dozens of persons volunteered information freely," one person "was interviewed seventeen times." Buzhardt surely seems to run a strong race for that top position.

The Boundaries of History

Critics who decry the lack of footnotes, then, are perhaps being a bit ungenerous as well as unrealistic. Ungenerous, because Woodward and Bernstein are straightforward enough in their narrative approach to enable careful readers to deduce the book's major sources. Unrealistic, because under the circumstances only a promise of anonymity enabled Woodward and Bernstein to get as much information as they did.

In part, however, the resentment of some critics seems to be focused on a different issue: the book's implicit pretension to being history. In crossing the line from the autobiographical prose of *All the President's Men* into the historical narrative of *The Final Days*, Woodward and Bernstein committed the cardinal sin of not knowing their place. They attempted a production beyond their means, and the result was "hot" history. So the critics would have us believe.

Is *The Final Days* history? Or to rephrase the question, are Woodward and Bernstein "doing" history? Since the bulk of this volume has been spent watching historians go about their business, we are in a better than usual position to answer.

The two reporters readily surmount the first and easiest hurdle. History is a narrative reconstruction of past events. The events of the Nixon presidency are past; *The Final Days* is a narrative reconstruction. So far, so good. But as has become clear, the key word in that definition is "reconstruction." It is reconstruction—the act of gathering, analyzing, and shaping raw information—that is at the heart of history. So let us look at a little more closely, first, at the raw information gathered by Woodward and Bernstein; and second, at the analyzing and shaping they do.

In terms of raw information, Woodward and Bernstein have gathered reasonably well. They make use of many of the sorts of documents that historians of the Nixon years will continue to draw upon: logs, memoranda, diaries, notes. There is, of course, a good deal of information the reporters did not gather because they could not. Classified materials were not available. Some actors in the drama refused to cooperate, including Alexander Haig, Henry Kissinger, and the man at the center of the action, Richard Nixon.

In the area of oral evidence, however, Woodward and Bernstein have collected more and better raw information than most historians could ever hope to find. As the case of the slave narratives collection demonstrated, oral evidence can be extremely valuable. Historians have made excellent use of the freed-men's stories, even though some may have been distorted by hindsight or blurred by time. In the case of *The Final Days*, interviews were conducted with subjects whose recollections were fresh, vivid, and close to the event—the ideal of oral historians. Indeed, the reporters recognized this closeness as their strong suit. They began interviewing only a week after the Nixon resignation because, as they put it, "We didn't want to give people a chance at hindsight."

The quality of Woodward and Bernstein's information is also noteworthy in terms of the people interviewed. Throughout this work we have seen historians expanding their research beyond the narrow coverage of society's elite to include the perspectives of middle and "bottom rail" people: the tobacco hands of Virginia, the villagers of Salem, the freedmen of Carolina, the white- and blue-collar Americans of Dedham and Braintree. In political history too, historians have moved beyond an analysis that focuses solely on "rational actors" and major decision makers to a recognition that anonymous bureaucrats and bureaucratic structures affect the political process.

Woodward and Bernstein have incorporated such perspectives into their narrative. Scores of secretaries, legal assistants, subcabinet officers, and personal aides have, in effect, left behind their own memoirs in *The Final Days*. The vast majority of such people would never publish recollections; yet their perspectives are important for historians wishing to piece together the dynamics of political Washington. Max Lerner notwithstanding, it may be valuable to know what the law clerks of Potter Stewart (not to mention Stewart himself) thought of Warren Burger's attempt to write a majority opinion on the Nixon tapes case. Similarly, it will be helpful to know how Henry Kissinger dealt with the inertial bureaucracy of the State Department—from the bureaucracy's point of view as well as the secretary's. And in terms of status dynamics and conspicuous consumption, we certainly are unlikely to learn from Ronald Ziegler's official memoirs that he demanded his coffee be served in a cup and saucer identical to the president's—cream-colored Lenox china with a silver presidential seal. Woodward and Bernstein's technique of beginning with the smaller fish and working up to the bigger ones has paid perhaps unanticipated dividends.

That raises the second part of our question—did the two reporters fully anticipate the dividends? History springs not from the raw material itself, but from the historian's ability to see its potential and shape it. How does *The Final Days* make use of its materials? What questions does it ask of them in order to extort significance? Throughout this book we have seen historians constantly analyzing individual documents and records. They have asked questions about perspective; about a document's context; or how its predispositions might affect its value as evidence.

Again, Woodward and Bernstein demonstrate that they have taken such questions into account. "In the course of over three years of reporting on the Nixon Administration," they note,

> we had learned to place extraordinary trust in the accuracy and candor of some sources. We had also talked regularly over the same period with a small number of people who consistently sought to give versions of events that were slanted, self-serving, or otherwise untrustworthy; we used information from them only when we were convinced by more reliable sources of its accuracy.

Carl Bernstein and Bob Woodward *(right) of the* Washington Post. *"Yesterday was for the history books. . . ." (Wide World Photos.)*

The prose of *The Final Days* confirms this assertion. For example, Ronald Ziegler appears to have contributed some material; yet Woodward and Bernstein obviously distrust his perceptions. Inevitably, some readers will disagree with the reporters' evaluation of their sources, but that is a matter of judgment. Such disagreements are everyday occurrences in the historical profession.

On a larger scale, however, Woodward and Bernstein's narrative asks relatively limited questions. This work has made clear that the broader concerns of historical inquiry are shaped by the theoretical concepts that historians bring to bear on an investigation. We have examined the pattern of land speculation and settlement in Tennessee because Frederick Jackson Turner asked provocative questions about the relation between democracy and the American frontier. We have gone beyond the question of guilt or innocence in the Sacco and Vanzetti case because John Higham and other historians have made us sensitive to the conflicts between immigrants and native-born Americans. We have explored the bureaucratic features of scientific research in the 1930s and 1940s because decision-making theories suggest that we may learn more that way about how the atomic bomb came to be used. Questions of such broad scope are not often suggested by the raw information itself. They are brought to the material by the historian.

This is where Woodward and Bernstein least resemble the researchers we have followed throughout this book. *The Final Days* is narrative history in its narrower sense, concerned primarily with laying out the who-what-where and describing it in a vivid, readable way. These are commendable goals, and ones not easily attained. But the broader questions remain unasked. What significance, for example, does the Watergate controversy have for the development of American political institutions? Perhaps Watergate should be regarded merely as one of the periodic scandals that embarrass administrations—like Teapot Dome of the twenties or the Credit Mobilier frauds of the Grant administration. On the other hand, President Nixon's behavior raises important questions about the constitutional division of power among the branches of the federal government. The Nixon administration continued a trend, begun during the New Deal years, of consolidating executive initiative and power at the expense of Congress and the courts. The president defied the Democratic-controlled Congress by refusing to spend money that Congress had appropriated for programs he disapproved. He engaged in wire-tapping and other clandestine intelligence activities for political gain as well as for national security.

Woodward and Bernstein discuss none of the issues raised by these actions, most likely because at heart, they are indeed journalists. The word itself reflects their perspective, sharing its Latin root with the French *jour*, or day. For the journalist, each day is a new deadline. *Washington Post* editors were in the habit of asking their reporters, "What have you done for me *today?*" Woodward and Bernstein were willing to write by that philosophy. "Yesterday was for the history books," they note in *All the President's Men*, "not newspapers." It was only natural that they were not inclined to step back and examine larger issues.

From the historian's point of view their decision, conscious or not, was wisely made. For we have seen that contemporary observers are usually not particularly well-positioned to evaluate the larger issues of their day. Was Teddy Roosevelt's compromise with the meat-packing industry an astute bargain or a sellout? The question was impossible to answer without knowing how the court ruled in later challenges to the Meat Inspection Act. Will the reform legislation passed during the aftermath of Watergate adequately restrain an imperial presidency? Even a trained historian would be loath to answer without hedging. Woodward and Bernstein chose to do the kind of history they knew best—an up-close, day-by-day narrative rather than detached, magisterial analysis.

To say that *The Final Days*, then, is only one kind of history is not to slight the book; merely to recognize the discipline's immense variety. History, after all, is perhaps the only profession that has the audacity to define its boundaries in terms of time rather than subject matter—to cast its gaze on anything that happened in the past. There is plenty of elbow room in this discipline; enough space to accommodate a wide variety of methods and subject matter. Woodward and Bernstein were not professional scholars, but that serves only to remind us of historian Carl Becker's insistence that we are all historians in one guise or another: young Sam Mitchell, the black freedman recounting the day the guns thundered over the Carolina Sea Islands; Bartolomeo Vanzetti, impelled to consider whether he would repeat the actions that brought him to final sentencing; even our own family members, passing tales from father to daughter, from mother to son, from older sister to younger brother. Watergate, which was "instant history" when Woodward and Bernstein encountered it, has slid inexorably into the past. But the episode serves to remind us that analytical tools used to analyze the past can serve equally well in making sense of the present.

ADDITIONAL READING

Woodward and Bernstein narrate their own pursuit of the cover-up in *All the President's Men* (New York, 1974), an account which focuses primarily on events through April 1973. *The Final Days* (New York, 1976) picks up chronologically where the first book left off. Press reaction to *The Final Days* can be found in the daily newspapers and newsmagazines of April 1976, as well as in book reviews and commentary such as Max Lerner, "Writing 'Hot History,'" *Saturday Review*, May 29, 1976; and John Osborne, "The Woodstein Flap," *New Republic*, April 24, 1976.

The most comprehensive history of Watergate thus far is J. Anthony Lukas, *Nightmare: The Underside of the Nixon Years* (New York, 1976, rev. ed. 1988). See also Stanley I. Kutler, *The Wars of Watergate* (New York, 1990). Richard Nixon sometimes claimed (and the record now shows) that other presidents pioneered the abuse of the power of their office in ordering government agencies to spy on citizens, political dissenters, and political enemies both real and perceived. Athan Theoharis, *The Boss: J. Edgar Hoover and the Great American Inquisition* (New York, 1988), and William W. Keller, *The Liberals and J. Edgar Hoover* (Princeton, N.J., 1989), are two studies that in a small way vindicate Nixon's claim by showing the historical roots of the FBI's domestic intelligence-gathering under Nixon's predecessors. By contrast, Stephen Ambrose, *Nixon: The Triumph of a Politician* (New York, 1989), the second of a three-volume political biography, lays the blame squarely with Nixon and his dark streak of paranoia and hate.

For another example of "hot history," readers may wish to compare Theodore White's *Breach of Faith* (New York, 1975) and Jonathan Schell's more interpretive study of the Nixon years, *The Time of Illusion* (New York, 1976). Some of the larger issues skirted by Woodward and Bernstein are aired in Frederick C. Mosher, *Watergate: Implications for Responsible Government* (New York, 1974); Ralph K. Winter, *Watergate and the Law* (Washington, D.C., 1974); and Philip B. Kurland, *Watergate and the Constitution* (Chicago, Ill., 1978).

Most accounts of Watergate that have appeared thus far are by the participants themselves, occasionally helped along by the ever-obliging "as-told-to" ghost writers. From the ranks of the co-conspirators have come the following books, listed roughly in diminishing order of administrative rank: *The Memoirs of Richard Nixon* (New York, 1978), in which Richard Nixon, after many pages, still seems puzzled over what the fuss was about; Harry R. Haldeman, *The Ends of Power* (New York, 1978); John Dean, *Blind Ambition: The White House Years* (New York, 1976), one of the more perceptive accounts; Charles Colson, *Born Again* (Old Tappan, N.J., 1976); Jeb Magruder, *An American Life* (New York,

1974): E. Howard Hunt, *Undercover: Memoirs of an American Secret Agent* (New York, 1974); James McCord, *A Piece of the Tape* (Rockville, Md., 1974); and G. Gordon Liddy, *Will* (New York, 1980). The last account seems to confirm the president's own assessment of Liddy. ("He just isn't well screwed on, is he?")

Other areas of the Watergate story have been recounted by those who brought the malfeasants to justice. "Maximum John" Sirica, as he was known in legal circles, gives the bench's perspective in *To Set the Record Straight* (New York, 1979). For the Ervin Committee, there is Senator Sam's version itself, perhaps somewhat ambitiously titled *The Whole Truth* (New York, 1981), as well as Samuel Dash, *Chief Counsel: Inside the Ervin Committee* (New York, 1976), and Minority Counsel Fred D. Thompson's *At that Point in Time* (New York, 1975). For the Special Prosecutor's office, see Leon Jaworski, *The Right and the Power* (New York, 1976); Richard Ben-Veniste and George Frampton, Jr., *Stonewall* (New York, 1977); and James Doyle, *Not Above the Law* (New York, 1977). Howard Fields, *High Crimes and Misdemeanors* (New York, 1978), covers the impeachment proceedings, as does a large part of Elizabeth Drew's perceptive *Washington Journal: the Events of 1973-1974* (New York, 1975).

We have not discussed the thorny and familiar issue of who Bob Woodward's most famous source, Deep Throat, was, since he appears only in *All the President's Men* and not *The Final Days*. We admit to having our own theories, though they require more legwork and researching to substantiate than we have had time, as yet, to spare. Perhaps a later edition of this book will have an epilogue. In the meantime, the most thorough detective work on the problem has been done by John Dean, in his book *Lost Honor* (Los Angeles, Calif., 1982). His choice for Deep Throat: Alexander Haig.

For readers wishing to investigate some of the primary documents of Watergate, several sourcebooks are available which make the task easier. For excerpts from the Ervin Committee hearings, consult *The Watergate Hearings* (New York, 1973), assembled by *The New York Times*, or else the full version issued by the Senate Select Committee on Presidential Campaign Activities, *Hearings, Watergate and Related Activities* (Washington, D.C., 1973). For the impeachment proceedings, see the House Committee on the Judiciary's *Impeachment of Richard Nixon, President of the United States* (Washington, D.C., 1974). Then, of course, there are the most notorious primary sources of the drama, the White House tapes and transcripts. The transcripts are available in convenient form either in *The Presidential Transcripts* (New York, 1974), as issued by the *Washington Post*, or in *The White House Transcripts* (New York, 1974), by *The New York Times*. Both texts are copied in full from the more unwieldy typescript edition issued by the Government Printing Office. But as *The Final Days* makes clear, the transcripts have been sometimes severely edited. The National Archives has made available for listening twelve and a half hours of the original tapes—those played at Congressional hearings. As of 1991, another 60 hours of transcripts have been released. They are stored, along with 5 million pages of files and documents from the Nixon presidency, in a no-frills

National Archives warehouse in Alexandria, Virginia, open to the public week-days. Listening to the recordings is a fascinating experience: the quality is uneven but usually understandable, at least with the help of FBI transcripts provided. The opportunity to analyze political decision making in terms of a blow-by-blow conversation, with inflection of voice to be weighed as well as syntax and content, is unprecedented.

CHAPTER FIFTEEN

Where Trouble Comes

POV: the abbreviation sounds military. It could be part of the shorthand used so often in the Vietnam War, either to label geographical areas (LZs are landing zones), to name armies (VC stands for Viet Cong), or even to list the status of soldiers (KIAs—killed in action, WHAs—wounded in hostile action). POV, however, is not military jargon. It is a screenwriter's abbreviation that stands for *point of view*. In films, a "POV shot" records a scene as if it were being viewed through the eyes of one of the actors. Where the director chooses to place the camera, to establish POV, determines to a large degree how the story is told.

Where should one place a camera in the Vietnamese village of Son My on March 16, 1968? When the artillery shells begin falling early Saturday morning, any camera angle would probably seem arbitrary. But for a moment, consider sorting them in terms of altitude: camera positions measured in feet above sea level.

POV, ground level: A dirt road, running past rice paddies not far from the South China Sea. Nguyen Chi, a farmer's wife, is already on her way to the market when she hears a series of explosions. She turns to see billowing smoke rising about a mile back, in the cluster of houses where she lives. Frantically she runs toward a hut by the road, whose occupants have just rushed outside, and follows them to a small underground bunker built for such occasions. After several minutes the boom of the artillery fades. Helicopters advance across the sky. As Nguyen Chi peers from the earthen shelter, she sees one of the choppers land in a rice paddy not far down the road.

POV, altitude 500 feet: Nine large army assault helicopters sweep over the countryside. At 7:30 in the morning the sun is already heating up their gleaming black bodies. Inside, men from Charlie Company sit nervously. They are launching a surprise attack on the Viet Cong's crack 48th Battalion, said to be holed up in the village below. Expecting heavy resistance, the men carry twice the normal load of rifle and machine-gun ammunition, as well as grenades and other ordnance. As the choppers descend, their blades change pitch for the landing, making a sharp, crackling *pop-pop-pop*. It sounds almost like rifle fire.

The nervous door gunners spray the surrounding fields with rockets and machine-gun fire. These last few moments of descent are the most vulnerable: with no troops on the ground and the choppers settling like clumsy ducks on the water, the men will be easy prey for an ambush. Scrambling, soldiers drop into the paddy and fan out, securing the landing zone. . . .

POV, altitude 1,000 feet: Lieutenant Colonel Frank Barker hovers in a smaller chopper. Charlie Company is part of his task force, assembled to root out the Viet Cong in the area. Barker watches the operation from his assigned air lane at 1,000 feet. After about twenty minutes, he sees the second wave of helicopters flying in below, unloading another fifty men. Charlie Company regroups and heads into the hamlet, where the vegetation is denser than in the open fields. At a thousand feet, it is difficult to see what's going on. But there is smoke and, over the crackling static of the radio, the sound of small-arms fire. At 8:28 Barker radios Captain Ernest Medina, the commander on the ground. "Have you had any contact down there yet?" he asks. When Medina replies that they have killed 84 Viet Cong ("Eight-four KIAs"), Barker's chopper banks and heads home for the unit's operations center.

The POVs could continue their upward spiral. The air corridor at 2,000 feet is reserved for the Americal Division's commander, Major General Samuel Koster, who flies over Son My several times that morning, well above reach of ground fire. At 2,500 feet the operations commander also monitors the action. Stacked in layers of airspace, looking on from higher and higher perches, these POVs provide increasingly wider views of the terrain. Yet the perspective also becomes more remote with the increase in altitude. Because these observers see more, they also see less.

The report of the morning's action becomes distorted not only by height but by distance, as it is relayed to the world at large. At the operations center, Press Officer Arthur Dunn telephones a two-page "after action" report into division headquarters. Dunn uses the statistics compiled by Colonel Barker's staff. The totals have risen since Medina's earlier report, to a final count of "128 enemy killed, 13 suspects detained and three weapons captured." The body count is the largest recorded for the task force since it began operations two months earlier. But one number makes Dunn uneasy: the three weapons captured. Could the Viet Cong retreat from a fierce fight taking along virtually all of their dead comrades' firearms? Unlikely. To Dunn, something seems "fishy."

In Saigon, more distant from the field of battle, the press officer has no time for such questions. He merely provides reporters with their story, which makes no mention of the number of weapons captured. Based on the briefing, *The New York Times* front page reports that "about 150 men of the American Division encountered the enemy force early yesterday. . . . The operation is another American offensive to clear enemy pockets still threatening the cities. . . ."

Another offensive to clear enemy pockets: As the *Times* recognized, this was neither the first nor the last of such sweeps. It amounted to one more confusing day in a war that, by 1968, was being waged with over half a million American troops. How important, really, was Charlie Company's assault? For journalists scrambling for a story, the picture remained unclear and there was little time to follow up. ("What have you done for me *today*?" Woodward and Bernstein's editors kept asking them.) None of the dispatches coming out of Vietnam gave any hint that the events at Son My, if told from the perspective of the men who entered the village that morning, might send tremors across America that would change how the nation thought about the war. For the time being, their POVs went unreported.

Cinematic Myths and Vietnam

During the same months that Charlie Company was conducting its search-and-destroy operations, Warner Brothers completed final work on *The Green Berets*, Hollywood's first dramatization of the war. The film's star and coproducer, John Wayne, had made a career of climbing into the boots of outsized heroes. For over thirty years "the Duke" had been the featured player in countless westerns, including *Stage Coach, Fort Apache*, and *The Alamo*. He had assaulted enemy-held islands in World War II dramas like *The Sands of Iwo Jima, Back to Bataan*, and *They Were Expendable*. In the midst of this new war, Wayne watched with dismay the growing domestic protest against American involvement in Southeast Asia. As a conservative patriot, he decided to fight back by directing and starring in a combat epic designed to show why Americans were at war.

The turbulent events of 1968, however, made patriotism a harder sell, even for an old hand like Wayne. In January, the Viet Cong had launched a series of surprise attacks during the Vietnamese celebration of Tet, the lunar new year. The strength of the Tet assault shocked many Americans, who began more and more to doubt the government's rosy progress reports. By the end of March (several weeks after Charlie Company's operation at Son My), the war had so divided the nation that President Johnson chose not to seek reelection. Events at home as well as abroad seemed increasingly violent and chaotic. In April, Martin Luther King was gunned down by an assassin; in June, so was Robert Kennedy, the candidate who seemed most likely to replace Johnson on the Democratic ticket. Both King and Kennedy had become outspoken opponents of the war.

In such tumultuous times, Warner Brothers became edgy about the prospects of its new film. Newspaper ads touting *The Green Berets* were almost defensive: "So you don't believe in glory. And heroes are out of style. And they don't blow bugles anymore. So take another look—at the Special Forces in a special kind of hell." Although antiwar demonstrators picketed the film's premiere ("John Wayne profits off G.I.'s blood," read one sign), an eager theater audience cheered as their hero, a tad paunchy at 61, led his Green Berets to a newly erected outpost "in the heart of VC country." At the end of more than two hours of action, U.S. Special Forces had tangled with mortar fire, nighttime raids, and poison punjee sticks, emerging triumphant in a fight for their embattled outpost. If newspaper stories like the one about Charlie Company seemed a bit distant from reality, *The Green Berets* presented instant history that was just the opposite. Its POVs were bold, colorful, larger than life.

The Green Berets was easy for the critics to dismiss. ("A film best handled from a distance and with a pair of tongs," sniffed *The New Yorker*.) But enough of Wayne's fans rallied round to make it a solid financial success. And while *The Green Berets* was the first feature film to use the war as its setting, it was hardly the last. Over the past quarter century, at least twenty-five films have portrayed aspects of the conflict. For better or worse, with more accuracy or less, far more Americans have come by their understanding of the war viewing dramatic films than by reading scholarly histories. In that sense historians and filmmakers have become rivals: revisiting the same battlefields, reconstructing similar dramas in rice paddies or small villages, delving for significance in an ambiguous past.

How should we approach films that purport to portray history, especially a subject as controversial as the Vietnam War? There are, of course, a number of straightforward ways to evaluate historical dramas. We can give each film a scrupulous fact-checking, to determine which parts are true and which false. Are the costumes right? Did a historical figure do the things he or she is said to have done on screen? If the characters are fictional, are they representative of historical figures in similar situations? This approach—administering a kind of historical lie-detector test—can reveal a great deal. But as we have seen, historians routinely use more imaginative ways to examine the past. If we can ferret out unspoken biases in the photographs of Jacob Riis, why not probe the cultural assumptions of *The Green Berets*? If the narrative perspectives in Woodward and Bernstein's writings can be dissected, why not explore the camera's points of view in a film like *Apocalypse Now*?

Still, a good deal of caution is needed when examining historical films for information about the past. The historical "reality" presented by dramatic films is radically different from that of a letter or diary, or even from a secondary account like *The Final Days*. At their best, movies have a visual and emotional immediacy more vivid than any reality evoked by the printed page. For Vietnam, they confront viewers with the *feel* of war—the oppressive heat of a jungle trail, the explosive chaos of a firefight. Yet even the best filmic realism is false or misleading. To begin with the obvious: the soldiers tramping across a rice paddy, machine guns in hand, are actors, not the original combatants. The location in which they appear is almost never that of the historical event. This is perhaps only another way of saying that any dramatic film sequence is an artful *construction of reality* rather than reality itself. Just as historians re-create their own versions of the past in prose narratives, so also do directors and their production crews on film.

But filmmakers and historians part company on their principles of reconstruction. A historian's first commitment is to remain faithful to the historical record. Of course, that commitment can be difficult to keep. As we have seen, any knowledge of what "really" happened in the past is conditioned by the primary sources available and the way we analyze them. We are not simply messengers between past and present, but active agents, doing our best to reconstruct an ambiguous past. Still, no matter how ingeniously historians tease meaning from the evidence, the source material remains their starting point.

For filmmakers, far different principles of construction are paramount. They involve questions of drama, not fidelity to the evidence. Does the screenplay move along quickly enough? Do the characters "develop" sufficiently? Does the plot provide enough suspense? These matters dominate the making of a film, even when that oft-repeated claim flashes across the screen: *Based on a True Story*. If historical sources cannot supply enough material to round out a tale, directors and screenwriters will tinker with the plot and characters until the story provides them with what they need.

The kinds of changes that are routinely made can be seen in Oliver Stone's *Born on the Fourth of July* (1989). Stone based his film on the memoir of a Vietnam veteran, Ron Kovic, who became involved in the antiwar movement. Kovic's faith in the war had been shaken by two traumatic events that overtook him in Vietnam: a nighttime firefight in which he accidentally killed one of his own men, and another night patrol during which his unit killed and wounded some Vietnamese women and children. According to Kovic's book, the two events took place several months apart, but the film combines them into a single incident. Similarly, Kovic describes a trip to Washington for an antiwar rally; in the film, he attends a protest at Syracuse University instead, where his high school sweetheart attends college. In fact, Syracuse had no violent demonstration and Kovic's book made no mention of a high school sweetheart. And there are many other similar alterations of detail.

Does this disqualify the film as history? In one sense, yes. By deliberately changing the historical record or inventing it out of whole cloth, Stone has done what no historian would do. No doubt he would defend the changes for dramatic reasons. Consider, for example, the most crassly commercial alteration: giving Kovic a girlfriend. To justify a budget of millions, a film must make money, and over the years box office receipts have proved that audiences are attracted to plots with an element of romance. For dramatic reasons, too, the idea makes sense. Young, innocent Kovic goes off to Vietnam a patriotic marine, while his sweetheart goes off to college and becomes an antiwar demonstrator. Now Kovic's struggle to come to terms with the war is intertwined with his search for a romantic relationship. Similarly, it makes dramatic sense to distill Kovic's traumatic war experiences into one vivid sequence, to leave time for the rest of the film to focus on his growing involvement with the antiwar movement. As for the decision to invent a protest at Syracuse rather than re-create the one in Washington, one suspects that Stone simply wanted to save on production costs. Recreating a full-scale march around the monuments of the nation's capital would have been much more expensive.

Even having made changes like these, Stone could argue that he has remained faithful to the essence of Kovic's story. If the goal of the film is to show the long, painful road from patriotic innocence to disillusionment and finally to a new commitment to political change, do the smaller details of the plot really matter? This is a dramatic film, not a scholarly monograph. Like novels or plays, films strive for an artistic standard of "truth" that resides less in the particulars of the historical record than in rendering situations and characters in authentic, human ways. In esthetic terms, Stone could argue that he respected the integrity of Kovic's story, and that *Born on the Fourth of July* reveals a great deal about many Americans who fought in Vietnam.

But the point remains. No matter how "true" a film tries to be to the emotions of its characters, the makers of feature films will always place dramatic considerations above strict fidelity to the historical record. And this recognition leads the historian to ask a more interesting series of questions. Instead of simply trying to discover which details of a film are based on historical facts and which are not, why not analyze the dramatic construction of the film itself? Accept, for the moment, that producers and directors are concerned with a different kind of artistic "truth" than historians. Grant that the search for profits often pushes Hollywood to distort the past in hopes of making films that its audiences need or want to see. This is another way of saying that dramatic films about history do not portray what actually happened in the past so much as what *ought* to have happened—at least in the minds of the audience or the film's creators. In short, we are leaving behind the reconstruction of a nation's history for an exploration of its myths.

A myth, to quote one dictionary definition, is "any real or fictional story, recurring theme, or character type that appeals to the consciousness of a people by embodying its cultural ideals or by giving expression to deep, commonly felt emotions." Most often, we think of myths as traditions that have survived from preliterate societies: tales of gods like Thor and Zeus, or hazy historical figures like Helen of Troy or Hiawatha. But the myths of modern culture are not simply derived from older traditions. Novelists and playwrights routinely create new narratives that speak to more recent hopes or anxieties. And Hollywood, an industry that markets the fantasies and fears of popular culture, inescapably finds itself in the myth business, creating stories, themes, and character types that embody the cultural ideals of its audiences and give expression to their deepest feelings.

What sorts of myths? Consider the story and characters in *The Green Berets*. Audiences already knew John Wayne as the star of films that embodied two well-established mythic traditions of American cinema. The first was the western, whose central tale is a saga of white settlers crossing the prairie in order to subdue the wilderness and supplant it with a new, more vibrant civilization. Wayne, whether playing a rangy cowpoke or a dashing cavalry officer, embodied the highest ideals of that new America. He was strong, independent, honest and fair, at once tender and tough. Equality and liberty were the watchwords of the West, contrasting sharply with the inequality of aristocratic Europe or even with the decadent, overcrowded cities of the East.

From John Wayne the hero of the West, it was only a short step to Wayne the Green Beret of Vietnam. Instead of hunting coppery-skinned Indians who menaced defenseless settlers, the Duke would now chase Asian guerillas who lurked in the jungle. Rather than commanding a fort in Apache country, he would defend an outpost near the Laotian border—this one conveniently nick-named Dodge City. Once again, the heroes of the West would have a chance to uproot the corruptions of the East, this time the infection of communism that had spread across Eurasia.

Wayne's previous roles reflected a second mythic tradition of American cinema: the combat epic that came of age during World War II. In the standard-issue World War II melodrama, an ethnically mixed assortment of recruits is thrown together in a front-line platoon, each soldier finding himself tested in the heat of battle. As the platoon shares the agonies and triumphs of a common experience, they are forged into a dedicated fighting unit. In effect, the story retells the classic myth of the American melting pot, in which immigrants from a multitude of ethnic backgrounds learn to live in a single nation. As the platoon unites to work for victory, it embodies the very democratic ideals that set America apart from other nations. Repeatedly, Wayne played the hero who made this myth so powerful. Like many others of his generation, Ron Kovic remembered viewing as a boy one of Wayne's classic Pacific combat films:

> Castiglia and I saw *The Sands of Iwo Jima* together. The Marine Corps hymn was playing in the background as we sat glued to our seats . . . watching Sergeant Stryker, played by John Wayne, charge up the hill and get killed before he reached the top. And then they showed the men raising the flag on Iwo Jima with the marines' hymn playing, and Castiglia and I cried in our seats. I loved the song so much, and every time I heard it I would think of John Wayne and the brave men who raised the flag on Iwo Jima that day. . . .

Combat films like *The Sands of Iwo Jima* and westerns like *The Alamo* and *Fort Apache* worked because the tales they told reinforced Americans' ideas about themselves as a people. Indeed, the mythic traditions of both the western and the World War II epic assumed that Americans were in many ways an exceptional people, set apart by their experience with democracy and liberty. This tradition of American exceptionalism could be traced back as far as John Winthrop's sermon to his fellow Puritans in 1630, that their new colony in Massachusetts would stand as "a city on a hill" and a shining example to the rest of the world. Winthrop's pride was motivated by a religious vision of the Puritans as a chosen people, but over the years that vision gained a political dimension as well, from the heritage of the American Revolution. It became overtly nationalistic during the nineteenth century, as the "manifest destiny" of western expansion transformed the United States into a continental nation. Wayne's films were among the many dramas that drew upon such themes.

In making *The Green Berets*, Wayne was well aware of the myths and messages he was constructing. In late 1965, knowing he would need army cooperation to help film battle scenes, he wrote President Johnson, making a successful pitch for the picture:

> Some day soon a motion picture *will* be made about Vietnam. Let's make sure it is the kind of motion picture that will help our cause throughout the world. I believe my organization can do just that and still accomplish our purpose for being in existence—making money. We want to tell the story of our fighting men in Vietnam with reason, emotion, characterization and action. We want to do it in a manner that inspires a patriotic attitude on the part of our fellow Americans—a feeling which we have always had in this country in the past during times of stress and trouble.

Wayne also recognized his own near-mythic stature in the American cinema. "Thirty-seven years a star, I must have some small spot in more than a few million people's lives," he told the president. "You cannot stay up there that long without having identification with a great number of people."

How does *The Green Berets* establish its myths? Since film is above all a visual medium, we should perhaps examine first the images conjured up by the characters in Wayne's drama. Wayne himself plays Colonel Mike Kirby: a tanned, tall, laconic officer who hates the bureaucratic hassles of his high rank and insists on joining his Green Berets in the field. Kirby's dramatic foil is George Beckworth (David Janssen), a liberal newspaper columnist who attacks American involvement in Vietnam. The visual images confirm his status as antagonist: Beckworth is a nervous chainsmoker, generally unwilling to look anyone in the eye.

At Dodge City, Colonel Kirby meets his South Vietnamese ally, Captain Nim, an able sort, but distinctly more bloodthirsty than the Green Berets. He has

Colonel Kirby (John Wayne) brings medical assistance *to a young Laotian girl while the skeptical liberal journalist (David Janssen) looks on. In this scene from* The Green Berets, *the visual message reinforces the film's mythic themes: that Americans are bringing order and democracy to a land threatened by an enemy as ruthless as the stereotypical Indians portrayed in Wayne's westerns.*

"personally greased" fifty-two Viet Cong that year, one of the men informs Kirby, and Nim hopes to double the number before another year goes by. (He keeps score on the wall of his "hootch," or thatched hut.) Like all the film's Vietnamese characters, Nim speaks a Hollywood pigeon English. "My home is Hanoi," he tells Kirby. "I go home too, someday . . . you see! . . . first kill all those stinking Cong . . . then go home."[1]

Beckworth is upset to find Captain Nim slapping around a captured VC spy. Indeed, Nim shakes the man so violently that Kirby feels called upon to restrain him. When Beckworth demands on explanation, Kirby reveals that the spy had killed an American medic on a mission of mercy in a nearby Montagnard village. The doctor was found in the jungle "beheaded, mutilated," says Kirby. "His wife wouldn'ta recognized him." Such contrasts of brutality and innocence defiled become the central stuff of Wayne's mythical Vietnam. While the Green Berets provide villagers with humanitarian aid, the Viet Cong assume the role of savages, raping young girls and torturing wives in front of their husbands.

To provide viewers with a heart-rending visual reminder of the war's horrors, the fort at Dodge City is also furnished with a lovable Vietnamese orphan whose parents have been killed during a VC raid. Named (of all things) Hamchunk, the orphan is followed about by a little puppy, apparently because the film's producers felt that an Asian orphan alone was not quite enough to melt the hearts of American viewers. In the climactic assault on Dodge City, the VC commit the ultimate atrocity: they grease poor Hamchunk's pooch, and the tearful orphan buries it as the bombs fall helter skelter around him. The valiant Captain Nim perishes too. "He bought the farm, sir," one of the men informs Wayne, but adds reassuringly, "he took a lot of 'em with him."

As so often happens when questions of drama are paramount, complex issues of geopolitics are reduced to intensely personal relationships and bold visual images. The can-do American colonel, the stalwart South Vietnamese ally, the hapless orphan—all reinforce the myths embraced by *The Green Berets*. Here is a war much like World War II (the so-called good war), in which decent Americans prevail over an unscrupulous enemy. The film ends with Hamchunk once again at loose ends, walking with Wayne along the beaches of the South China Sea. "What will happen to me now?" he asks plaintively. Wayne sets a Green Beret atop the boy's head and then (as in so many earlier westerns) walks into the sunset with his pal. "You let me worry about that, Green Beret," he says. "You're what this war is all about." No matter that Vietnam's beaches face *east* (this sun would have to be rising); the message of these visual images is strong and clear. Americans have come to Vietnam to protect innocents and promote democracy just as they had in Hollywood's previous wars.

---

[1] Like the other Vietnamese characters, Nim is not played by a Vietnamese. The role was filled by a Japanese-American, George Takei, known to many as Mr. Sulu of *Star Trek* fame. In 1968, allowing Asian-Americans of any sort to take principal speaking roles was a measure of progress compared with the days of World War II, when a WASP like Katherine Hepburn played one of the noble Chinese peasants in *Dragon Seed* (1944). The mythic image Takei projects in *Star Trek* stands rather humorously at odds with his character in *The Green Berets*: Sulu the navigator, ever the cool head in an interstellar crisis, versus the bloodthirsty, inarticulate Nim.

While visual images help establish mythic themes, the structure of a film's narrative can be equally revealing. As we have seen, filmmakers are constantly constructing their versions of history with dramatic considerations uppermost. Is a soldier wounded fatally in a firefight? We must ask ourselves, why at that point in the screenplay and not earlier? Does a woman discover something unsettling about the personal background of her lover? We must wonder, why now? Or why at all? For historians, questions about why events happened in a particular order can be resolved only by analyzing the primary sources. In the case of films, characters are killed off or lovers jilted because the screenwriters, the director, or the producers wish these events to happen. Thinking about the way a story is put together, in other words, can expose the intentions and the values of the film's creators.

In this light, the plot of *The Green Berets* is tantalizingly odd. Its various parts don't quite fit together. Most of the film focuses on Colonel Kirby's defense of his border outpost. But tacked onto this tale is a second, unrelated story. As he prepares the defenses of Dodge City, Kirby is suddenly flown from his outpost to attend dinner at "Le Club Sport," a fancy nightspot in the port city of Da Nang. There, he sees an Asian beauty dining with a Vietnamese companion. Before we can learn more, a couple of Green Berets appear and yank Wayne from his dinner: the VC attack has begun.

Only after Dodge City is safely retaken do we discover that the mysterious lady in Da Nang is a double agent ready to lure the Viet Cong's highest-ranking general into a trap. The film then embarks on a plot in which Wayne infiltrates a commando team armed with drug-tipped arrows and crossbows deep into enemy territory. Sneaking into the general's bedroom, the Green Berets drug him and pack him off in a body bag to a rendezvous where he is lofted on high by a helium balloon and whisked away by an American airplane dragging a hook. The whole concoction is sheer, implausible fantasy, with no relation to the rest of the film. Even worse, the extra length makes *The Green Berets* drag interminably.

Why tack on the extra plot? Any Hollywood script doctor could have seen that the obvious way to shorten an overly long film was simply to eliminate it. But if the producers considered that option, they never carried it out. Why not?

Put yourself in the place of the screenwriter. Try eliminating the second plot and walk with John Wayne through what has now become the final scene of your new, shorter epic. Everything remains as before—the same dialogue, same camera angles. See how the new ending plays.

The Green Berets stand victorious outside Dodge City, thanks to an air attack which has strafed and killed nearly every VC in the fort. "We can probably move in there tomorrow," says Wayne, "God willin' and the river don't rise." Sounding like he's back in sagebrush country, Wayne does move in. The VC flag, fluttering over the outpost, is cut loose and blows away. As Wayne surveys the territory, one of his sergeants walks up hesitantly:

SERGEANT: What do we do now, sir?
KIRBY: First we get some sack time . . . [Pause. Looks grimly around.] And then we start all over again.

And then we start all over again? Can this be the climax to all the tragic bloodshed, the anguished deaths, the carnage? We start all over again? When the flag went up at Iwo Jima, it *stayed* up. But in 1968, the course of fighting in Vietnam was different—as even Wayne and his coproducers recognized. American armed forces did not try to capture territory; instead they attempted to kill as many enemy as possible, in a war of attrition. When American search-and-destroy missions cleared an area, they usually either moved on in another sweep or returned to their base, leaving the territory once again to the enemy. In Vietnam, the victories never quite stayed won.

Suddenly, the reason for the awkward second plot becomes clearer. In 1968 the real war in Vietnam could provide no prospect of a definitive victory. Yet unlike history, an action-adventure film demands a climax that will satisfy audiences that the hardships and deaths of its heros have not been in vain. The only finale Wayne's writers could devise was a second, wholly implausible victory. *The Green Berets* clings valiantly to the cinematic myths of World War II and the wild West, but only by abandoning even tenuous links with reality.

Son My: At Ground Level

The realities of the war, however, were becoming harder to evade. John Wayne's film demonstrated that although myths might distort history, they could not ignore it entirely if they hoped to speak to audiences in lasting and satisfying ways. The tension between the ideal and the real, between *what should have been* and *what was,* made *The Green Berets* an unconvincing film for many Americans. And already in the summer of 1968, the seemingly routine search-and-destroy mission at Son My was beginning to catch up with the myths in which Wayne sought to clothe American involvement in Vietnam.

Several days after Charlie Company returned from Son My in March, another helicopter from the 11th Brigade swept low over the area. Ronald Ridenhour, a door gunner, was struck by the desolation. Nobody seemed to be around. When Ridenhour spotted a body, pilot Gilbert Honda dropped down to investigate. It was a dead woman, spread-eagled on the ground. As Ridenhour recalled later

> She had an 11th Brigade patch between her legs, as if it were some type of display, some badge of honor. We just looked; it was obviously there so people would know the 11th Brigade had been there. We just thought, "What in the hell's wrong with these guys? What's going on?"

As the chopper continued its sweep, several Vietnamese caught sight of it and ran to a bunker. Ridenhour wanted to flush the men out with a phosphorus grenade, but the pilot refused to come in low enough. Ridenhour was angry. Why hadn't Honda pursued? The pilot was evasive; all he would say was, "These people around here have had a pretty rough time the last few days."

At first Ridenhour forgot the incident. Then a friend mentioned Charlie

Company's operation. According to the word going around, Charlie Company had eliminated the entire village. Astonished, Ridenhour talked over the next few months with a number of soldiers who had been at Son My. The more he heard, the more outraged he became.

When he returned home to Phoenix, Arizona, Ridenhour could not let the matter rest. In March 1969, he summarized what he had learned in a letter and sent copies to the White House, the Pentagon, the State Department, and members of Congress. Prodded by several members of Congress, the Army began an inquiry. By the end of August 1969 the Criminal Investigation Division had interviewed more than seventy-five witnesses. Many of Charlie Company's members had already finished their tours of duty and were technically beyond reach of Army discipline. But the investigators' attention centered increasingly on the leader of the first platoon, Second Lieutenant William Calley. On September 5 the Army charged Calley with the premeditated murder of 109 "Oriental human beings . . . whose names and sexes are unknown, by means of shooting them with a rifle." Because of regulations, the charges had to be filed by the commanding officer where Calley was currently stationed. That was Fort Benning, Georgia, a location used two years earlier by John Wayne to film much of *The Green Berets*.

To the surprise of some Pentagon officials, newspapers did not feature the story. But one or two reporters became interested. Following a tip, journalist Seymour Hersh interviewed first Calley and then other Charlie Company veterans in Utah, California, New Jersey, and Indiana. One, Paul Meadlo, agreed to tell his story to CBS Evening News on November 21. His revelation sent reporters scrambling. Both *Time* and *Newsweek* ran cover stories. These new accounts referred less often to Son My, the name of the village used in the newspaper accounts of 1968. Instead they used the name of the smaller hamlet within the boundaries of Son My. On the army's map, that was labeled My Lai.

Inevitably, the memories that surfaced were fragmentary, imperfect. Some members of Charlie Company preferred not to talk with anyone. Others felt an aching need to speak out. In the end, there were only partial points of view: wrenching, disjointed perspectives from which to piece together what happened that March morning as the men disembarked from their helicopters.

POV, on the ground, at hamlet's edge: The soldiers high strung, advancing nervously. They expect return fire at any minute—or the concussion of a booby trap exploding underfoot. A sergeant turns, sees a man near a well. "The gook was standing up shaking and waving his arms and then he was shot," recalls Paul Meadlo. Another soldier: "There was a VC. We thought it was a VC." As the platoons reach the first houses, they split up and begin pulling people out of the hamlet's red brick houses and its hootches.

Below ground; a bunker: Pham Phon hears the artillery stop. When he pokes his head out, several American soldiers are about 200 feet away. Telling his wife and three children to follow, he crawls out. Phon knows how to act when the Americans come. Above all, one must never make a sudden movement, running away from the soldiers or toward them—they will become suspicious and shoot. One must walk slowly, gather in small groups, and wait quietly. As Phon approaches the Americans, his children smile and call out a few words of English: "Hello! Hello! Okay! Okay!"

The Americans are not smiling. The soldiers point their rifles and order the five to walk toward a canal ditch just outside the hamlet.

A group of infantry: There is noise, suddenly, from behind. One of the men whirls, fires. It's only a water buffalo. But something in the group seems to snap, and everyone begins firing, round after round, until the buffalo collapses in a hail of bullets. One of the soldiers: "Once the shooting started, I guess it affected everyone. From then on it was like nobody could stop. Everyone was just shooting at everything and anything, like the ammo wouldn't ever give out."

Soldiers began dynamiting the brick houses and setting fire to the thatched hootches. Private Michael Bernhardt: "I saw these guys doing strange things. . . . They were setting fire to the hootches and huts and waiting for the people to come out and then shooting them. They were going into the hootches and shooting them up. They were gathering people in groups and shooting them."

At the center of the hamlet, about forty-five Vietnamese are herded together. It's about 8:15 a.m. Lieutenant Calley appears and walks over to Paul Meadlo. "You know what to do with them, don't you?" Meadlo says yes. He assumes Calley wants the prisoners guarded. About fifteen minutes later Calley returns. "How come you ain't killed them yet?" he asks. "I want them dead." He steps back about fifteen feet and begins shooting. Meadlo is surprised, but follows orders. "I used more than a whole clip—used four or five clips."

Ronald Haeberle follows the operation into the hamlet. Haeberle is a photographer from the Public Information Detachment. Since the Army anticipates this will be a major action, he is there to cover the engagement. He comes upon some infantry surrounding a group of women, children, and a young teenage girl. Two of the soldiers are trying to pull off the top of the girl's black pajamas, the traditional Vietnamese peasant garb. "Let's see what she's made of," says one. "Jesus, I'm horny," says another. An old woman throws herself on the men, trying to protect the girl. The men punch and kick her aside. One hits her with his rifle butt.

Suddenly they look up: Haeberle is standing there with his camera. They stop bothering the girl and continue about their business. "What should we do with 'em?" one soldier asks. "Kill 'em," says another. Haeberle turns away as an M-60, a light machine gun, is fired. The women and children collapse on the ground, dead.

As he makes his way through the hamlet, Ronald Grzesik comes upon Paul Meadlo, crouched on the ground, head in his hands. Meadlo is sobbing like a child. Grzesik stoops and asks what's the matter. Calley made me shoot some people, Meadlo replies.

Pham Phon and his family wait nervously at the top of the canal ditch. By now perhaps 100 villagers have been herded together. At first they stand, but soon the Americans make them sit, to prevent them from running away. Phon hears gunfire in the distance and has a horrible premonition. He tells his wife

Army photographer Ron Haeberle's searing photographs *of the events at My Lai, published in* Life *magazine in December 1969, provided shocking counterimages to those in* The Green Berets*. The older woman is being restrained by other villagers after she attacked soldiers who had been molesting a younger woman (right rear, buttoning her blouse). "Guys were about to shoot these people," Haeberle recalled. "I yelled, 'Hold it,' and shot my picture. As I walked away, I heard M16s open up. From the corner of my eye I saw bodies falling but I didn't turn to look." (Ron Haeberle,* Life *Magazine © 1969 Time Warner.)*

and children to slip down the bank into the ditch when the soldiers are not looking.

Lieutenant Calley orders some of the men to "push all those people in the ditch." Calley begins shooting and orders Meadlo to follow his lead. Meadlo: "And so I began shooting them all. . . . I guess I shot maybe twenty-five or twenty people in the ditch . . . men, women and children. And babies." Another GI, Robert Maples, refuses to use his machine gun on the crowd. But other soldiers fire, reload, and fire again, until the villagers in the ditch lay still.

Underneath the mass of bodies, Phon and his family lie terrified. They are unhurt, except for one daughter, wounded in the shoulder. As the hours pass,

Phon says nothing, praying his daughter will not moan too loudly from the pain; praying the soldiers will move on.

By 11:00 the guns have fallen quiet. At his command post west of the hamlet, Captain Medina has lunch with his crew and several platoon leaders, including Lieutenant Calley. Two girls, about ten and eleven, appear from out of nowhere. Apparently they have waited out the siege in one of the rice paddies. The men give the girls cookies and crackers. After lunch, Charlie Company blows up a few underground tunnels they have discovered, demolish the remaining houses, and move out of My Lai.

Or more precisely, they move out of what on army maps is labeled "My Lai (4)." Actually, the map gives the name My Lai to six different locations in the area. To outsiders, Vietnamese place names can be confusing. "Villages" such as Son My are really more like American counties or townships. Many hamlets exist within each village; and even these are divided into subhamlets, each with its own name. The Army has not successfully transferred all the names onto their maps. Thus when friendly Vietnamese informants tell Army Intelligence that the Viet Cong's 48th Battalion is based, say, at "My Lai," they do not realize that the Army shows six My Lais on their maps. On this morning of March 16, Americans have attacked the wrong hamlet, one approximately two miles away from the reported stronghold of the 48th Battalion.

The people who live in this settlement do not call it My Lai. Its official name is Xom Lang—merely, *the hamlet*. For years, though, residents have also referred to their home by a more poetic name, Thuan Yen. A rough English translation is *Peace*, or *The Place Where Trouble Does Not Come*.

Denial

By the time the facts about My Lai became known, the wider debate over the war had forced Lyndon Johnson from office. Richard Nixon began a lurching, four-year course of scaling back the conflict. Antiwar protests flared when Nixon sent American troops into neighboring Cambodia, but they tapered off again as the president carried out his policy of "Vietnamization," steadily withdrawing American troops, leaving South Vietnamese forces to absorb the brunt of the fighting. By 1973, American and North Vietnamese negotiators had hammered out a treaty allowing Nixon to claim "peace with honor." But this was largely a face-saving gesture. Despite all pretenses, the war's outcome was a defeat for the United States. Few knowledgeable observers were surprised to see the North Vietnamese complete their conquest of South Vietnam two years later.

As the war wound down by fits and starts, so did the controversy over My Lai. The details of the attack had been so repellent, many Americans at first found them hard to accept. A poll taken by the *Minneapolis Tribune* revealed that nearly half of the 600 persons interviewed believed that the reports of mass murder were false. Other citizens angrily defended the accused. "It sounds terrible to say we ought to kill kids," said a woman in Cleveland, "but many of our boys being killed over there are just kids, too." At the end of a lengthy military trial, Lieutenant Calley was found guilty of "at least twenty-two murders" and sentenced in 1971 to life imprisonment. Following appeals and a forty-month stay in federal custody, Calley was paroled in 1976. Four other soldiers were court-martialed, but none convicted.

Supporters of the war resented the publicity given My Lai. They pointed out that only months before, Communist forces had massacred several thousand civilians at the provincial capital of Hue. Then too, they noted that since the late 1950s, the Viet Cong had engaged in a campaign of political terror, assassinating village officials appointed by the American-backed South Vietnamese regimes. In contrast, they portrayed My Lai as an aberration in American policy: "the actions of a pitiful few," in the words of General William Westmoreland. President Nixon admitted that there "was certainly a massacre," but believed it to be "an isolated incident."

In one sense, historians have confirmed that judgment. The available records for the war reveal no other mass executions of similar magnitude. At the same time, congressional hearings as well as conferences sponsored by Vietnam Veterans Against the War produced testimony of other GIs that on many occasions, civilians or suspected Viet Cong had been treated harshly, shot indiscriminately, or tortured to extract information. Those opposing the war pointed out that even in the case of My Lai, where misconduct had occurred on a large scale, the story had not come to light until a soldier entirely outside the Army's chain of command had prodded high officials to push for an investigation. How many other, lesser incidents went routinely unreported? Historians themselves have not yet undertaken any systematic investigation of such incidents, in part because the task would be so daunting.

Although the ultimate significance of My Lai remained unclear, one thing was certain. The encounter became a defining moment in the public's perception of the war. It did so, a historian might suggest, because it left shaken the long-cherished myth of American exceptionalism. As defenders of a democratic culture, Americans were supposed to behave differently from the rest of the corrupt world. They were not the sort, *The Green Berets* suggested, who would rape young girls or execute innocent civilians. Furthermore, My Lai attracted so much attention because it made the issue concrete and personal, in just the way that film dramas strived to do. John Wayne had reduced complex political and economic issues to visual, intensely personal images ("You're what this war's all about," Kirby tells little Hamchunk). Similarly, Ron Haeberle's searing photographs, reproduced in *Life* magazine, served as counterimages that shattered the mythic stereotypes of *The Green Berets*. Henceforth it would be impossible to take the plot and themes of a western or a World War II epic and merely re-create them in Vietnam. The old myths could no longer be used unchanged.

For nearly a decade, Vietnam remained a subject too hot to handle in feature films. Hollywood dared approach the war only indirectly, as in the irreverent comedy *M*A*S*H* (1970), set during the Korean War. By 1978, however, attitudes were changing. A new wave of Vietnam movies were scheduled for release, encouraged by reports of Francis Ford Coppola's epic under way, *Apocalypse Now*. "When I started," Coppola recalled, "basically people said, 'Are you crazy? You can't make a movie on Vietnam, the American public does not want it.'" Coppola was prudent enough to hire two presidential pollsters to undertake a survey before he committed to the project. The results indicated that the public would indeed buy a "nondidactic" film. "The movie doesn't make you feel guilty," Coppola explained about his work in progress, "but it attempts to be cathartic."

Before Coppola could fulfill his lofty ambitions, however, Michael Cimino beat him in the race to capture Vietnam's mythic high ground. "Ready for Vietnam?" asked *The New York Times*, as *The Deer Hunter* opened in December 1978. Cimino told the *Times* that he had joined the Army about the time of the Tet offensive. "For me, it's a very personal film. I was attached to a Green Beret medical unit. My characters are portraits of people whom I knew." Judging from the first reviews, Americans were indeed ready to confront Vietnam head-on. "The film dares to say that things have come down to life versus death, and it's time someone said this big and strong without fear," enthused *Newsweek*. "What really counts is authenticity, which this movie has by the ton," raved *New York* magazine.

But what was meant by "authentic?" To a historian viewing the film, the characters do seem less stereotyped than those in *The Green Berets*. The dialogue is more natural, less stilted. Yet the film's story and images seem just as mythic. The first third of the drama takes place not in Vietnam but in Clairton, a steel town nestled in the foothills of the Alleghenies. Michael (Robert De Niro), Nick (Christopher Walken), and Steven (John Savage) are leaving their mill jobs in this Russian-American community, off to serve in Vietnam. Steven is married after his last day at work; then he and his buddies head into the mountains for one last deer hunt together. Michael, the obvious leader of the group, regards the hunt as a defining, purifying moment. One must do the job right, he tells Nick: bring down a buck with only one shot. Like Natty Bumppo, James Fenimore Cooper's nineteenth-century hero of *The Deerslayer*, Michael embodies America's noble ideals. The film's visual images emphasize the deep, almost ritualistic ties binding these men: at work, the fiery flames of the blast furnace; after hours, the enveloping dark of the neighborhood bar; at the wedding, glittering icons of the Russian Orthodox church; out hunting, the misty, other-worldly peaks where Michael fells his buck.

Moving and bold—yes. But authentic? The answer to that question is less clear. Cimino went to extreme lengths shooting these sequences, not so much to re-create historical reality as to obtain the proper "look" for his myths. Clairton is an imaginary town, created by shooting in eight different locations spread over four states. Its imposing Russian Orthodox Church is from Cleveland and is twice the size of anything a town like Clairton might afford. The hunting scenes were shot not in the Alleghenies but on the other side of the continent, in the Cascades of Washington. When the deer proved too small for Cimino's taste, he airlifted in larger animals from a New Jersey preserve. "We needed big deer," he said. "I told them there would be a revolution in the theaters if we killed Bambi." Audiences *expect* big deer and overwhelming mountain peaks. And because myth deals with expectations rather than reality, Cimino obliged.

Images of the "one-shot kill" *are central to* The Deer Hunter. *Michael (Robert De Niro, left) embodies the frontier ideals of America. For him, the encounter with a buck on the mountainside is a defining, purifying moment. In contrast, the Viet Cong are depicted as inhuman torturers who pervert the idea of a "one-shot" kill into Russian roulette, which Michael and Steven (John Savage, right) are forced to play.*

The first third of the film ends with the men sitting quietly in an empty bar, one of them rather implausibly playing a melancholy bit of Chopin on a piano. Still in semidarkness, we hear the first faint *whump whump whump* of helicopter blades. In a flash we are in Vietnam—the lush vegetation, the smoke, choppers bearing down on a hamlet. Things now happen quickly, confusingly. A Viet Cong guerilla throws a grenade down a bunker, wounding the peasant inside. We see Michael lying, perhaps stunned, in the grass nearby. Suddenly he springs up and incinerates the VC soldier with a flame-thrower. Reinforcements appear, among them Steven and Nick.

After a firefight, the scene shifts abruptly to a Viet Cong camp, where Steven, Nick, and Michael are being held with other prisoners. Sadistic guards force them to join a hideous game of Russian roulette, in which a prisoner places against his temple a pistol loaded with a single bullet, spins the cylinder, and fires. The losers die; the winners play the next challenger. Nick is nearly unmanned by the experience but survives. Michael one-ups his tormentors by daring to play with not one bullet but three. When he wins, he uses the bullets to kill the guards and then escapes with Nick and Steven.

The three men manage to reach American lines, but Steven loses both legs, while Nick, his sanity shaken, disappears into the underworld of Saigon, where casinos offer the same ghastly game of roulette. The final third of the film follows Michael back to Clairton, where he attempts to reconstruct the lost world of loyalty and community that the war has shattered. Finally he returns to Vietnam in a last attempt to rescue Nick, now a dazed, drug-addicted professional on the roulette circuit. The two face each other over the table—Michael, hoping that one final game will jolt Nick into returning home. But in his haze Nick plays on, and this time loses. Back in Clairton, his friends gather after the funeral. As the film ends, they sing "God Bless America"—tentatively at first, then with feeling.

The roulette scenes "act as a central metaphor of this film," noted Jean Vallely, a writer who interviewed Cimino for *Esquire* magazine. Certainly the scenes are emotionally wrenching, impressively acted, and vividly shot—far more powerful than anything in *The Green Berets*. "I wanted people to feel what it was like to be there, to be in jeopardy every moment," Cimino explained. "How do you get people to pay attention, to sustain twenty minutes of war without doing a whole story about the war?" For Cimino, authenticity seems to revolve around dramatic *feelings*, constructing an emotionally arresting moment rather than a re-creation of the war's historical context. ("How do you get people to pay attention?") When Vallely probed for more information about the roulette scenes, Cimino seemed reluctant to talk, admitting only that he had read about such games "in a newspaper report."

Journalists who covered the war were less reticent. None of them had read any reports of Viet Cong forcing prisoners to play roulette, to say nothing of Saigon casinos practicing the sport. The best *Time* magazine could dig up was one or two unnamed "old hands" who were said to have recalled "a few episodes" from the 1920s and '30s. Peter Arnett, a journalist awarded a Pulitzer for his reporting from Vietnam, complained, "I am now discovering that increasing numbers of Americans believe the last act of the war took place in a sinister back room somewhere in Saigon, where greedy Oriental gamblers were exhorting a glazed-eyed American G.I. to blow his head off." Seymour Hersh, who had helped bring the crimes at My Lai to light, walked out of a screening of *The Deer Hunter* in disgust.[2]

But if *The Deer Hunter* is not authentic in terms of historical details, do the film's myths in some way reflect a kind of emotional truth about the war? To answer that, we need to consider what emotions are being called forth by the plot of *The Deer Hunter*. Just as we did with *The Green Berets*, it may be worth asking what meanings can be deduced from the way that the film is constructed.

The Deer Hunter is an even longer film than *The Green Berets*: three hours and four minutes, to be exact. Yet how much of it concerns the actual experiences of American GIs in Vietnam? If we eliminate the scenes about the games of roulette—events that bear no relation to the real Vietnam—the answer is, *less than four minutes*. In that brief interval, we see a Viet Cong guerilla drop a grenade into a bunker; Michael retaliate; and he, Nick, and Steven become prisoners. The structure of the film, in other words, suggests that very little of

---

[2] Apparently, Cimino's mythmaking was not limited to the movies. Reporter Tom Buckley discovered that the filmmaker had fudged his age in the *Times* interview, claiming he was 35 instead of 40. He had never been a Green Beret, had spent most of his six months of active duty at Fort Lee, New Jersey, with about a month thrown in for medical training in Texas, where he might have met a few of the Special Forces. All this occurred not in 1968, but 1962—well before the heaviest American involvement in Vietnam.

The Deer Hunter had *anything* to do with Vietnam. Yet of course it does. We need only imagine our Hollywood script doctor rewriting the plot to eliminate the war entirely. In the new version, Michael, Nick, and Steve are leaving Clairton to dig for gold in the jungles of Venezuela. Once there, they are captured (in about four minutes) by rival prospectors, who force them to play roulette . . . and so on, until Nick tragically blows his brains out in a backroom bar in Caracas. The structure of this new plot is precisely the same as the old one. The dramatic tension should be every bit as gripping. Yet would such a film have received the attention lavished on *The Deer Hunter?* Obviously not.

Clearly, Cimino intended that audiences come away believing they had experienced something of the war's agonies: the haunting trauma of shattered communities, friendships, and lives. But in suggesting how that trauma came about, the film's plot amounts to a comforting, even racist fantasy. By spending only four minutes considering American actions in Vietnam, *The Deer Hunter* deflects attention away from the real traumatic events of the war and onto stereotyped villains. *They* did it to us, the film suggests: we were shattered by swarthy, inhuman tormentors. In their evil hands, the holiest myth of the West—the ritual of the one-shot kill—was perverted into an evil game of torture. This was a message tailored perfectly for those filmgoers who, as Coppola said, didn't want to "feel guilty," and who could now leave the theater singing "God Bless America," believing that the myths at the center of Michael's world (and theirs) remained intact. Not surprisingly, *The Deer Hunter* received the Academy Award for Best Picture at ceremonies in April 1979. As Michael Cimino bounded to the podium to collect his Oscar, the man who handed it to him, now gaunt from a bout with cancer, was none other than John Wayne.

And in one final irony, the realities of Vietnam once more stood cinematic myth on its head. For there *was* at least one documented case of roulette that remained unnoticed by *The Deer Hunter's* critics. The day after My Lai, Captain Ernest Medina flushed out another Viet Cong suspect as Charlie Company continued south. When the man refused to talk, Medina took his thirty-eight caliber revolver, placed it at the man's temple, and spun the barrel. Medina later insisted that the gun was empty, but several of his men disagreed. When the villager still refused to talk, Medina "grabbed him by the hair and threw him up against a tree," said one eyewitness. "He fired two shots with a rifle, closer and closer to the guy's head, and then aimed straight at him." The suspect broke down and began babbling; he was indeed a communist province chief. Pleased, Medina posed for a picture. Drinking from a coconut held in one hand, with the other he brandished a large knife at the prisoner's throat.

The Search for New Myths

By using the same techniques of analysis that we brought to bear on *The Green Berets*, it becomes clear that the anguished experiences of Vietnam made it impossible for *The Deer Hunter* to follow the older, patriotic myths of the western or the combat dramas of World War II. Cimino's film won critical

Mythical images of the West are twisted *in Francis Ford Coppola's*
Apocalypse Now. *In place of the can-do Colonel Kirby of* The Green
Berets, *Colonel Kilgore, played by Robert Duvall, conducts a harrowing
raid on a Vietnamese village. Duvall's cavalry hat and spurs make the
connection with the cinematic genre of the western, but the tragedy at
My Lai has given this gleeful colonel a grim undertone: "I love the smell
of napalm in the morning," says Kilgore after his conquest is complete.*

acclaim because it acknowledged the pain of Vietnam. Yet for all that, it refused
to come to grips with the actual circumstances of the war. In 1979, director
Francis Ford Coppola's *Apocalypse Now* provided a rival portrait that faced the
realities of Vietnam more squarely.

Though the central plot of *Apocalypse Now* was as fictional and almost as far-
fetched as *The Deer Hunter*'s, it did portray the kind of stresses laid bare at My
Lai. Coppola's audience could never confuse his soldiers with the fresh-faced
GIs who followed John Wayne or with Cimino's injured innocents abroad. In a
sequence some critics hailed as the most thrilling battle scene ever filmed,

Colonel Kilgore (whose name reflects his temperament) leads a helicopter assault nearly as ruthless as the one at My Lai. Though immensely harrowing, the assault seems almost surreal because the choppers descend on their target hamlet blasting Wagnerian opera from huge loudspeakers. (This is to "scare the shit out of the slopes," Kilgore explains, reflecting the casual racism so often a part of the war.)

Just as the troops at My Lai left an 11th Brigade patch between the legs of a prominently displayed corpse, so Kilgore deals out playing cards of death on the bodies of his slain villagers, to serve both as boast and warning to the VC. Just as Charlie Company set up camp after the massacre and went swimming along the beaches of the South China Sea, Kilgore eagerly unpacks a surfboard to ride the waves offshore. The resonances with My Lai are unmistakable. Yet audiences may have been so swept away by the sheer firepower of the chopper assault that they failed to realize how much the scene undermined the cherished myth that Americans invariably preserved their humanity in the heat of battle. Often enough, viewers embraced the scene's affirmation of America's technological supremacy. In a chilling example of life imitating art, some American assault helicopters in the Gulf War of 1991 attacked Iraqi positions as loudspeakers aboard boomed out recordings of Wagner.

Colonel Kilgore's excesses, however, are only a prelude to a more metaphysical confrontation with the realities of My Lai. Captain Willard (Martin Sheen) has been sent on a mission to eliminate a Green Beret colonel named Kurtz, who has deserted and is operating independently just across the Laotian border. As Willard journeys farther into the jungle, he himself becomes more ruthless, more like Kurtz. When the boat taking him upriver is sidetracked by a needless attack on a peasant sampan (the jittery crew opens fire prematurely), Willard shocks the other soldiers by cold-bloodedly killing a wounded woman, so that his mission will not be delayed while they take her downriver for medical attention.[3] Willard recognizes the hypocrisy of the situation: "It was a way we had over here of living with ourselves. We'd cut 'em in half with a machine gun and give 'em a bandaid. It was a lie; and the more I saw of them, the more I hated lies." But instead of disavowing the war, Willard pushes deeper into the jungle toward the immoral Kurtz. He is descending, it seems, toward the same elemental savagery that characterized My Lai.

But in the end, *Apocalypse Now* is defeated by its own literary pretensions. In trying to make the film more than just another war picture, Coppola modeled his story on Joseph Conrad's literary classic, *Heart of Darkness* (1902). Set along Africa's Congo River at the height of European imperialism, Conrad's tale concerns a man sent to investigate a colonial ruler gone "native"—also named Kurtz. Coppola's implication—that Vietnam is America's own imperialist nightmare—was an intriguing notion. But as played by an overweight, eccentric Marlon Brando, Kurtz only distracts from the grittier horrors of the real war. His

---

[3] In a no doubt unintended parallel with *The Green Berets*, the sampan firefight is triggered by a woman moving toward a crate which the Americans suspect contains weapons. In fact, the crate holds yet another puppy—a rather unlikely pet for this Vietnamese family. This time, of course, the irony is reversed: it's the *Americans* who are the wanton killers.

lunacy is so otherworldly, it has no connection with the experiences of ordinary American GIs in Vietnam, or to the earlier scenes in *Apocalypse Now* that gave the film its mythic power.

Meanwhile, many Americans remained reluctant to examine the causes or context of the brutality demonstrated at My Lai. It was simpler to embrace again the traditional myths of American valor, honor, and decency. The most prominent advocate of this approach was Ronald Reagan, a Hollywood actor turned politician, who understood well how cinematic myths were made. As a presidential candidate in 1980, a year after the release of *Apocalypse Now*, Reagan called upon Americans to "stand tall" and praised the war in Vietnam as a "noble cause." Reagan's views were in tune with a number of studies appearing in defense of the American role in Vietnam.

Hollywood too revised and burnished its views of the war. Two of the most popular films of the Reagan years starred Sylvester Stallone as the smoldering, half-Indian, half-German, entirely musclebound John Rambo. In *First Blood* (1982), Rambo seems to resemble yet another damaged and deranged vet from films of the 1970s. But times have changed: underneath the antisocial shell of this misunderstood ex–Green Beret lurks a noble savage. When Rambo is challenged by the sadistic sheriff of a corrupt town in the Pacific Northwest, he undertakes a private war against the establishment, leaving the town in ruins. In terms of Hollywood myths, this is a revenge fantasy, in which the innocent warrior, in tune with the land, vents his rage against the weak-kneed politicians and bureaucrats who refused to let him fight to win in Vietnam.

The relation of this revenge myth to the war was made clearer in a sequel, *First Blood, Part 2* (1985). A "Special Operations" unit from Washington wants to send Rambo back into Vietnam, to discover whether Americans listed during the war as MIAs (missing in action) are still being held as prisoners. (For nearly two decades, North Vietnam's refusal to provide information on the status of missing Americans has led some relatives of MIAs to press the government to discover whether any MIAs were left alive.) In the film's entirely fictional plot, Rambo located an MIA prison camp with the help of an Asian beauty he encounters deep in enemy territory. ("Too much death—death everywhere— maybe go America—live the quiet life," she remarks hopefully, to the one American who has proved himself utterly incapable of settling down peacefully anywhere.) But treachery is afoot: when Rambo radios in the camp's location, the "stinking bureaucrat" from Special Operations calls back the rescue helicopter. He had assumed Rambo would fail, thus allowing the controversy over MIAs to disappear. Needless to say, Rambo manages to fight off entire detachments of Vietnamese and their Russian allies, rescuing the American prisoners and piloting them safely home.

Once again, consider the film's dramatic structure. How does the film's plot reflect a mythic rather than a historic reality about Vietnam? To begin with, although the producers clearly supported the notion that Vietnam was a "noble cause," the plot is not about the war itself. Why? In an escapist adventure, Rambo must be allowed to win. And even in Hollywood, where producers rewrite history to their taste, there was no way audiences would accept a rewritten war in which the United States won. By focusing instead on the issue of MIAs, "victory" was defined in terms of the far simpler task of rescuing a dozen prisoners. And like *The Deer Hunter*, the film's motivation centers on what *they* did to *us*, rather than on the more ambiguous question of American involvement in Vietnam.

Furthermore, the mythical Green Beret of the 1960s has been transformed. In 1968, when real lives were being lost and real atrocities committed, *The Green Berets* was careful to show John Wayne restraining his bloodthirsty South Vietnamese allies. By the 1980s, however—a generation away fom the real horrors of the war—Rambo's new version of valor is a muscular superman whose body becomes a well-oiled, finely tuned killing machine. (During the years when the war was actually fought, Stallone himself was spending his draft-age years teaching at a private girl's school in Switzerland, as an acting student in Miami, and acting in a soft-core porn film titled *A Party at Kitty and Stud's*.)

The villains of the eighties have changed too. The Vietnamese still conform to the Hollywood stereotypes of Asian soldiers (they shout a lot and run around ineffectively), but Stallone's real opponent becomes a blond Russian sadist named Colonel Petrovsky. Vietnam had faded from the front pages, after all, while President Reagan was still referring to the Soviet Union as an "evil empire." Perhaps most revealing, the climax of the film occurs not when Stallone rescues the MIAs, but when he stomps into the American intelligence operations center and, in righteous wrath, machine-guns the files, computers, and radio equipment of the quaking traitor from Washington. "Do we get to win this time?" Rambo asks at the beginning of the film. By the time the last credits roll, he *has* won: not only defeating the Vietnamese and the Russians, but also the greatest villain of Ronald Reagan's domestic evil empire—the government bureaucrat.

In part, the passage of time and fading memories made it possible for a wide audience to accept Rambo's fantastic myths. Americans no longer had to face the war every night on the news. But greater distance had also drained the political debate of some of its old divisiveness. That opened the door, by 1986, to a very different film about Vietnam. The director of *Platoon*, Oliver Stone, had served in Vietnam for fifteen months and had been wounded twice. Returning home he wrote a screenplay about the war, but in 1976 no one would produce it; memories were too fresh. A decade later, producers were willing to take the risk.

Platoon became one of the first commercially successful films to look at the war itself; to see Vietnam as history. As the opening credits roll, Chris Taylor (Charlie Sheen) steps out of the giant maw of a cargo plane into the oppressive heat of Vietnam. But the raw sounds of jet engines, jeeps, and airport clatter are muted. Over them, a serenely sad melody fills the soundtrack, a technique that distances us from what we are seeing. The music is Samuel Barber's *Adagio for Strings*, a composition that first received widespread attention in 1945, when it was broadcast following the announcement of Franklin Roosevelt's death. In *Platoon*, its elegaic melody mourns men and times past, a feeling reinforced by an epigraph on the screen: "Rejoice, O young men in thy youth." Taken from the Bible's Book of Ecclesiastes, the words are not those of celebration but of warning, spoken by one whose youth has long vanished. ("I have seen every-thing that is done under the sun, and behold, all is vanity and a striving after wind.") As Taylor and other GIs cross the runway, they see the body bags of dead servicemen being loaded into the plane, heading home—those who have striven, perhaps, in vain.

At the outset, *Platoon*'s format seems much like the old World War II dramas, with their ethnically balanced mix of soldiers learning the hard lessons of war. But this is Vietnam, and *Platoon* recognizes the differences. We meet Bunny, the violent redneck who takes bites out of beer cans; Rhah, the tough-minded Puerto Rican; King, a black draftee from the rural hills of Tennessee; Lerner, a naive white recruit; Junior, a street-smart black soldier from the urban north; and Chris Taylor—the observer, newcomer, and college-educated odd-man-out who has volunteered for service. Because of the war's duty rotation system, recruits stayed in Vietnam for only one year. Thus the composition of fighting units was constantly changing, as each grunt in the field served out his 365 days and departed. Under such a system, morale was more difficult to maintain, since newcomers were treated suspiciously as greenhorns, whose mistakes were likely to get the old hands killed. And the old hands had every incentive to duck tough assignments that might send them home in a body bag.

Platoon also dramatizes the anguish of fighting in Vietnam. Sheen is tor-mented by ants that crawl over him; he faints from the heat and humidity of a hard march; he stares anxiously into a rainy, impenetrable dark, trying to spot the invisible enemy. Then on New Year's Day 1968, the platoon comes upon an enemy bunker complex. At the center of the jungle camp a fire still burns—evidently the VC have fled only moments earlier. Sergeant Elias (Willem Dafoe) probes a tunnel complex, inching along in the dark, hoping not to be blown away by a waiting guerilla. Others in the platoon are spread out along the camp's perimeter, each nervous about being isolated. Suddenly a booby trap explodes, killing a soldier.

From out of the jungle the men march to a nearby village. The Viet Cong have retreated here, haven't they? Along the way, another soldier is found brutally murdered, leaving the platoon in a dangerous mood. The villagers go placidly about their farm work; yet the Americans realize that at the very least the hamlet's residents have been helping the guerillas, and perhaps are VC them-selves. The scarfaced Sergeant Barnes (Tom Berenger) stalks angrily through the settlement, finding concealed ammunition, herding some of the women into a pigpen. Taylor flushes one man from a bunker and, temporarily enraged, shoots at the feet of a peasant, making him dance in fear. Then Bunny crushes the man's skull with his rifle butt. Outside other women and children are crying as Barnes questions the village's headman. The hysteria, the fear, and the rage clearly upset many of the men, who are on the verge of opening fire indiscriminately. Sergeant Barnes shoots one woman who has been yelling at him; then points his rifle at the headman's daughter and is about to execute her when Elias physically attacks him and tells him to stop. Barnes backs off, but fixes Elias with a steely eye. "You're dead," he says. The platoon's lieutenant gives the order to torch the village and then the soldiers move out.

The amoral Sergeant Barnes threatens to kill a young villager
in Platoon. *Contrast this scene with the one of John Wayne in* The Green
Berets *on page 363. The events at My Lai have obviously altered
dramatically the cinematic images of Americans at war in an
ambiguous conflict.*

What makes this sequence remarkable is that, unlike *The Green Berets, The
Deer Hunter,* or Rambo's fantasies—even unlike *Apocalypse Now*—it provides
an answer to a question that is at bottom historical rather than mythical. What we
see unfolding before us is My Lai—or rather, a My Lai in the making, averted
only because Sergeant Elias steps in. But because the film has followed the
platoon's mission over the course of several months, we are seeing the incident
in context—a context that closely mirrored the Vietnam experience of many
American GIs. The trauma of Vietnam becomes not merely a question of what
they did to *us*. Nor is it even a question of what we did to *them*, which is the
equally distorted reverse-angle perspective. *Platoon* makes it easier to see that
in a civil war, where the civilian population is divided, war becomes an ambiguous, dangerous occupation, especially for foreigners who understand little of
Vietnamese culture. The women who protest "No VC! No VC!" may be cooking
enough rice to feed an entire unit hiding nearby; and the children who accept
candy from GIs and call out "Okay! Okay!" may turn around and lob a grenade.
"I used to like kids," said Herbert Carter, one of the soldiers at My Lai, "but I
can't stand them any more. . . ."

    In a war where territory was never gained permanently, how could victory
be measured? Body counts were one way. "Anything that's dead and isn't white

is a VC," went one Army joke making the rounds. A member of Charlie Company recalled being shocked, shortly after he arrived in Vietnam, to see a troop carrier drive by with "about twenty human ears tied to the antenna." Even Lyndon Johnson could not resist exhorting troops in Vietnam to "come home with the coonskin on the wall." When GIs began to measure victory in terms of bodies counted, when friend and foe looked alike, and when more than a half-dozen men in Charlie Company had been killed by exploding booby traps, the ingredients for trouble were present. "It just started building," recalled Ronald Grzesik. "I don't know why. Everybody reached the point where they were frustrated. . . . I remember writing a letter home saying that I once had sympathy for these people, but now I didn't care." Two days before My Lai, Gregory Olsen, a devout Mormon in Charlie Company, wrote his father about what happened after another booby trap incident.

> . . . it all turned out a bad day made even worse. On their way back to "Dotti" [other members of the company] saw a woman working in the fields. They shot and wounded her. Then they kicked her to death and emptied their magazines in her head. They slugged every little kid they came across.
>
> Why in God's name does this have to happen? These are all seemingly normal guys; some were friends of mine. For a while they were like wild animals.
>
> It was murder, and I'm ashamed of myself for not trying to do anything about it.
>
> This isn't the first time, Dad. I've seen it many times before. I don't know why I'm telling you all this; I guess I just want to get it off my chest.

To its credit, *Platoon* reflects these realities. Yet it reaches no hard conclusions about the issues it raises. Having made reference to My Lai, the scene in the hamlet ends with an image of American innocence. Against the backdrop of burning huts, the platoon escorts frightened villagers to safety. GIs who moments earlier were ready to murder and rape now cradle children in their arms—just as, at the real My Lai, Colonel Medina and Lieutenant Calley shared cookies and crackers with two girls from the village. Repeatedly, *Platoon* returns to this tension between good and evil. During another mission, the violent Barnes makes good his threat to kill the saintly Elias. The mythical overtones are strong: with a church in the background, Elias dies like Christ, his arms stretched out as if in crucifixion. But here, good and evil do not boil down to *us* versus *them*. The good Elias is every bit as much a soldier as the evil Barnes. The experience of My Lai has forced *Platoon* to give up the myth of American exceptionalism—that Americans are more virtuous, thanks to their special circumstances. They must wrestle with the evil within themselves as all people do.

Elias as a Christ figure, Barnes as an amoral realist . . . These are mythological, dramatic concepts rather than historical ones. But they reflect the circumstances of the war in far different ways than the myths of *The Green Berets* or *The Sands of Iwo Jima*. *Platoon*'s ambiguities reveal the difficulty of imposing traditional myths on Vietnam, a war that demanded myths of its own.

In the end, it will not do to say that *Platoon* is better history than *The Green Berets*—although most historians might conclude that it more accurately portrayed the conditions of the war. Myths of the cinema will always reflect the needs of drama more than the requirements of historical evidence. For their part, historians must remain faithful to their own creed: to examine the images of the silver screen rationally and with the same skepticism they bring to any primary or secondary source.

But is a rational, skeptical approach enough? If truth be told, people do not often make love or die for their country on rational grounds alone. The best history recognizes those deep-seated emotions that myths address. For that reason we have examined not only the facts of My Lai but the more intangible effects the event has had on our self-image as a nation. In their eagerness to become mythmakers for the millions, the magicians of Hollywood have offered us not one but many myths with which to shape our lives. The power of history to undertake a reasoned analysis of the past offers hope—and perhaps a method by which we may come to appreciate the authentic truths that the best myths reveal.

So let us return one last time to Son My. As historians, we cannot expunge the painful record of what took place; but it may be worth reiterating that My Lai stood as an extreme of the American experience in Vietnam. If the booby traps, the ambushes, the frustrations of an unseen enemy worked on all soldiers, not all chose to behave in the same way, even at My Lai.

POV, above the hamlet in an observation helicopter: Chief Warrant Officer Hugh Thompson, of Decatur, Georgia, is sweeping the area. He spots a wounded girl by the side of a rice paddy and decides to mark her location with a smoke grenade so that the men on the ground can provide medical help. Thompson is astonished to see a captain walk over to the girl and shoot her. Turning north, Thompson sees a small boy bleeding along a trench and marks *his* location with smoke. Casually, a lieutenant walks up and empties a clip into the child.

Beside himself with anger, Thompson tries to contact ground forces. When he cannot get through, he radios a loud protest to brigade headquarters. Then, circling over the hamlet's outskirts, he sees a canal ditch with "a bunch of bodies in it." A pilot nearby is reminded of "the old Biblical story of Jesus turning water into wine. The trench had a grey color to it, with the red blood of the individuals . . ." Thompson spots some children still alive among the mass of bodies. Nearly frantic, he lands his small chopper and picks up a child about two years old, dazed with shock. He calls in another gunship for a dozen more youngsters. In the air once again, he sights the same lieutenant who shot the child he had marked earlier. The lieutenant—Thompson later identifies him as Calley—is in the process of destroying a bunker where women and children are huddled.

This time Thompson lands, gets out of the chopper, and stalks over to Calley and tells him to remove the civilians. The only way to get them out, responds Calley, is to use hand grenades. "You just hold your men right here," Thompson retorts angrily, "and I will get the women and kids out." Thompson orders one of the waist gunners in his chopper to aim his machine gun "at that officer" and shoot if he tries to interfere. Then Thompson walks back and places himself physically between Calley's troops and the women and children, until a chopper arrives to evacuate them.

For his actions, Thompson was belatedly awarded the Distinguished Flying Cross. The curious historian may consult the citation in Army records; it is less than direct in describing the conditions under which Thompson had been "disregarding his own safety." It notes only that he found the children "between Viet Cong positions and advancing friendly forces." As usual, the raw material of the past is neither as clear-cut nor as comforting as the larger-than-life deeds of the cinema. It remains for historians, sifting through such telltales, to fashion narratives that are not only worth dying for, but living with.

ADDITIONAL READING

At least twenty-five feature films have been made about the American experience in Vietnam. Many others touch tangentially on the war. Rather than provide a comprehensive survey, we chose to explore a few films in depth. We strongly recommend that students view for themselves at least some of those films we have analyzed. All are available on videocassette. For broader coverage of the films of Vietnam, see Albert Auster and Leonard Quart, *How the War Was Remembered: Hollywood and Vietnam* (New York, 1988), Linda Dittmar and Gene Michaud, eds., *From Hanoi to Hollywood: The Vietnam War in American Film* (New Brunswick, N.J., 1990), and Pat Aufderheide, "Vietnam: Good Soldiers," in Mark Crispin Miller, ed., *Seeing Through Movies* (New York, 1990). Nor did we discuss documentary films about Vietnam. *Hearts and Minds* (1974) illustrates how the format can convey a highly interpretive message; *Vietnam: A Television History* (1983) is a thorough thirteen-part series originally aired on the Public Broadcasting System. Both pay far more attention to the Vietnamese side of the war than most American accounts. Another PBS series, *Frontline*, has examined the My Lai incident in *Remember My Lai* (WGBH Television, 1989).

For those unfamiliar with the technology of filmmaking, James Monaco provides an excellent introduction to understanding how the medium shapes its message, in *How to Read a Film* (New York, 1972). Another good introduction is Louis Giannetti, *Understanding Movies* (3d ed., Englewood Cliffs, N.J., 1982). For a look at the ways historians can approach film, see a collection of essays sponsored by the American Historical Association, John E. O'Connor, ed., *Image as Artifact: The Historical Analysis of Film and Television* (Malabar, Fla., 1990).

Two journalists have provided detailed reconstructions of the events at My Lai: Richard Hammer, *One Morning in War: The Tragedy of Son My* (New York, 1970), and Seymour Hersh, *My Lai 4: A Report on the Massacre and Its Aftermath* (New York, 1970). Both authors also examined aspects of the military investigations and trials: Hersh in *Cover-up: The Army's Secret Investigation of the Massacre at My Lai 4* (New York, 1972), and Hammer in *The Court Martial of Lieutenant Calley* (New York, 1971). Psychiatrist Robert Jay Lifton places the soldiers' experience in a broader perspective in *Home from the War: Vietnam Veterans: Neither Victims nor Executioners* (New York, 1973), while Peter Goldman and Tony Fuller profile a single company (not the one at My Lai) in *Charlie Company: What Vietnam Did to Us* (New York, 1983). On the issue of war crimes, see the contemporary discussion in Edwin Knoll and Judith McFadden, eds., *War Crimes and the American Conscience* (New York, 1970); also *The Winter Soldiers Investigation: An Inquiry into American War Crimes* (New York, 1972), issued by Vietnam Veterans Against the War.

The number of books on the war itself is vast. A judicious introduction is George Herring, *America's Longest War: The United States in Vietnam, 1950-1975* (2d ed., New York, 1986). Two other useful jumping-off points are

Stanley Karnow, *Vietnam: A History* (New York, 1983), and George Kahin, *Intervention: How America Became Involved in Vietnam* (New York, 1986). For a dissenting view, see Dave Richard Palmer, *Summons of the Trumpet: A History of the War from a Military Man's Viewpoint* (New York, 1978).

A number of memoirs vividly recall the life of the ordinary grunt in the field, including Tim O'Brien, *If I Die in a Combat Zone* (New York, 1989), Philip Caputo, *A Rumor of War*, (New York, 1977), and Ron Kovic, *Born on the Fourth of July* (New York, 1977). Kovic's book, of course, invites comparison to Oliver Stone's film of the same title, and provides an interesting example of how filmmakers change stories for dramatic reasons. Three oral histories survey a range of GIs' experiences: Al Santoli, *Everything We Had* (New York, 1981), Mark Baker, *Nam: The Vietnam War in the Words of the Men and Women Who Fought* (New York, 1983), and Wallace Terry, *Bloods: An Oral History of the Vietnam War by Black Veterans* (New York, 1984). Finally, Michael Herr's *Dispatches* (New York, 1978) is a personal history of the war that captures its extremes almost better than anything else.

Among other films worth seeing but not discussed in this chapter: *Coming Home* (1978), an early attempt to explore the struggle of returning vets, and *Go Tell the Spartans*, based on a novel by Daniel Ford (*Incident at Muc Wa*). This low-budget film was eclipsed in 1978 by *Coming Home* and *The Deer Hunter*, but it portrayed the war's gritty ambiguities far more accurately. A more recent pair worth comparing are *Casualties of War* and *Born on the Fourth of July*. Both were released in 1990, both featured well-known stars, both dealt with painful experiences of the war. Yet one film succeeded at the box office, while the other did badly. Based on the principles set forth in this chapter, it should be possible to explain why, in terms of myths and audience expectations. In charting the effects of Vietnam on American cinematic myths, John Wayne's earlier westerns and war epics are worth viewing. Lifton's book (cited above) notes how many eager recruits went off to war with images of John Wayne in their heads.

Finally, it may be interesting to track the use and abuse of history in films relating to topics covered in earlier chapters. The experience of free African Americans and freed slaves during the Civil War can be seen in *Glory* (1990). *Hester Street* (1975) is a vivid look at one aspect of the immigrant community Jacob Riis photographed. *All the King's Men* (1949) adapts to the screen the Robert Penn Warren novel inspired by the career of Huey Long, while *Little Boy and Fat Man* (1990) chops, slices, and dices the history of the Manhattan Project in typical Hollywood style. *All the President's Men* (1976) offers a more straightforward translation of Woodward and Bernstein's book.

Index